Daniel White Hodge

Heaven Has A Ghetto

Daniel White Hodge

# Heaven Has A Ghetto

## The Missiological Gospel & Theology of Tupac Amaru Shakur

VDM Verlag Dr. Müller

## Impressum/Imprint (nur für Deutschland/ only for Germany)

Bibliografische Information der Deutschen Nationalbibliothek: Die Deutsche Nationalbibliothek verzeichnet diese Publikation in der Deutschen Nationalbibliografie; detaillierte bibliografische Daten sind im Internet über http://dnb.d-nb.de abrufbar.

Alle in diesem Buch genannten Marken und Produktnamen unterliegen warenzeichen-, marken- oder patentrechtlichem Schutz bzw. sind Warenzeichen oder eingetragene Warenzeichen der jeweiligen Inhaber. Die Wiedergabe von Marken, Produktnamen, Gebrauchsnamen, Handelsnamen, Warenbezeichnungen u.s.w. in diesem Werk berechtigt auch ohne besondere Kennzeichnung nicht zu der Annahme, dass solche Namen im Sinne der Warenzeichen- und Markenschutzgesetzgebung als frei zu betrachten wären und daher von jedermann benutzt werden dürften.

Coverbild: www.purestockx.com

Verlag: VDM Verlag Dr. Müller Aktiengesellschaft & Co. KG
Dudweiler Landstr. 99, 66123 Saarbrücken, Deutschland
Telefon +49 681 9100-698, Telefax +49 681 9100-988, Email: info@vdm-verlag.de

Herstellung in Deutschland:
Schaltungsdienst Lange o.H.G., Berlin
Books on Demand GmbH, Norderstedt
Reha GmbH, Saarbrücken
Amazon Distribution GmbH, Leipzig
**ISBN: 978-3-639-20763-7**

## Imprint (only for USA, GB)

Bibliographic information published by the Deutsche Nationalbibliothek: The Deutsche Nationalbibliothek lists this publication in the Deutsche Nationalbibliografie; detailed bibliographic data are available in the Internet at http://dnb.d-nb.de .

Any brand names and product names mentioned in this book are subject to trademark, brand or patent protection and are trademarks or registered trademarks of their respective holders. The use of brand names, product names, common names, trade names, product descriptions etc. even without a particular marking in this works is in no way to be construed to mean that such names may be regarded as unrestricted in respect of trademark and brand protection legislation and could thus be used by anyone.

Cover image: www.purestockx.com

Publisher:
VDM Verlag Dr. Müller Aktiengesellschaft & Co. KG
Dudweiler Landstr. 99, 66123 Saarbrücken, Germany
Phone +49 681 9100-698, Fax +49 681 9100-988, Email: info@vdm-publishing.com

Copyright © 2009 by the author and VDM Verlag Dr. Müller Aktiengesellschaft & Co. KG and licensors
All rights reserved. Saarbrücken 2009

Printed in the U.S.A.
Printed in the U.K. by (see last page)
**ISBN: 978-3-639-20763-7**

## DEDICATION

To my wife, Emily White Hodge for enduring through this process with me. Thank you babe!

To my mother for raising me up to be a strong man who never takes no for an answer.

To Dede. The person who was my spiritual rock throughout my entire life. She prayed for me even when I didn't want prayer. Thank you for loving on me and showing me a glimpse of God's love. Rest in peace.

To Tupac, for an inspiring life that has encouraged me to study even harder and to continue seeking the truth.

This book process did not come without much struggle. At first, I did not even plan to write as a profession, but, after some encouragement from my wife, Emily, and some other people, I knew it was the right choice. This work is dedicated to those people such as Dr. Mel Donalson, Ms. Beverly Tate, and Bakari Kitwana who help young Black scholars, like myself, get off their feet. Thank you!

I would like to thank Roberta King for being open minded enough to take me on as a PhD student with a subject matter that is not exactly orthodox mission studies. Roberta was a great mentor and gave me rich material in which to apply to Tupac's music. She was a great help in advocating for me and my project too.

I would also like to thank the blazing pioneer in urban mission, Jude Tiersma-Watson. Without the path she carved out beforehand, none of us "urban folk" would have a strong voice at Fuller. She has been a great help and confidant in times of great need. Thanks to her and John, her husband.

I would also like to thank Daniel Shaw for all of the great advice, direction, mentoring, and wise guidance he gave. Without him, the methods of this book would not be where they are at now. He is committed to each of his students and gave me the time I needed to finish this unique project.

I would also like to acknowledge the Los Angeles Hip Hop community that gave me countless hour's worth of insight and material in which to connect to Tupac. They provided for me a great praxis of material and engagement.

I cannot leave this page without deeply thanking my wife, Emily. While writing this book, I had been in school for four and a half years of our five year marriage. She has endured the late nights, and the editing points, and has encouraged me with abundant grace when I was too tired to go on. I can only hope to model such loving grace in return. Thank you so very much!

Without God's directional help, I would not be here. While I do not think God "called" me in the traditional sense to write this book, I do feel as though God and I have grown so much closer because of this. And, as a result, I have grown in God's word and God's image just a little more; especially as it relates to God's connection to not only me, but Tupac. I thank God for the insight into my own life to see the profane and sacred both in paradox; all the while God loves me and continues to walk next to me, even when I cannot feel God or am too weak to go on. This has truly been an amazing faith walk, and God has brought me through the other side!

To all the peeps in the 'hood that do not get this type of platform to voice their message, keep ya head up ya'll, your time is coming!

## TABLE OF CONTENTS

DEDICATION ..................................................................................................... ii
TABLE OF CONTENTS ................................................................................... iv
LIST OF TABLES .............................................................................................. ix
LIST OF FIGURES .............................................................................................. x
INTRODUCTION: WHICH WAY IS UP? ........................................................ 1
    Tupac's Enigma ............................................................................................ 2
    Missional Approaches .................................................................................. 3
PART I   SETTING UP THA STAGE: APPROACHING THE STUDY OF
TUPAC SHAKUR AS THE URBAN PROPHET ............................................... 5
CHAPTER 1  MY OWN BAPTISM IN DIRTY WATER .................................. 7
    Comin' Up .................................................................................................... 7
    From the Rural to the City ........................................................................... 9
        Police in the 'Hood of Seaside .............................................................. 10
        L.A. Riots ............................................................................................. 11
    Jesus and the Hip Hop Prophets ................................................................ 12
    Towards a Theology of Hip Hop Culture .................................................. 13
CHAPTER 2  STUDYING TUPAC: LEARNING THE ICON ........................ 16
    Introduction: Tupac .................................................................................... 16
    The Book Structure .................................................................................... 20
        Purpose and Goals ................................................................................ 22
        Significance .......................................................................................... 22
        Central Research Issue ......................................................................... 23
        Definition of Terms ............................................................................. 24
CHAPTER 3  BRINGING TUPAC'S GOSPEL TO LIFE ................................ 27
    Tupac as a Study ........................................................................................ 27
    Ethnohistory as a Method .......................................................................... 28
        Ethnolifehistory as a Method ............................................................... 35
        Longitudinal Cultural Process Compared to a Person's Cultural
        Process .................................................................................................. 38
        Qualitative Content Analysis and Lyrical Case Studies ..................... 39

Weaknesses ................................................................................................ 42
The Context for the Study ....................................................................... 44
Summary .................................................................................................. 46

CHAPTER 4  TOWARD A THEORY OF TUPAC'S MUSIC ........................... 47
Physical Behavior .................................................................................... 48
Social Behavior ........................................................................................ 50
Verbal Behavior ....................................................................................... 51
Three Intersecting Areas in Tupac's Music ............................................. 53
    Inspiration ........................................................................................ 54
    Improvisation and Composition ...................................................... 55
    Life Events ....................................................................................... 56
Connecting Tupac's Music for Study ....................................................... 59
Summary .................................................................................................. 63

PART II: HIP HOP CULTURE and THE 'HOOD: THE CONTEXT FOR TUPAC ...................................................................................................... 65

CHAPTER 5  THE CONTEXT OF TUPAC HIP HOP CULTURE ................... 67
So, What is Hip Hop Culture? ................................................................. 69
Identity of Hip Hop Culture Among Hip Hop Youth ............................. 78
    Rhythm and Audio .......................................................................... 83
    Language and the Verbal ................................................................ 85
    Spatial .............................................................................................. 87
    Written ............................................................................................. 89
Hip Hop's Rootz ....................................................................................... 91
Summary ................................................................................................ 101

CHAPTER 6  THE 'HOOD COMES FIRST: THE URBAN CONTEXT ......... 103
The Rootz of The 'Hood ......................................................................... 103
    Jazz Music ..................................................................................... 106
    The Rise of Black Popular Culture .............................................. 108
    The Civil Rights Movement ......................................................... 109
    Malcolm X ..................................................................................... 111
    Martin Luther King Jr. .................................................................. 113
The 1970's and The Rise of 'Hood Culture .......................................... 115
    Postmodernity and Hip Hop Language ....................................... 117
    The Niggarization of a Nation ..................................................... 119
Spirituality in the 'Hood ........................................................................ 122
Summary ................................................................................................ 124

CHAPTER 7  TUPAC, BLACK POPULAR CULTURE, AND HIP HOP ....... 126
Tupac and Black Popular Culture ......................................................... 131
Themes in Black Popular Culture and Tupac ....................................... 133
    Sex   136
    Economics ..................................................................................... 138

| | |
|---|---|
| Cultural Values | 141 |
| The Value of Words | 142 |
| The Value of Being Real | 144 |
| Summary | 148 |

**PART III:** ................................................................................ 150

**TUPAC'S ETHNOLIFEHISTORY** ........................................... 150

**CHAPTER 8 TUPAC'S LIFE ERAS** ........................................ 152
| | |
|---|---|
| Military Mind (1971-1980) | 152 |
| The Black Panther Party | 153 |
| Afeni | 156 |
| The Music and Arts | 159 |
| Criminal Grind (1981-1988) | 162 |
| Growing Up in Different Hoods | 162 |
| Marin City | 165 |
| The Political Economy of Crack Cocaine | 166 |
| Ghetto Mindset | 168 |
| The Ghetto Is Destiny (1989-1992) | 172 |
| The Era: Sources of Tupac's Passion and Vision | 172 |
| Death | 174 |
| Digital Underground | 175 |
| 2Pacalypse Now | 176 |
| T.H.U.G. L.I.F.E | 177 |
| Exodus 18:11 | 180 |
| Outlaw (1992-1995) | 181 |
| The Long Arm of the Law | 181 |
| Hollywood | 183 |
| THUG LIFE and Hollywood | 186 |
| Prison and Me Against the World | 187 |
| Ghetto Saint (1996-Present) | 189 |
| All Eyez on Him | 189 |
| Deathrow Records | 192 |
| I Wonder if Heaven Got A Ghetto | 194 |
| Hold on Be Strong | 195 |
| September 13, 1996 | 195 |
| Summary | 196 |

**CHAPTER 9 TUPAC'S MUSICAL MESSAGE** ........................ 197
| | |
|---|---|
| Tha Social and Political Message | 198 |
| The Social Message within 2Pacalypse Now | 198 |
| 'Hood Matters | 201 |
| Tupac's Politics | 203 |
| Tha Familial and Communal Message | 206 |
| The Women of the Family | 206 |

   Community .................................................................................. 208
  Tha Class Message ............................................................................ 212
   'Hood Poverty ............................................................................. 212
   Niggaz ........................................................................................ 216
   The Marginalized ....................................................................... 218
  Tha Spiritual Message ...................................................................... 224
   The Suffering Jesuz .................................................................... 225
   The Profane ................................................................................ 229
   Sinner's Prayer ........................................................................... 233
   Hope and Vision: Gospel ........................................................... 237
  Summary ............................................................................................ 240

## PART IV HERMENEUTICAL SHIZNIT: TUPAC'S GOSPEL ..................... 243

## CHAPTER 10 INTERPRETING TUPAC'S THEOLOGICAL MESSAGE .... 245
  Theological Frameworks .................................................................. 245
   Reversing the Hermeneutical Flow ........................................... 245
   Nitty Gritty Hermeneutics ......................................................... 248
   Jesus and Hip Hop ..................................................................... 250
  Black Jesuz ........................................................................................ 251
  The Image of Black Jesuz ................................................................. 253
  Sorrow, Misery and God for Tupac .................................................. 255
  Summary ............................................................................................ 257

## CHAPTER 11 THE GOSPEL OF CHRIST ACCORDING TO TUPAC: REVERSING THE HERMENEUTIC WITH TUPAC .............................. 259
  Hold On: Matthew 11:27-30 .............................................................. 260
  Keep Ya Head Up: Matthew 28:20 .................................................... 262
  Heaven's Got a Ghetto: John 3:16-17 ................................................ 264
  The Paradox of the Sacred in the Profane ......................................... 268
  Summary ............................................................................................ 270

## CHAPTER 12 BLASPHEMY: TUPAC AS A PRE-EVANGELIST .............. 272
  Tupac Explaining Culture ................................................................. 274
  Nit Grit 'Hood Theology ................................................................... 278
   Thug Life Theos ......................................................................... 282
  The Narrative of Christ ..................................................................... 284
  Summary ............................................................................................ 286

## CHAPTER 13 CONCLUSION: FINAL THOUGHTS ON OUR GHETTO SAINT ......................................................................................................... 288
  Missional Essentials .......................................................................... 289
   Preparing the Way ...................................................................... 289
   Announcing Good News ............................................................ 290
   Identify With Sinners ................................................................. 291
   Confronting Social Injustice ...................................................... 291

      Power of the Holy Spirit ............................................................ 292  
      Accepting and Dealing with the Nature of the 'Hood .............. 292  
      From Street Sainthood to Jesus ................................................ 293  
      Concluding Remarks .................................................................. 296  

APPENDIX A  PICTORIAL VIEW OF TUPAC .............................................. 299  

APPENDIX B  T.H.U.G. L.I.F.E. CODE .......................................................... 300  

APPENDIX C  BLACK PANTHER 10 POINT PROGRAM and PLATFORM 302  

APPENDIX D  TUPAC'S TATTOO'S ............................................................. 305  

APPENDIX E  TUPAC'S MUSICAL CONNECTION TO SLAVE MUSIC ... 307  

APPENDIX F  CONTENT ANALYSIS OF: 2PACALYPSE NOW (1992) .... 310  

APPENDIX G  TUPAC'S AFFECT ON THE HIP HOP CULTURAL  
    CONTINUUM ........................................................................... 313  

APPENDIX H  SONG: SO MANY TEARS ..................................................... 314  

APPENDIX I  FIVE STAGES OF RACIAL IDENTITY ................................ 316  

APPENDIX J  MATERIAL USED IN TUPAC ETHNOLIFEHISTORY ......... 317  

APPENDIX K  TUPAC'S INVOLVEMENT WITH THE LAW ...................... 318  

GLOSSARY OF HIP HOP LANGUAGE .......................................................... 320  

SELECTED BIBLIOGRAPHY .......................................................................... 321  

INDEX ................................................................................................................ 339

## LIST OF TABLES

TABLE 1: THE DIFFERENCES BETWEEN RAP AND HIP HOP ............................... 70
TABLE 2  BLACK POPULAR CULTURE SOCIETAL THEMES ............................ 134
TABLE 3  TELEVISION THEMES ON ECONOMICS ............................................... 139
TABLE 4  LANGUAGE USED ................................................................................... 142
TABLE 5   TUPAC'S MUSICAL POSITIONS .............................................................. 169
TABLE 6  TUPAC'S DISTINCTIONS OF THE FEMALE GENDER ........................ 208
TABLE 7  TUPAC'S CLASS ORDER IN THE 'HOOD ............................................... 214
TABLE 8  TUPAC'S DEFINITIONS FOR THE WORD NIGGA ................................ 217
TABLE 9   LYRICAL CONNECTION TO THE LORD'S PRAYER ........................... 235
TABLE 10  TAXONOMIES OF TUPAC'S MUSICAL MESSAGE ............................ 241
TABLE 11  NIT GRIT 'HOOD THEOLOGY KEY PRECEPTS ................................... 281

## LIST OF FIGURES

FIGURE 1  FLOW OF THE BOOK PART ONE .................................................. 6

FIGURE 2  CROSS SECTIONAL APPROACH ............................................. 31

FIGURE 3  INSTITUTIONAL SYNTHESIS ................................................... 32

FIGURE 4  CULTURAL CONTINUUM PROCESS ...................................... 34

FIGURE 5  PROCESS OF ETHNOLIFEHISTORY IN CONTEXT .............. 43

FIGURE 6  FLOW OF EVENTS TOWARDS A SONG .................................. 57

FIGURE 7  TUPAC'S MUSICAL AREAS CONNECTION ........................... 60

FIGURE 8  FLOW OF BOOK PART TWO ..................................................... 66

FIGURE 9  THE SUB-GENRE'S OF HIP HOP CULTURE ........................... 72

FIGURE 10  THE INTERCONNECTION OF THE FOUR IDENTIFICATION FACTORS WITHIN HIP HOP CULTURE ` ............................ 91

FIGURE 11  PERCEIVED REALITY AND FANTASY WITHIN THE MEDIA ......... 145

FIGURE 12  FLOW OF BOOK PART THREE............................................... 151

FIGURE 13  TUPAC'S SOCIAL INFLUENCE ............................................. 164

FIGURE 14  TUPAC'S MUSICAL FOUNDATION....................................... 171

FIGURE 15  TUPAC'S THUG LIFE CODE'S MESSAGE ........................... 192

FIGURE 16  CULTURAL IDENTIFICATION PROCESS THROUGH TUPAC ........ 223

FIGURE 17  NEW THEOLOGICAL FOUNDATIONS THROUGH TUPAC'S LYRICS............................................................................ 230

FIGURE 18  FLOW OF BOOK PART FOUR................................................. 244

FIGURE 19  TUPAC'S GREATER CONNECTION IN THEOLOGY ......... 268

FIGURE 20  REVERSING THE HERMENEUTIC USING TUPAC ............................ 276

FIGURE 21  TUPAC'S LIFE'S AFFECT ON THE HIP HOP CULTURAL
            CONTINUUM ..................................................................................... 313

# INTRODUCTION:

# WHICH WAY IS UP?

> Here on Earth, tell me what's a black life worth
> A bottle of juice is no excuse, the truth hurts
> And even when you take the shit
> Move counties get a lawyer you can't shake the shit
> Ask Rodney, LaTasha, and many more
> It's been goin on for years, there's plenty more
> When they ask me, when will the violence cease?
> When your troops stop shootin niggaz down in the street
> Niggaz had enough time to make a difference
> Bear witness, own our own business
> Word to God cause it's hard tryin to make ends meet[1]

These are rapper Tupac Shakur's lyrics. He was considered a Hip Hop saint and theologian. Though he is dead, his words, lyrics, and life still live on as a symbol of hope for many in the urban community. Tupac was the ghetto saint who set a precedent for reaching inner city youth. He did so with such relentless passion, that many deem him a prophet and leader. Tupac was the irreverent Reverend for many, in the inner city as well as the suburbs.

Exactly who, or what, is Tupac Amaru Shakur? Is he as bad as the media makes him out to be? What made him so popular? What made him so controversial? What makes his life worth studying? Is he still relevant today? Moreover, what makes him a prophet of the 'hood?[2]

These, and more, are questions that this book will deal with as a central area of investigation. Tupac Amaru Shakur was one of the most prolific figures within Hip Hop

---

[1] Tupac, "I Wonder if Heaven Got A Ghetto?" R U Still Down (1997).

[2] See the glossary for complete definition of the word.

culture and American mainstream pop culture.[3] If you were to walk down any 'hood shopping center or market, Tupac is there in the form of a T-shirt, a piece of artwork or any variety of pop culture items. To this day, young people who were not even alive during most of Tupac's life value and honor Tupac as one of their most important figures and role models.[4]

### *Tupac's Enigma*

Another phenomenon that arises with Tupac's image is the fact that his music remains a central force within Hip Hop culture. In a music genre that has a bench life of 4-6 months before it is considered "old-school,"[5] Tupac's music remains "new" for many, and it is not uncommon to hear his music (that dates over a decade) played in car stereo systems throughout America's cities. Tupac continues to have his presence felt not only within the 'hood, but also in suburbs and rural areas too.

In 1992, the artist and producer Dr. Dre released his now infamous album "The Chronic." That was the first hard-core Hip Hop album to be sold to suburban youth and marketed outside the 'hood.[6] With the album's sale, came the rise of the Gangsta Rap era in American mainstream popular culture, where Tupac was given a new audience of

---

[3] Dyson (1996, 2001, and 2004), Bastfield (2002), Cendedive (2003), and Lazin (2003) all regard Tupac as the "ghetto-Saint." He remains a figure that dealt with spiritual matters and concerns, according to these scholars.

[4] This is seen in the research that I did for my MA thesis (2003). Ninety-five percent of the young people interviewed related a spiritual experience to Tupac and how he had helped them, in some way or another through his music.

[5] That which is concerned with any style, music, or language that is older than 6 months to 1 year within Hip Hop culture. The term can also refer to a person, if that person's personality, style, dress, and language are that of "old" and dated over a decade old.

[6] See the sales statistics and the projected demographics that this album was marketed to by studying Sound Scan documents and Dr. Dre's album on http://www.allmusic.com/ (last accessed on December 5th, 2004).

suburban youth. This monumental date took Hip Hop into the living rooms of upper middle class American homes. For one of the first times, suburban youth were gaining a deeper understanding of Black[7] culture, including Tupac's portrayal of Black urban culture.

Tupac's music was not only attractive to urban youth, but also to suburban youth—who were typically White.[8] Tupac's music reached an even broader audience.

Tupac attained iconic status with his murder on September 13, 1996. His image as a ghetto saint went from theoretical to real, and rumors of him still being alive began to grow. Even today, there are groups of people who believe that he is still alive and is planning his return to the music scene.

### *Missional Approaches*

Keeping this in mind, how does the church[9] respond to someone like Tupac? Another question immediately comes to mind, how does the church respond to Hip Hop culture in general? How does the church respond to such seemingly profane lyrics, lifestyle, and life?

In general, the church has not had a very good record of engaging popular culture (e.g. Detweiler and Taylor 2003; Lynch 2005). The Church has had an "us" vs. "them" approach to engaging popular culture, in particular Hip Hop culture. Hip Hop, for the church, is Mammon's evil twin, and must be avoided. However, a full engagement with

---

[7] The word Black will be capitalized in this book. The capitalized word refers to the ethnic group African Americans. When the word is in lower case it will refer to the color black.

[8] The word White will be capitalized in this book. The capitalized word refers to the ethnic group commonly referred to as Anglo, Caucasian, or Euro American. When the word is in lower case it will refer to the color white.

[9] In this book, I will be using this term "church" as the urban church. This church includes, but is not limited to The Black, Latino, emergent, White, protestant, and multicultural church's that exist within the 'hood.

theological and academic rigors must mean that we engage pop culture, and more importantly Hip Hop culture (Lynch 2005: ix).

If we are going to engage with any level of culture then we must first recognize what culture is already telling us. Craig Detweiler and Barry Taylor state, "popular culture must be investigated theologically because it is already studied by the broader culture" (2003: 20). In this case, I ask the question, "what is Tupac already telling us, society, young people, urban culture, and the church?" In addition, how does that translate into a broader understanding of who Jesus is?

Tupac is an enigma for many, including me. Caught between a handgun and the sacredness of the Cross, Tupac was an activist that took his work to heart. Moreover, Tupac was a rap artist that lived his music, and did not merely "rap" it. I desire to know more about why so many young people I have worked with in the past fifteen years have seen Tupac as their "pastor" unlike traditional pastors. I desire to know the theology behind tracks like "Is there a Heaven for A G?," and "Black Jesus." More importantly, I wish to know how to use Tupac's message (within his music, diaries, and videos) to better reach young urban people in greater Los Angeles.

## PART I

## SETTING UP THA STAGE: APPROACHING THE STUDY OF TUPAC SHAKUR AS THE URBAN PROPHET

This book deals with the transformational and theological aspects of Tupac Amaru Shakur. I use ethnohistorical methodologies in understanding Tupac's life and mission, as this opens up new vistas for approaching, understanding, interacting with, responding to and transforming the 'hood (and ourselves).

A few characteristics set this book apart from other missiological studies. First, the focus of this book is on one person, and not a culture as a whole. While Hip Hop culture will be discussed, the focus is not on the culture alone, rather on how the individual, Tupac, influenced and was influenced by the culture as a whole. Along with how that influence translates back to the church and ensuing evangelism from that church. Second, this book deals with the reality of the profane and the harsh living conditions of the 'hood. This includes using language and images that would not traditionally be seen in most theologically based books. Third, this book uses the methodology of ethno-life-history. This is a new method developed with Daniel Shaw that is based on the ethnohistory method. This method focuses on the significant eras in a person's life and how those events translate into the broader context of culture. Since this process is essential, this book also has an autobiographical element.

In Part I, I set the stage as we prepare to investigate the life of Tupac and enter his definition of the 'hood. First, I describe my own approach to the 'hood. I describe my perspective, as I begin to introduce myself and my context and how I came to this topic.

Part I is an introduction to the study so that the "stage" may be set for the rest of the book.

The rest of Part I will focus on the mechanics of the book; program structure, methods, and central research focus. This will then set up the rest of the book which will focus on the Tupac's theological message as derived from Black popular culture, Hip Hop culture, the 'hood, and his own message.

The bold letters in Figure 1, illustrate the area that Part I will be focusing on. Part I connects my own personal life history to Hip Hop, the 'hood, and Black popular culture. It will further illustrate how those areas come together to form the overall structure of the program.

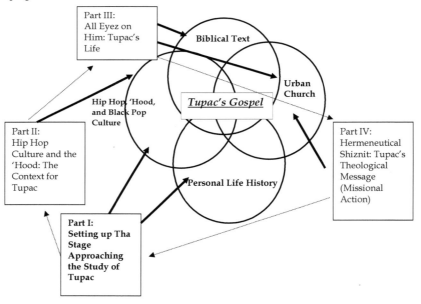

**FIGURE 1**

**FLOW OF THE BOOK PART ONE**

# CHAPTER 1

# MY OWN BAPTISM IN DIRTY WATER

Much of this book revolves around the ethnolifehistory of Tupac. In addition, there is a large amount of research and findings that arise out of my lifelong love affair with Hip Hop. Further, I have spent over ten years ministering and serving in the urban community.

In this chapter, I give the reader a brief insight into my own ethnolifehistory to elaborate on how I am also connected to Hip Hop culture, urban youth, and Tupac. In other words, I give the reader some insight into my history: when I fell in love with Hip Hop and how I came to want to study the life of Tupac. I will briefly discuss my own life and how it connects to the broader scope of Tupac's missiological and theological message.

## *Comin' Up*

I was raised in a Christian home. I grew up in Menard, a small town in central Texas. I was the only "mixed" kid. By that, I mean I was the only kid that was half Mexican and half Black. I looked Black. The Mexican gene must have skipped me. I had the krunk[1] and a strong afro. My skin color was darker than most Mexicans, yet I was lighter than many Blacks. This made for some confusion among both myself and Whites who did not know whether to call me a "nigger" or "spic."

---

[1] A natural look in hair as opposed to the process Jerry Curl or waves.

I still remember the first day of school in Menard. I was wearing Wrangler jeans, Kangaroo shoes, and a Lacrosse multi-colored striped shirt. My hair was slamming[2], and I was ready. When I walked in the classroom, I expected to be greeted and welcomed. Instead, it was a scene right out of a Hollywood film. Everyone was talking and carrying on, the teacher was getting students settled, and then I walked in. It was as if each person in that room was about to die, and they had a second or two to think about it. You could hear a pin drop. I heard one kid say, "Is that a nigger?" While still another said, "What the hell is that?"

Grasping for words—since obviously no one had ever seen someone from "my-kind"—the teacher came up to meet me while she encouraged the other students to carry on. From that day forward, I knew there was something different about me. At the time, I could not put my finger on it nor would I truly appreciate that difference until later in life, but I knew that I was different and that life, as I knew it, would no longer be the same.

Living in Menard, I was constantly reminded of how different I was and how much society did not really value me nor care for me. To give you an example of the type of culture that existed in Menard, when I was in the sixth grade, we had a Halloween party. Students were encouraged to dress up and compete for a prize. A friend of mine decided to dress up as a Ku Klux Klan member. Yes that is right, a Ku Klux Klan member. To make matters worse, he won first place! Not to mention my principal was a former Grand Dragon for the Klan.

My baptism took place in a small Seventh Day Adventist church. I attended a church that said they "loved" everyone and that "all" were created equal in the eyes of God. But, I saw things differently. I was constantly told that the anger that boiled inside of me and took only a small lifting of that lid to be released, was evil and of the Devil. As my pastor told me, "You need to forgive White people Dan. After all, it's because you

---

[2] Meaning, my hair looked really nice and neat.

coloreds do not know how to handle yourselves that you make us Whites upset." Rap music, in its early stages then, became a positive outlet for the rage and anger I felt. I did not know it at the time, but I was being baptized into another culture, a culture that would take me on a journey far larger and longer than I could expect.

The first time I truly fell in love with Hip Hop was on a clear night in 1980 while riding in the back of my mom's car. I was listening to the radio, or lack thereof, and while trying to find my favorite radio station, I came upon a song where someone was actually speaking over the music. They were talking about how great they were, and how bad[3] the other person was. I could not believe what I was hearing. I later came to realize that it was the group Run-DMC. From that point on, I knew I needed more.

When I got back home to tell my friends, I was shunned even more, and told, "That nigger monkey music will never sell, that's all shit!" My love for the music genre grew even deeper.

### *From the Rural to the City*

Those early days in Texas will remain forever etched in my mind. But, after a failed marriage and the strong desire to get me out of that town, my mom decided to move out to California around 1988. It was one of the best decisions she would ever make for the family.

We moved out to Central California into the Monterey Bay area—Seaside to be exact. I always enjoyed the city, and what it had to offer. And even though most people who are born in a small rural town typically prefer that lifestyle, I always wanted the city. There was just more to offer, and Seaside was just that.

By this time in my life I was involved in various extra curricular activities that did not involve Denzel Washington and the Boys and Girls Club. I got involved in gangs.

---

[3] I use the term "bad" here to mean the literal definition, not the street term meaning good.

Ice-Cube's 1990 album, "AmmeriKKKa's Most Wanted," had been released, and I was hooked on the political conscious edge of rap music. I had seen Tupac in concert several times with Digital Underground, and knew even then, that there was something different about him.

At last, the city and urban culture could embrace my unique musical style that made me who I was. Hip Hop opened up the doors and I came running in. Moreover, the city had embraced my "mixed" ethnicity and could deal much better with the fact that I was "mixed" than Menard, Texas ever could. I knew the city was the place for me.

Still, with all this good stuff going on, gangs were an issue, along with urban societal issues, broken homes, drug abuse, and police violence. I was raised to distrust the police and never to go near them, even if they called you. They were not to be trusted. And, for good reason. Until the age of 22, I never met a cop that was not crooked, racist, violent, a liar, or a murderer. In my neighborhood, police were worse than the gangs themselves.

### Police in the 'Hood of Seaside

My first beating from a police officer came on the evening of July 6, 1989. I was walking home with some of my friends after a party, when four cop cars rushed up on us. They placed us against the wall, patted us down and asked us questions about a robbery that took place ten minutes prior. We had not seen it, nor been near. More importantly, we were not involved in it. Still, the officers hand-cuffed us, took us down to the docks, and beat us with their night sticks while still hand-cuffed in the back seat of their patrol car. We were left for dead on the opposite side of town, where we were then arrested for being drunk and disturbing the peace.

N.W.A.'s[4] song, "Fuck The Police," on their "Straight Outta Compton" album, was our ghetto anthem. Moreover, N.W.A. set the tone for urban youth interacting with the police. Ice Cube, Ice-T, Public Enemy, KRS-One, and Too-$hort all set the pedagogy in the late 1980's and early 1990's on how to interact with the police. They also warned the nation of the impending explosion that happened on April 29, 1992—the riots.

## L.A. Riots

When we saw the beating of motorist Rodney King, we all finally felt as though we could rest a little easier. Up until that point, no one believed that police beatings were a common thing in the 'hood. Most people—typically Whites—responded, "Oh those people are just resisting arrest, what else can a policeman do?" We actually believed that the officers would be found guilty—the first time! When we heard the "not guilty" verdict, all of the anger, frustration, hate, and rage exploded within us and discharged into the streets for the nation to see that this was the last straw that any group of people could take. We took all those emotions and let them out on Korean-owned stores, White motorists, security guards, and anyone who represented the White hegemony that we had come to despise.

The L.A. riots were a rupture of societal, economical, and communal networks that had been far too long neglected in the 'hood. The riots demonstrated that there was a deep need in America's ghettos, and that someone needed to pay closer attention. Hip Hop culture was one of the main leaders in this voice.[5]

---

[4] The 1980's gangsta rap group named Niggas With Attitude. Arguably the godfathers of gangsta rap on the West Coast. Originating out of Compton and South Central California. N.W.A. caused much controversy from many of their songs as they discussed urban politics, societal structures, economics, sex and the gangsta lifestyle from a ghetto's perspective.

[5] In this voice, Tupac's first album, "2Pacalypse Now," was released that dealt with the struggles and seriousness of the young Black male in American society. Tupac also highlighted how this problem could not be ignored for much longer.

Sanyika Shakur (A.K.A. Monster Kody Scott) clearly states what happened on that day:

> On April 29, 1992, the world witnessed the eruption of the Crips and Bloods. The scar of over twenty years that had been tucked out of sight and passed off as "just another ghetto problem" burst its suture and spewed blood all across the stomach of America. People watched in amazement as "gang members," soldiers of the Crip army, pelted cars with rocks, sticks, and bottles, eventually pulling civilians from their vehicles and beating them. This was hours after they had routed a contingent of LAPD officers. Troop movements escalated, and Los Angeles was set ablaze. All this began on Florence and Normandie in South Central, the latest Third World Battlefield (1993: xii).

As a participant in the riots of 1992, I can say that it was one of the most cathartic, spiritual, and frightening events of my life. On the one hand, I had the release of over a decade's worth of anger, and on the other, I had the reality that we were destroying our own communities. Having Korean store owners shoot at you while you look for clips to reload your AK-47, is not something that will quickly escape my mind. The riots were hell, but a necessary one to give a stronger voice to the 'hood, and to give Hip Hop a broader audience. Moreover, the riots were important because we as ghetto dwellers had endured the iron fist of police brutality for way too long—police brutality that was relentless; hence making the riots inevitable; it was one racist police beating too many. Now people were beginning to listen.

### *Jesus and the Hip Hop Prophets*

After seeing a good friend of mine shot in front of me seventeen times, and having detectives come to my house to investigate the credit card fraud ring I was in, I decided I needed a change. One of two things would happen to me: I would end up like my friend, or I would end up in jail. Both of those options were not what I wanted.

By 1994, I knew I needed a change. I needed to deal with the anger inside me and deal with my own demons. An older – and much wiser—man was hanging out with us at the time. We all knew he was a pastor, and that he wanted to effect change in the community. Of course, he dressed "funny" and always told "corny" jokes. We would laugh at him, but inside we knew there was something different about him. After my friend was killed, he decided to have a citywide revival. He invited all of us to this event, and in true Black teenage male fashion, we rejected his offer the first time. Still, I knew I needed a change. And I told my friend "Andre" that I would go and see what the meeting was about, just to "be nice." A week later, I was walking down to the front of the church to re-receive Christ and be baptized for the third time in my life. From that point forward I knew I would work in the 'hood with young people.

Hip Hop played a role in all of this. For the first four years of my walk with Christ, Hip Hop was the enemy. In fact, I did not see Tupac as a "prophet" but as a blasphemer and poor role model who needed to be ignored. Sadly[6] enough, I preached this message to many youth. Even worse, I taught that Hip Hop was from the Devil and was not useful in the church because of its initial surface appearance and connection to "worldly influences."

### *Towards a Theology of Hip Hop Culture*

My "fundamental" days were too long for me, but, necessary in order to understand "both sides." Hip Hop remained a friend when I was not. After I was married in 2001, my community of fifteen years decided that my wife was too White, and from the wrong denomination. We were forced out of our community for asking too many questions, and for questioning the elders.

Hip Hop was there. I re-opened the book I had closed on Hip Hop and re-discovered that there was a deeper message within the music, genre, and people that were

---

[6] Meaning, this concept of condemning an entire culture because of a few "bad apples" is preposterous. There is not one single culture that is neither totally evil nor totally righteous. Sadly, refers to the fact that many ministers, pastors, and reverends preach this message and people believe them.

involved in the culture. Tupac, for me, lead the way. The very person I had condemned and taught against became a best friend, and every one of his songs etched itself deeply into my soul as I rediscovered myself and came to an enlightened understanding of who Jesus is.

Hip Hop has always been there. Gordon Lynch argues that Hip Hop culture has permeated almost every facet of American mainstream culture (2005). Bakari Kitwana suggests that there needs to be a critical examination of the culture in order to better understand the current trends and styles within youth culture (2004). Kanye West, in "The College Dropout" album, argues that God loves the hustlers, pimps, killers, prostitutes, and people that society would otherwise not deal with. Tupac questions if there is a Heaven for real Niggaz. Tupac changed the letter "S" to "Z" to indicate a deeper meaning of the word suggesting a "Class" status rather than the person. Robin Kelly (1994: 207-212) agrees, and further suggests that the term can permeate skin color as well. This is an area we will discuss further in the book. Big Syke asks if the church can even handle him, while KRS-One has suggested that Hip Hoppers need to start their own church (2003). God loves the Hip Hoppers.

These are missional and evangelistic recommendations from characters that would not typically be considered "prophets" or even pastors. However, Hip Hop culture has been ignored by the church far too long and now needs attention. Moreover, I believe that it is part of Jesus' mission and that He Himself is involved in the culture.

To engage this culture means that we will have to get past the "F" word and thong underwear—these are merely symptoms of a deeper issue. To be stuck in this arena of language and style will only hinder the Gospel message being preached. A war is happening today in our city streets, Tupac was one of the first to illuminate it, bring light to the darkness, and put a voice to the fact that it needs to be dealt with. Hip Hop matters.

More importantly, Tupac deserves discussion because of his martyr image and prophet persona. As we move deeper into the 21$^{st}$ century, a more progressive, aggressive, and non-oppressive theology of the 'hood is needed in order to evangelize urban youth—Tupac has a message for us. This is his message.

# CHAPTER 2

## STUDYING TUPAC:
## LEARNING THE ICON

In this chapter, I will introduce the scope and structure of the book. Further, this section will deal with the arrangement and/organization of the book.

As stated prior, I did not care for Tupac in my early years as a Christian. I was a fan of his in my young years, but when I became a Christian I lost my culture and identity. While doing field research for my Masters degree, I was interviewing urban youth. The name Tupac was the single name that kept coming to the surface. Youth continually told me that he was their "mentor" and "prophet." It became clear to me that Tupac needed a second look and a broader study completed than that done by Michael Eric Dyson (2001).

There are significant theological issues that arise from Tupac's life that push me to ask deeper questions. How do we contend with Jesus and the F word in the same sentence? Does God deal with the profane? Did God design language, and if so, what about its profanity? Is Tupac "saved?"

### *Introduction: Tupac*

I shall not fear no man but God
Though I walk through the valley of death


I shed so many tears (if I should die before I wake)

Please God walk with me (grab a nigga and take me to Heaven)[1]

Every culture has its icons. Here in America, there are many icons: Marilyn Monroe, Elvis Presley, John F. Kennedy, John Wayne, Martin Luther King, Malcolm X, Johnny Carson, Michael Jackson and many others like them have etched their own philosophy on our lives in one way or another. Tupac is an American icon too.

He was iconic in his style, life, language, and messages. Tupac lived the life he talked about[2] and was true to his word. Further, Michael Eric Dyson, in the documentary Tupac VS. (Peters 2001), discusses how Tupac's music was like Gospel music; he lived the life he talked about in his music. If you are a gospel singer, this is great, but if you are a rapper, then it becomes a problem, being further complicated if you are a gangsta rapper. Moreover, Tupac was one of the few rappers who put meaning and passion to every one of his songs. Most artists have two-three tracks they really work on, and the rest of the album is just filler music. But Tupac put heart and soul into every song. More importantly, each one of his songs told a story and had purpose.[3]

Michael Eric Dyson states,

> Tupac is perhaps the representative figure of his generation. In his haunting voice can be heard the buoyant hopefulness and the desperate hopelessness that mark the outer perimeters of the Hip Hop culture he eagerly embraced, as well as the lives of the millions of youth who admired and adored him (2001: 13).

Further, as one young man put it to me, "This was the realest nigga you could find. I mean, he was a pastor to me. He helped me through some deep shit in my life" (Hodge 2003: Interview 9 "Miguel").

---

[1] Tupac, "So Many Tears" from the album "All Eyez on Me' (1995).

[2] For a deeper understanding of this see *Tupac Vs.* (Peters 2001).

[3] See Appendix A for a pictorial view of Tupac.

Michael Datcher, Kwame Alexander, and Mutulu Shakur further state that, "Tupac Amaru Shakur was ours. He presented himself to our generation like a gift offering. No ribbons, no bows, no paper. He came in a plain box and he came opened" (1997: Introduction). Tupac was relevant to many, and gave voice to a generation that for years had been underrepresented: the Hip Hop generation.

This Hip Hop Generation concept was developed by Bakari Kitwana (2003: 3-25) in which he parallels the Hip Hop generation with Generation X. He argues that Generation X is predominantly White, male, and upper middle class. For Kitwana, the Hip Hop generation represents the same generation, but is more contextual for the urban culture. Further, to date, Tupac's album sales topple sixty-five million and continue to grow.[4]

For me, as a follower of Christ and missiology, I am compelled to study and understand Tupac's theological message. What makes Tupac have a theological message as compared to 50 Cent? Tupac was one of the first rappers to conjoin the profane and the sacred. Tupac's scandalous union of these two concepts made him into a controversial figure for some, but also made him a hero for others.

This union intrigues me. As a result, a theology of the profane emerges. Tupac embodied both the theological and the profane, while still embodying a Christ-like image that permeated many of his songs. This is one reason why so many young people loved him. More importantly, Tupac was a man of his word, he was credible. When he spoke of 'hood violence, you knew he had lived it, "been there, and done that." Teresa Reed states:

> Tupac's experiences afforded him the credentials to preach about the social decay that gave rise to his tragic and famous persona. While Marvin Gaye could sing about war, he had never actually been on a battlefield, on the front line, in the direct line of fire. Tupac, on the other hand, had been there. His

---

[4] As seen from Billboard archives and www.allmusic.com.

descriptions of ghetto life are so disarmingly graphic because they are often his accounts of situations he knew of first hand (2003: 156).

Tupac had lived a life that matched the life of his listener. Even if the listener was White and lived in the suburbs, he could still relate to certain elements—be it the party, the money, or the women.

Tupac argued for a spiritual revolution and for community building (Dyson 2002: 204-206). Tupac was concerned with 'hood matters and for 'hood youth—Black, Latino, White, Asian, and women. In that same vein, many women loved Tupac. Tupac was both a father and sex image to them (Ardis 2004; Dyson 2001: 21-46; and Reed 2003: 151-152). Tupac clearly defined the different elements of women, for him there were three types of women; (1) a woman, (2) a Ho, and (3) a bitch. Many women would come to agree with him and define women in these three categories themselves.

Tupac was also concerned with social justice and for bettering the community as a whole, righting social injustices, bettering the person, helping the young and gaining wisdom from the older generation.[5] Tupac connected with people and gave to people out of his heart. This was evident in his connection to the audience and how the audience would respond to him during a concert or in public. To take this a step further, Tupac would frequent clubs without security and would just be "hanging out." This was something that made him an even more popular figure—someone who was powerful and popular, but could "hang" with the normal people.

I did not know this about Tupac. I, along with many others, was fooled by the media's analysis of Tupac. I fell into the public raging rapids of fear that floods the mind with images of a thug, a murderer, and hooligan. As I have developed an understanding of Tupac's life, I have found that his life was much deeper and connected to God than I

---

[5] This is seen in his giving amounts and his own fan letters (Sims 1999). Tupac was a community activist, but many did not know this because the media typically followed Tupac only when he was in trouble.

had ever imagined. But many have not taken the time to study to understand the person. Rather, many have torn down the person. This is one of the primary reasons why I have chosen to study the theological message of Tupac for a stronger evangelism within the 'hood.

### *The Book Structure*

The thrust of this book is an overview of Tupac Shakur's spiritual and missiological gospel message. The data for this book was gathered using a variety of methods focused on Tupac's life, music, poetry, and writings. This book utilizes the ethnolifehistory method and uses qualitative content analysis, as well as case studies to bring validity and reliability to the study.

Ethnolifehistory is an excellent method to study the life of a person. First, the method is narrative, based on stories in the urban context. By examining the story, how that story is shaped by different events in culture and then observing the major cultural eras, we are able to grasp a deeper understanding of that culture—or in this case, a person. Tupac told stories and his life was a story. By using this method, we will be able to better see the deeper meanings that underlie Tupac's life.

Second, this methodology combines other methodologies and is by nature more well rounded. It can utilize interviews, active interviews, case studies, ethnographic data, and even surveys. It has both a qualitative and quantitative quality to it. In the urban context, the story is what matters. Ethnolifehistory allows for that to happen, and allows the person's life to be seen in all aspects—the good, the bad, and the ugly.

Lastly, I like developing new concepts. This method is new, and I plan to use it again for further research. I adapted this method from ethnohistory that observes cultures and their major eras (Tippett 1973; 1980). However, this method focuses on the culture and not the individual person. I was able to adapt this, and make it relevant for the urban context.[6] I have also adapted it to fit this book so that every part of Tupac flows out of the different eras within his own life.

This book is largely centered around Judeo Christian philosophies and mantras. While Tupac himself embodied theologies from The Nation of Islam, the Five Percent Nation, and Rastafarianism time did not allow me to engage further into these theologies. However, Tupac was connected to those faiths as well and it deserves noting. Please understand I mean no disrespect to these faiths or am I ignoring their rich traditions and histories. I am simply focusing on one particular faith tradition.

The book is divided into parts. A diagram will begin each part, to enable the reader to follow the process. Part I—Setting Up tha Stage: Approaching the Study of Tupac. I began this process by setting the stage with my own story, and the major eras in my life. Every book has a personal element. In this case, I will be using my own story to set up the study and to help the reader see how I came to this topic. This section will detail the book structure and give the skeletal dynamics of my research project.

Part II—Hip Hop Culture and the 'Hood[7]: The Context for Tupac. In this section, I will be discussing the broad context in which Tupac operated. Hip Hop culture, rap music, Black popular culture, and Thug Life will be discussed in this section. This will have two different views: macro and micro. Hip Hop and Black popular culture will be the macro, while Tupac's own view will be the micro.

Part III—All Eyez on Him: Tupac's Life. This section will deal with Tupac's life, his eras[8], how his life was shaped by outside forces, that eventually led to his death. I will

---

[6] I will further this explanation in Chapter 3.

[7] Throughout this book I use non-standard spelling for some words to reflect their pronunciation and emphasize their use both from Tupac and Hip Hoppers.

[8] The different life stages that can last for months or years. For the purpose of this book, Tupac's eras lasted years; they consisted of significant life stages and seasons.

22

also be analyzing certain major eras in Tupac's life, providing insight into both their societal and theological meaning. This section will present the major findings from my research in this section.

Part IV—Hermeneutical Shiznit: Tupac's Theological Message. In this section, I examine Tupac's message by drawing from his music and poetry. This section offers new theory to the field of missiology. Further, I will provide practical insights into new evangelical methods, appropriate for the 'hood, developed from Tupac's life. It will also provide the conclusions and recommendations from my research.

## Purpose and Goals

The purpose of this research is to explore the missiological significance of Tupac Shakur in order to better reach Hip Hop youth.[9] Tupac's theological message deserves to be studied in order to gain a broader understanding and provide new direction for evangelism in the 21$^{st}$ century in the urban context.

The goals of this book are to utilize my understanding of Tupac's lyrical messages to reach Hip Hop youth and to present an evangelistic tool for the urban and multicultural church as a whole.

## Significance

Personally, I believe this research will better serve theological studies as the field develops for the 21$^{st}$ century. A stronger understanding of Tupac will help urban youth workers serve the young people they are ministering to.

---

[9] These can be a variety of ethnicities and from different socioeconomic status'. This term is not limited to just Black or ghetto youth. Hip Hop youth are a vast and growing population that embodies an ample variety of ideologies, ethnicities, lifestyles, and pedagogies.

Missiologically speaking, little to no work is being done from an "insiders" perspective on Hip Hop culture, particularly on the life of Tupac. Ultimately, there will be a theology of the profane that can benefit urban missions as a whole, as well as the Christian academic community.

As a researcher, I am biased towards Hip Hop music, postmodernism, and inner city youth. Questioning authority is a trademark of my life. These all compose my biases that influence this particular research project.

## Central Research Issue

The central research issue is to explore Tupac Shakur's missiological message within his music and life. The main research questions this book seeks to answer are:

1. What was Tupac's life about?
2. How do urban youth identify with and view Hip Hop culture as it relates to Tupac?
3. What is the theological and societal framework for Black Popular Culture in which Tupac operated within?
4. What is Tupac's theological message?
5. What was Tupac's gospel message?

This book will focus on the life of one person: Tupac Shakur. Further, this project is concerned with Tupac's life within each era and how it relates back to culture for a broader understanding of theology within the urban context.

I am limiting my study to one of Hip Hop's better-known artists, Tupac Shakur. While Hip Hop encompasses a variety of cities, Los Angeles is the scope of study when looking at popular culture.

This book is not an in-depth study of the ethnomusicological aspects of Tupac's music. Rather, it focuses more on a missiological perspective within an urban context. Ethnomusicology brings new concepts and dimensions to the discussion.

Black popular culture will remain at the center of the main culture studied for Tupac; which is not limited to just Black people—Asians, Latinos, and Whites are included in this culture as well. Blacks, Whites, and Latinos will also be a focus in this study.

While many other youth listen to rap music and Tupac, the nature of this study will delimit youth from ages 15-22 in the inner city.

## Definition of Terms

Since the study of Hip Hop culture is relatively new in theological institutions, it is necessary to define some key terms that will be used in this book. I have laid out some of the more relevant terms that I will be using so that the reader is aware of the language being used. The urban context has a language all its own. Therefore, I will define exactly what I am discussing in this book.

- Tupac Shakur: is defined as, the ghetto theologian and renowned Hip Hop artist that passed away on September 9, 1996 from gunshot wounds. His songs and life inspired many to see him as a saint, prophet, and ghetto messiah that would provide insight for many. Tupac, in his lyrics, presented many different messages about who Jesus was, the personhood of Jesus, new directions for the church, and a new understanding of the cross and suffering. Tupac's death only heightened his fame and made him into a martyr of Hip Hop culture and urban community. His is the central figure of this study.

- Inner city youth culture: is the youth culture that represents the "ghetto" or neighborhoods that have been traditionally impoverished, oppressed, and typically within city limits. It is the lifestyle and worldview that exists within these ghetto enclaves that comprises inner city youth culture. Now, This term is rapidly changing and is in flux, however, Edward Soja (2000), Bakari Kitwana (2005), and Andreana Clay (2003: 1346-1350) argue that the 'hood is rapidly changing geographic locations into a suburban setting. Soja (2000) argues that within the next fifteen years there will be fundamental geographic upheaval of the ghetto to what we now know as suburbia (Soja 2000: 396-405). In other words, what we think of as "urban" now—inner city, 'hood—will soon be associated with geographical regions that resemble the suburbs.

- The Urban Postmodern: can take on many different meanings. For the purpose of this study it refers to the culture of people that resemble the characteristics of Postmodernity: communal, holding no absolute truths, meta-narrative related, and the acute ability to question authority all within an urban context.

- Theology of the Profane: In an attempt to gain an understanding of the profane, or that which is negative, foul, perverse, irreverent, sacrilegious, and blasphemous there must be a biblical perspective in which to gain a deeper theological, spiritual, and saintly message from these "profane" issues.

- The Niggaz: This is a contested word, but it was part of Tupac's vocabulary. Moreover, it is in the vocabulary of many urban youth. This term, as it is used in the literature, identifies a class and socioeconomic position. A Nigga, as described by Boyd (2002) Kelley (1994), is a person from the working class generation of Blacks; the blue-collar and street dwelling person that also represents Tupac's Thug Life image: the downtrodden and marginalized. For Tupac it also meant, Never Ignorant Getting Goals Accomplished. This term can also supersede racial arenas and be used to solely describe class and socioeconomic positions.

- Thug Life: (The Hate U Give Little Infants Fucks Everyone). The Thug, for Tupac and in this study, did not mean the literal definition of the word. Thug for him meant the marginalized, the gang member, the pregnant teen mom, and/or the person that does not "appear" to be the normal. Tupac gave the 'hood a new "Gospel" message within the Thug Life mantra. This "Gospel" message was about hope, vision, and acceptance. Tupac also emphasized that Heaven does accept you as you are through Christ, despite what the traditional church may state. This is the theological discussion I will have at the conclusion of my book based on the research findings on Tupac.

- Hip Hop Youth: this is a variety of ethnicities that encompasses many different backgrounds. While Hip Hop is global and is in almost all levels of society in the United States, I am primarily concerned with youth that are from an inner city background and who are involved in Hip Hop culture; ages ranging from thirteen to twenty.

- Urban and Multicultural Church: this church could encompass the Black church, the Pentecostal church, the Latin Church, and/or multicultural urban emergent churches.

- Ghetto Saint: I will be using this term to focus on part of Tupac's character. Now, I am not suggesting that Tupac was a "model" Christian for everyone. However, he did present an image of a person who had aspirations of a Holy life and Holy virtues as they related to the 'hood. In other words, Tupac was a saint in that he was able to articulate different theological matters such as death, love, and salvation. Tupac also aspired to live a virtuous life, even though he did not succeed at it many times. In his heart, he was aspiring to live a better life and be an example for others to follow. This was seen in both his music and his poetry which connected deeply to people. The Catholic Church defines saint as, "holy people and human people who lived extraordinary lives. Each saint the Church honors responded to God's invitation to use his or her unique gifts. God calls each one of us to be a saint."[10] Based on this definition, I will argue that Tupac was a saint within a Hip Hop context.

- Natural Theologian. Michael Eric Dyson refers to "Natural Law Theologians" (2001: 210-211), a person from the street that fashions themselves after the Old Testament creed of death, life, God, and love (Dyson 2001: 211-212). However, I use this term to refer to Tupac as an unrefined, organic, grassroots, pre-evangelistic type of 'hood preacher that can begin conversations about God with hard core Hip Hoppers in which most traditional pastors cannot. Tupac was just that.

- Tupac's Spirituality: This term refers to Tupac's spiritual connections. In other words, Tupac's everyday association with God, life, the search for meaning, love, and salvation as seen in his music, poetry, and interviews.

This is the grounds for this study. In the next chapter, I will be discussing my methods that will be utilized in this study.

---

[10] Taken from http://www.americancatholic.org/Features/SaintofDay/default.asp Last accessed on Tuesday December 19, 2006.

# CHAPTER 3

# BRINGING TUPAC'S GOSPEL TO LIFE

In this chapter, I discuss the process used to gather the data for this book and ultimately arrive at Tupac's gospel message. While ethnolifehistory is the main method being utilized, two other methods are used. Qualitative content analysis and case studies are also employed to support ethnolifehistory and to bring validity to the results. The overlying method used in this book is ethnolifehistory which also embodies other methods that I will illuminate in this chapter. I did not originally plan to use ethnolifehistory. I felt that more conventional methods such as interviews and case studies were more appropriate. However, for studying a person's life and discovering the events that shaped that person's life, ethnolifehistory was chosen.

### *Tupac as a Study*

To approach a person's life and to study it, one must take special care that the individuals themselves are not "lost in translation." In other words, the person's true words and content must be used, and the researcher's own personal opinion must be minimized. Tupac was not someone who could easily be understood. His life, character, language, and philosophy were complex. Yet, there remained a simplistic way to his life.

Due to such variety in Tupac's life, I needed a method that could encompass the entire scale of his life, while still paying homage to his needs and views as they pertain to the 'hood and broader context: The United States. The ethnohistory method suited this almost perfectly. However, it needed some modifications if it were to work on a person.

For example, what sets this method apart from life narrative and an ethnographic study? Moreover, what makes this method strong enough to stand on its own when the researcher could use life narrative and ethnographic studies? Ethnolifehistory is a method that deals with the events and life eras that occur within a person's life and uses those events to see how they shaped the broader culture. In contrast, Yamaguchi (1999) discusses the event history method. This method looks at the life of a society, but uses a quantitative approach in gathering the number of times a certain event happens. Ethnolifehistory studies how the broader culture and context have shaped a persons life (e.g. Tippett 1980). Life narrative focuses more on a person's life story without encompassing the eras and how each of those eras was significant. Jude Tiersma (1999) does a similar study in her book project using life narrative for her methodology. In contrast, the ethnographic study deals with a familial approach to the culture and/or a family, and therefore not dealing with eras of one particular person (Silverman 2000: 32-36; Bernard 2000: 190-193).

This method, the ethnolifehistory, is a combination of the life narrative and ethnographic study, but now the researcher can look at the significant eras in a single person's life and analyze their influence. Ethnolifehistory became the method of choice in looking at Tupac' life. In this fashion, we are now able to look into Tupac's life and see what drove him, shaped him, made him laugh, cry, who he loved, how he loved, and what his epistemological views were of life and society were.

## *Ethnohistory as a Method*

Ethnohistory is neither a discipline in itself nor an interdisciplinary field. Rather, as William Fenton asserts, "Ethnohistory is a way of getting at certain problems in culture history" (1962: 2-3). It is neither an anthropological view of history nor an historical view of anthropology (Tippett 1973:1). Once again, this method is not to be confused with the method event history analysis. Event history analysis method is concerned with the patterns and correlates of the occurrences of events within a culture (Yamaguchi 1991). While there are similar aspects of this method to ethnohistory, even history analysis is more concerned with means, medians, and modes of a culture while emphasizing the statistical analysis rather than the qualitative aspects of the culture.

Alan Tippett argues that ethnohistory is a vehicle for understanding different aspects of a culture (Linton 1936: 403), he states,

> Ethnohistory is a technique for considering cultural data spatially and sequentially. The data itself is organized into traits or elements, and these in turn into spatial patterns which we term complexes and maybe into even larger configurations sometimes called activities (Tippett 1973:1).

In using ethnohistory, the researcher attempts to look at the significant moments in a culture and how those moments interact, relate, differ, interrelate, and ultimately come together to shape and form that particular culture. Philip Dark states that to reconstruct the culture of an ethnic group, the ethnohistorian is faced with first examining their data analytically before turning to synthesis (1957: 231).

Analysis and synthesis are reserved until the proper data has been collected from the culture and its informant. The ethnohistorian's goal is to produce a type of historical "trail" that highlights the significant events in a culture's history. Philip Dark states:

> The ethnohistorian has to construct a picture of things as they really were and of events as they really happened. The investigators sense of coherency and continuity rests on a feeling for the way in which the dimensions of time and space are structured and form a framework for the exposition of the culture of the ethnic group. All data must be carefully related, and not to an imaginary picture. For the picture to make sense its relation to the evidence must be apparent (1957: 231-232).

The method takes on three types that the ethnohistorian may use. The first is cross sectional (see Figure 2), the second is institutional, and the third is the cultural continuum (e.g. Tippett 1973: 2-3; Dark 1957: 231-278). The first, cross sectional, is a type of scheme that consists of a series, or functionally related, picture of the institutional aspects and variations of the ethnic group (Dark 1957: 233). In this type, the sense of the culture's development is largely obtained by period following period (Dark 1957: 233-234; Fenton 1962: 8-9). "The emphasis in the Cross-sectional type is the synchronic" (Dark 1957: 234). Susan Rasmussen (1999) is an example of how the cross sectional type is used. She uses the type to examine the slave narrative in Tuareg Culture. In Rasmussen's study she asks a central question for her study,

> What is the role of the classic "slave narrative" in a society characterized by contradiction and ambiguity: internal precolonial stratification on the one hand, and on the other, external marginality in relation to the postcolonial nation-state(1999: 2)?

In this study, Rasmussen uses the method in the similar fashion, but begins to see how different native's lives are affected by cultural change, and how their lives affected culture as well.

In Figure 2, each of the periods of the culture are sectioned off. The researcher then analyzes each period in relation to the entire culture's existence. In this way, the researcher is able to identify significant moments within each of those periods.

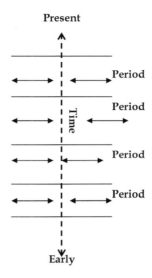

**FIGURE 2**

**CROSS SECTIONAL APPROACH**
(Dark 1957:258)

The second type of ethnohistory is institutional (See Figure 3), the development aspects over time are prominent and synchronic aspects are minor (Dark 1957: 237; Tippett 1973: 2-3). The subject might be social, economic, and political; the data only being employed as a means of developing fully the main theme (c.f. Dark 1957: 238). This type might be thought of as a functional study in time. In practice, the main theme is sub-divided into necessary descriptive components forming a configuration developed synchronically and diachronically (Dark 1957: 238). Dark further states:

> Another modification of this type would be that where a group of institutions were treated relatively equally in their development aspects but related to the total cultural setting at certain periods. The larger the number of such units chosen the greater the descriptive difficulty of developing the relationships

between them at the synchronic level. This leads to a choice of convenient periods at which to relate the various institutions under consideration, and finally to the device of considering such relationships under a separate descriptive section (1957: 238).

Both Tippett (1973,1980) and Terraciano (1998) used this type in their studies.

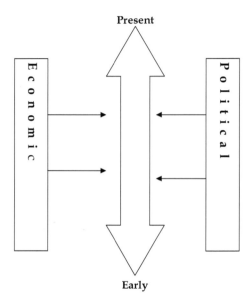

**FIGURE 3**

**INSTITUTIONAL SYNTHESIS**
(Dark 1957: 262)

The third type of ethnohistory is cultural continuum, (Figure 4), which focuses more on spatial and temporal aspects of a culture. This cultural continuum is a concept derived from Ralph Linton's "The Study of Man" (1936). Linton suggests that cultures in general have a continuum that is changing continually. He states, "Throughout the length of the cultural continuum, therefore, traits are constantly being added and other traits lost" (Linton 1936: 295). For the purpose of this study I am focusing in on Hip Hop culture's continuum and how Tupac affected that continuum. This continuum, as suggested by Linton, is present in every society and culture throughout the world. The continuum is therefore made up of many different traits. These traits thus leave a mark and the culture begins to define how each trait affects it; "Every culture is not only a continuum but a continuum in a constant state of change" (Linton 1936: 295-296). Figure 4 presents a basic understanding of the cultural continuum process in ethnohistory. Both the cross sectional and institutional types aim to study the whole cultural unit; the former tends to sacrifice temporal continuity for structural unity while the latter emphasizes temporal development to the loss of structural uniformity (Dark 1957: 243). However, with the cultural continuum type the scheme maintains an even balance between synchronic and diachronic aspects of the culture (Dark 1957; Tippett 1973). "The culture of the ethnic group is shown developing over time, expanding or contracting spatially, its contents and structure altering and readjusting as it changes" (Dark 1957: 243). For the cultural continuum type, synthesis is spatial and temporal (e.g. Tippett 1973).

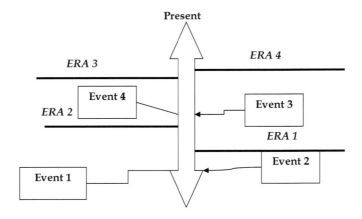

**FIGURE 4**

**CULTURAL CONTINUUM PROCESS**

Figure 4 illustrates that within the cultural continuum, you are looking at moments, eras, and periods in the culture's life and how those events affected the culture as a whole. I asked questions such as:

- How did this particular event in Tupac's life develop over time?
- How might this event have affected and influenced Tupac and/or Hip Hop culture as whole?
- How long did this period last for Tupac?
- Why did it come about?
- How did the context in which the culture is in, affect this period?

In Alan Tippett's (1980) study of Fijian culture, he looked at Fijian culture between the periods of 1835-1905; studying the key eras and events that influenced the culture and how those events formed and shaped the over all culture. Tippett uses the data gathered to form his conclusions and recommendations (1980:62-64). The cultural continuum is the part of ethnohistory that I have incorporated in to ethnolifehistory because of its overall analysis.

Another dimension of the cultural continuum process is called Upstreaming. This term was innovated by William Fenton (1962) who describes it as restructuring the sequence of events "against the tide of history going from the known present to the unknown past" (Fenton 1962:12). In other words, the researcher would trace the single event sequentially, to determine the causes, effect, and affects on the culture overall. Upstreaming has its benefits because it allows the researcher to trace an event and gain an overall scope of the event and its significance.

## Ethnolifehistory as a Method

The ethnohistory method is an ideal method for studying different aspects of a culture's development over time. However, with the advent of postmodern study and research (c.f. Gubrium and Holstein 2003), a more specific and narrative method is needed when approaching a person's life. Gubrium and Holstein argue that postmodern research is a more community and communal feel. The researcher must be in touch with their audience and see them more than just "subjects and objects" (2003: 22-25). Therefore, *ethnolifehistory* is the preferred method. This method also allows the researcher to investigate the significant changes in that particular ethnic culture. However, all of the uses of this method have been on cultures as a whole.[1] For this study,

---

[1] This is not to suggest that I have done an exhaustive search for the uses of the method. Merely in the amount of time that I have done this research, I have found no one using this method to study a single person in a culture.

I focused using the method to study the aspects and significant eras in a persons life; the person being Tupac Shakur.

I focused on the cultural continuum type, for the method *ethnolifehistory*, as I felt that it provided me with the best use of the entire method. I am able to investigate Tupac's life while focusing on the moments, eras, and significant changes that affect Hip Hop and contemporary American Popular Culture as a whole. This type is also diachronic, meaning that I am able to study different moments across periods of time and how those moments developed.

Tupac's complex life affected Hip Hop culture's continuum.[2] That affect is still felt today—even after ten years since his death. The ethnolifehistory of Tupac gives me the researcher adequate room to investigate how Tupac became such an enigma. Moreover, it allows me to ask why so many young people are still enamored by what Tupac's music.

Another important aspect of using ethnolifehistory to study the life of Tupac is to better understand the phenomenon as to how his music continues to remain "fresh" and new. By Hip Hop cultural standards of music, and due to Tupac's time period (mid 1990's), he can be considered "old-school."[3] Most Hip Hop artist's music during this period, are now viewed as "old school." However, Tupac's music and lyrics are still considered relevant today as during his lifetime. Moreover, his lyrics have been reconfigured with contemporary beats from Hip Hop producers such as Eminem and Kanye West.

The cultural continuum of the ethnolifehistory of Tupac will show that Tupac affected many different dimensions of Rap music genres such as: gangsta rap, political

---

[2] See Appendix G to see how Tupac affected Hip Hop cultural continuum.

[3] In other words out of date, old, old fashioned, and/or classic.

rap, party rap and Christian rap. Tupac is one of the only Rap artists that has influenced all sub-genres of rap music and remains a Hip Hop social and political figure. Ethnohistory will help to uncover why this is so.

In this study, I used archival, book, and interview material (from archival DVD's and interviews) to gather the data necessary to investigate Tupac's cultural significance. As Allan Tippett states, "A good ethnohistorian must have a wide knowledge of the language of the documents he is studying" (1973:7). In Tippett's study (1973, 1980), he had to have knowledge of Fijian language; especially ancient Fijian language. For this study, language is no different. Even though English is used, Hip Hop language is different from proper contemporary American English. Moreover, Tupac influenced the language through his lyrics as well. For this reason, I focused on fifty-two archival poems from Tupac's life.

These were then combined with other archival information found on seven DVD's about Tupac's life.[4] They then were labeled and given significance in order to view the different eras in Tupac's life. I attempted to interview Tupac's family, however I was unable to contact them directly. The interviews were only used as a supplement to the other data gathered about Tupac.

Therefore, for this book, I have identified Tupac's life eras as follows:[5]

- Military Mind (1971-1981)
- Criminal Grind (1981-1988)
- The Ghetto Is Destiny (1989-1992)
- Outlaw (1992-1995)
- Ghetto Saint (1996-Present)

---

[4] See Appendix J for a complete list of the material used in Tupac's ethnolifehistory.

[5] These categories are adapted from the documentary film *Tupac Vs.* (Peters 2001).

## Longitudinal Cultural Process Compared to a Person's Cultural Process

As seen in the ethnohistory studies I have researched, each uses a longitudinal process. For example, Keener (1999) addresses and describes the warfare tactics used by the Iroquois against fortified settlements using ethnohistory as his method. Dark (1957) argues that ethnolifehistory is a multidimensional method. Fenton (1962) argues against ethnolifehistory and makes substantial arguments that the method is overall weak and very similar to ethnography (1962:2-23). Rasmussen (1999) uses a longitudinal ethnohistory approach to analyze narratives about past servitude not only with micro issues of social stratification or African slavery, but also with broader issues of inter-textuality, motivations, and the relationship between oral accounts of past servitude by two persons.

This means that entire cultures were studied and observed to see how different traits in the cultural continuum have affected the culture as a whole. However, as previously stated, I have found no work that has used ethnolifehistory to study a person and/or a person's cultural significance.

I would argue that ethnolifehistory could be used to study many different individuals that have been significant in different cultures. For example, Gandhi could be seen to have affected the cultural continuum for many different cultures and would warrant an in-depth study of his ethnolifehistory. Elvis is yet another popular culture icon that has affected many to this date as well. Martin Luther King Jr., Malcolm X, Hitler, and even Jesus are all examples of potential ethnolifehistory studies using the cultural continuum trait.

Since the cultural continuum trait looks at the contributions, eras, and significant moments in a culture, it is the perfect fit to look into a person's life and use the same process one uses to investigate an entire culture except on the micro level of a person's life. Because the method is formed around qualitative data, the researcher is free to gather major data from interviewees, archival material, family members, local data, and even media data. In the end you will arrive at a complex set of results that will begin to unwind the significance of this person's life. This is what was done in my current study of Tupac.

For Tupac I was able to rely on oral history mainly gathered from seven DVD archival documentaries, and two archival CD audio interviews. Most of the data from the Hip Hop world is not written, but spoken. The use of current technology such as DVD, emails, and electronic documents make it easier for the ethnolifehistorian to gather accurate data and import it into their research. Key words, phrases, and sentences were then taken from the material to analyze Tupac's ethnolifehistory.

## Qualitative Content Analysis and Lyrical Case Studies

Qualitative research is largely engaging with people. David Altheide states, "Research is a social process. The social and cultural environments in which one operates as an investigator contribute to how one views research problems, data sources, and methodological approaches" (1996: 4). To gather data from eight television, ten musical, and eight film sources I modified the quantitative content analysis method to fit a qualitative study, and invite that "social-process" in, as Altheide would argue. I performed a qualitative content analysis of Black popular culture. This content analysis focused on examining themes that arose from Black popular culture based on several criteria. These criteria were derived from two sources: literature and Tupac's own life history.[6] These criteria are societal frameworks (the key theme in the social structure and/or social focus within Black popular culture), class and socioeconomics (those cultural systems that are concerned with money, power, and class position), sexuality

---

[6] Learned on earlier research on Tupac's ethnolifehistory.

(this includes male and female roles within Black popular culture and sexual communications between people), cultural exposition (those areas that are unique to Black popular culture and the politics of identity, representation, and gangstaism), and spirituality (those elements in the culture that are concerned with God, Christ, the Holy Spirit and theology). The data for these five areas was derived from three key areas of Black popular culture: music, television, and films.[7]

Studying the key areas of Black Popular culture is an important step in the methodological process which helps inform me how Tupac's relationship is connected to the broader aspects of Black popular culture and Hip Hop culture.[8] This is important in understanding how culture affects Tupac, and how he affected those cultures.

This data on the relationship between Tupac and Black popular culture was gathered using methods that were derived from Riffe, Lacy, and Fico (2005) and Altheide (1996). These authors argue that qualitative data analysis of media content is just as effective as quantitative. Furthermore, researchers are able to gain a deeper insight into meanings outside of a quantitative analysis (Riffe, Lacy, and Fico 2005: 173-174).

Qualitative content analysis is a relatively new qualitative method being used in the social sciences (A.Turner 2004; James 2004; Altheide 1996; Riffe, Lacy, and Fico 2005). While this method does not utilize the popular quantitative aspect, the qualitative facet allows the researcher to grasp themes as opposed to singular events or words that are then used to correlate numerical meanings. These themes are also tied into narrative—narrative is a staple within Black popular culture and can be traced back to Africa (Lincoln and Mamiya 1990: 300; Loeterman and Kalin 2004). Qualitative content

---

[7] Black literature—such as the poetry and writings by Maya Angelou—were not used as sources for this study on Black popular culture due to time constraints.

[8] These are two separate cultures, while Hip Hop is a part of Black popular culture; Hip Hop is much larger and not relegated to merely Blacks.

analysis allowed me to gain a broad scope of the major themes that arose from television, music, and film.

Building upon Tupac's life eras from his ethnolifehistory, I have investigated Tupac's musical message by studying his music between the years 1988-2000.[9] The different themes in Tupac's life were used to gain a broader knowledge of each song, poem, and musical piece to gain further perspective on the theology of the profane. In addition, this was the method used to gather Tupac's theological message from his music.

Listening to Tupac's music, between 1988-2000, gave me deep insights into Tupac's theological message. Hidden deep within every song is a message of his life, philosophy, epistemology, and understanding of God. For Tupac, each song took on one of three different themes: the participant, the watcher, or allegorical narratives from his life or lives around him. Using Altheide's (1996: 23-42) method for gathering qualitative media, I was able to gather up all of Tupac's songs,[10] analyze them, and place them into 6 different categories: social, class, communal, familial, political, and spiritual.

These six areas were then used to fit into the larger scope of Tupac's theological framework.[11] Tupac's theological framework, derived from his musical message, is listed below:[12]

- Eucharistic Persona
- Existential Humanity
- Apotheosis Disposition

---

[9] See Appendix F for a sample of the content analysis of Tupac's music.

[10] From the website http://www.ohhla.com/YFA_2pac.html last accessed on April 14, 2006.

[11] This framework is implied by me, the researcher. Having not been able to interview Tupac—for obvious reasons—I used existing data and archrival data to formulate these categories in a tutorial with Ralph Watkins in Winter 2006 at Fuller Seminary.

[12] These terms will be defined at length later in the book.

- Hermeneutical Method
- Epistemology

To achieve reliability and validity, the ethnolifehistory method utilizes three separate methods to arrive at its conclusions: qualitative lyrical research, archival interview data, and qualitative media analysis. Figure 5 demonstrates that in the process of the ethnolifehistory, validity and reliability are achieved by the three methods that help arrive at life eras. Further, to distinguish one era from the last I used three qualifiers:

1. Was there a major change in lifestyle and life patterns? (Major being: a death, prison, birth, geographical change)
2. What new lifestyle patterns were established?
3. How long did these new patterns last?

## *Weaknesses*

While all of these modifications are good, there remain some problems with the Ethnohistory method. William Fenton states:

> The practice of Ethnohistory is about as difficult to outline and make explicit as it is impossible to tell how an ethnologist goes about field work in the society of a living culture. The point of view and the method is suggested by the problem, and a lot of what we call theory is a rationalization for kinds of experimental or research situations. Materials impose very definite limits on what can be done, whether they are informants or documents (1962: 11).

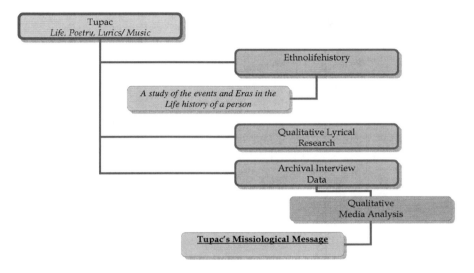

**FIGURE 5**

**PROCESS OF ETHNOLIFEHISTORY IN CONTEXT**

Ethnohistory, because of its varied uses, poses various problems. In several cases, the method can be seen as a hybrid of narrative analysis, sometimes making the reader wonder where exactly they are going (e.g. Fenton 1962). Additionally, the ethnohistorian has to prove to many researchers—who focus on statistical data—that their study is worthwhile and that this method is as equal as event history analysis (minus all the mathematics involved). Rasmussen (1999) had this issue with the slave narrative study she did. This is a common problem for many qualitative researchers vs. quantitative results. In any case, the ethnohistorian must be able to cover each area well in the research (c.f. Tippett 1973 and 1980).

More importantly, this is a new method, and has not been field tested by other researchers. This being the case, there could be certain flaws that I might have missed initially when doing this study. While looking at Tupac's life, I was only able to focus on using qualitative content analysis and case studies for external methods.

This ethnolifehistory of Tupac would have been further strengthened if I had been granted an interview with Tupac's mother, Afeni Shakur.[13] In addition, I was not able to directly contact any family members regarding Tupac. I relied solely on archival material from public tapes, CD's, and DVD's. The gathering of this necessary data would have immensely strengthened this study.

Lastly, Tupac's interview and personal insights into his own life would have been an enormous help. However, Tupac is deceased, and the only information left is found in poetry, his music, and his past interviews. In doing an ethnolifehistory, Tupac's poetry, music, and past interviews are key in discovering eras in his life.

### *The Context for the Study*

The gathering of data was done in Pasadena, California between the months of May and June of 2006. I was able to utilize the University of California Los Angeles' archival television shows to gather data for Black popular culture.

Qualitative content analysis allowed me to gain a broad scope of the major themes that arose from television, music, and film. Qualitative content analysis is a relatively new qualitative method being used in the social sciences (Turner 2004, James 2004). While this style of the method does not utilize the popular quantitative aspect, the qualitative facet allows the researcher to grasp themes as opposed to singular events

---

[13] This was a long process. I spent two years attempting to reach her and no one ever got to me. She is a protected person, being that many do try to reach her, and she has not had good interactions with the public.

and/or words that are then used to correlate numerical meanings. These themes are also tied into narrative—narrative is a staple within Black popular culture and can be traced back to Africa.

To review Tupac's relation to Black Pop Culture I looked at:

Between 1980-1995

TV:
- The Jeffersons
- Fresh Prince of Bel Air
- Different Strokes
- Dave Chappell Show (Supporting)
- What's Happening (Supporting)

Film:
- Boyz in the Hood
- Scarface
- Do the Right Thing
- Juice
- Which Way is Up?
- American Me
- Menace II Society
- 8-Mile (Supporting)

Music:
- Ice T
- Ice Cube

- NWA
- Public Enemy
- Yo Yo
- Ray Charles
- Quincy Jones

Past research from Tupac's ethnohistory was used to formulate the five criteria that were used in the content analysis. Within Tupac's life, these five areas arose constantly. Moreover, these five criteria exist within Black popular culture as seen in the data gathered.

The data gathered here allowed me to gain a broader view of Tupac's social and theological connection to Black popular culture in order to enter the next phase of my research project and to develop a theology of the profane from Tupac's music, life, philosophy, and examples. This research allows me to add a new element into understanding some of the reasons why Tupac might have done what he did.

For Tupac's music, I was able to attain all of his published songs online. This enabled me to print them to allow for data analysis and to attain correlations from them.

*Summary*

In this Chapter I have discussed the methods used in this book project. I have used the method ethnolifehistory to discover the missiological message of Tupac. I focused on the cultural continuum of ethnolifehistory and used several supporting media sources to connect Tupac to Black popular culture and Hip Hop culture. In the next Chapter I lay out a basic theoretical framework for approaching Tupac's music.

# CHAPTER 4

# TOWARD A THEORY OF TUPAC'S MUSIC

Approaching Tupac's music is not without a discussion on ethnomusicology. Tupac's music is just that: music. There are two parallel bodies of work that discuss ethnomusicology. The first, discusses it from a more mainstream European perspective. The second discusses it from a more Black and "urban" perspective in which better fits Tupac and his body of music. However, the two are important and deserve equal treatment.

Mark Slobin and Jeff Todd Titon contend, "every human society has music. Music is universal; but its meaning is not" (1984: 1). Tupac's music evokes different meanings for different people all over the world (c.f. Nettl 1983; Grout 2001). Terry Miller and Andrew Shahriari assert that music is not a language because it is not governed by the rules of language (2006:13). They further argue that, "it is questionable whether music really can transcend linguistic barriers and culturally determined behaviors, through some form of emotional communication so fundamentally human that all respond the same way" (Miller and Shahriari 2006: 13). While I agree with the fact that *all* music is not a language, and *all* music cannot have humans respond the same way, I challenge their position on language and music as it relates to rap music. Rap is words and follows certain set of language rules.[1]

---

[1] This does not mean that rap music is grammatically correct, it simply means that rap music is more about the words than the actual music, those words convey different meanings to different people, Russell Potter argues that rap music, is in fact, a postmodern language (1995: 55-80). I find it troublesome that Miller and Shahriari title a book "World Music: A Global Journey" and do not even discuss the affects of rap and Hip Hop on the world music scene.

My problem with their statement and argument is that a rap artist such as Tupac uses language, the sampled lyrics of other artists, and complex lyrical scores to grab his listeners and stir up deep meaning within different people. In addition, while music is not a standard language for all humans, rap music evokes deep meaning with its language to the people that listen to it (Potter 1995:1-24; Pincus-Roth 2005). Tupac's lyrics were laced with deep, complex, and intrinsically composed musical scores that reached into the soul of the person listening.

In order for Tupac's music to reach such a broad audience, there needed to be a platform for that message to be preached. This is what makes an ethnomusicologist come alive: discovering the meaning behind the artist within the music (Nettl 1983:22). Alan Merriam argues that music has a system, but that it cannot exist without human beings, "music sound must be regarded as the product of the behavior that produces it" (1964: 32). In other words, for Tupac's behavior, worldview and personal ethos shaped his lyrics and musical score. Tupac's music had human interaction. Tupac's music connected to Merriam's three musical behaviors; physical, social, and verbal (1964:32-34). These concepts are part of a larger framework, which comprises labeling the music concept, behavior, and the sound that the music embodies (Nettl 1983:22-25; Merriam 1964: 30-35). Tupac's music was also connected to this conceptual framework. Therefore, we enter into this discussion.

### *Physical Behavior*

Merriam states that the physical behavior is, "the physical tension and posture of the body in producing sound, and the physical response of the individual organism to sound" (1964: 33). Tupac's music fully embodied this. One need not look any further than a high school dance when a Tupac song is played. The subtle nodding of the head, the tapping of the foot, the shaking of the hand, the closure of eyes while the body effervescently moves to the rhythm are all evidence that Tupac's music connects to the physical part of the "organism," the person.

Tupac himself would have to "feel" the rhythm before he placed his lyrics over it. Tupac wrote consistently and kept material coming for days. Many of his songs were once poems that were converted into songs (Hodge 2005). These songs connected with the physical and reached deep into the psyche of the person listening. In other words, Tupac's music was something that you could "feel" in your heart. When I interviewed young people regarding Tupac I was consistently told that Tupac was someone that you could "feel" all inside your body (Hodge 2003). Part of that physical behavior also came in the form of physically moving out to action in the community as a result of that "feeling" in your heart. Craig Watkins states, "Hip hop's evolution launched a revolution in youth culture" and continues to do as a result of both the music and message (2005: 148).

This feeling of the rhythm is also heightened with the use of video. Cheryl Keyes states, "Rap music videos draw on physical and intellectual references—encoded culture—that augment the message the rap artist delivers" (2002: 210). Videos adversely affect this physical behavior in that now the audience has a visual on what the verbal—rap—is (e.g. Morgan 1998: 282-300).

For many Hip Hoppers, they must have a song move them physically (Clay 2003: 1348). If you cannot at least bob your head to the rhythm, the song is labeled "whack," or not worthy of Hip Hop culture. Tupac's music connected people to both the physical and the spiritual. His music was able to make you move physically, while also evoking grander thoughts about life and God.

In the song "Black Jesuz" with the Outlaws, the rhythm is simple and steady, while summoning great questions about church, life, and society.[2] This is an excellent

---

[2] See Appendix B.

example of having both the physical and spiritual connect. The interesting question that then arises is, does the physical need to happen first? I would suggest that within Hip Hop culture the physical would need to transpire first in order to reach the spiritual.

### *Social Behavior*

The social behavior that comes from a song is concerned with the social environment around the musician (Merriam 1964: 33). Few other artists are able to connect with the social environment like Tupac. Tupac was socially conscious; mainly because of his upbringing and familial environment. Tupac was aware of the social realities of living in the ghetto.

For music to take shape, the social element must be present (e.g. Merriam 1965; Nettl 1983). In fact, the social aspect of music is a key tenet of postmodern music, which, I would argue, Tupac's music was (Kramer 2002: 13-26).

Social behavior is also concerned with what action you will take after hearing the music. Imani Perry suggests that Hip Hop music can inspire social change and social political action (2004: 41-51). Tupac would continually urge his listeners to take action. In "2Pacalypse Now" (1992), Tupac raised the question of "Why mo niggas in the pen than in college?"[3] For Tupac, there needed to be a major social change, this was evident in 90 percent of his music.

In the same album, Tupac also addressed the social behavior of Black men:

> You know they got me trapped in this prison of seclusion
> Happiness, living on tha streets is a delusion
> Even a smooth criminal one day must get caught
> Shot up or shot down with tha bullet that he bought
> Nine millimeter kickin' thinking about what tha streets do
> to me

---

[3] Ice Cube (1991) also raised this extremely important question regarding social action in the inner city.

> Cause they never talk peace in tha black community
> All we know is violence do tha job in silence
> Walk tha city streets like a rat pack of tyrants
> Too many brothers daily heading for tha big penn
> Niggas commin' out worse off than when they went in
> Over tha years I done a lot of growin' up
> Getten drunk thrown' up
> Cuffed up
> Then I said I had enough
> There must be another route, way out

For Tupac, the Black male was an "endangered species" that needed social attention and help. In this particular song, entitled "Trapped," Tupac raises social issues, and suggests that we—the urban community—must take social action; a behavior. Tricia Rose asserts that rap arose in a post industrial city context in which artists and listeners are able to shape their own social community through the music (1994 b: 78-85).

## *Verbal Behavior*

In this behavior, Merriam suggests that it, "is concerned with expressed verbal constructs about the music system itself" (1964: 33). For Tupac, this was central to all of his music. For Tupac, the verbal message was just as important as the overall message of the song that was being proclaimed. The verbal part of the music was the heart of the song.[4]

This area is part of Hip Hop culture as a whole. What you say is a key feature of Hip Hop culture. Language, whether verbal or non verbal, is a large part of any culture. How you communicate, both verbally and non-verbally, are important and it is how your own message will be received.

Further, the verbal aspect of Hip Hop culture is nothing original to Black culture in general. Cheryl Keyes states, "Black poetic speech is fluid and predicated on what

---

[4] Tupac discussed how he put his music together in interviews on the DVD *Tupac Vs.* (Peters 2001).

communication scholars call nommo, 'the power of the word,' a concept derived from the Dogon of Mali" (2002: 22). This "power of the word" is fundamental in rap music. However, rap music and Hip Hop culture are not the only aspects of Urban and Black culture that utilize verbal communication to convey its message. Keyes once again asserts, "in the black traditional church, preachers occasionally interject rhyming in their sermons" (2002: 26).

The verbal aspect of Black culture also plays a large role in rap music. Unique linguistics are part of this "power of the word" within rap music. Geneva Smitherman suggests it, "reflects the dynamic, colorful span of language used by African Americans from all walks of life" (1998: 204). This colorful use of language finds its way into rap music, and the verbal behavior connects with the listener. Smitherman (1998: 203-224) discusses at length this lexicon of African American Vernacular English and connects a historical aspect to the verbal behavior.

Tupac understood this, coming from an oral tradition.[5] Tupac made it a point to be certain that all of his lyrics could be understood even though many times when he recorded songs he would slur words. To correct this problem, he would lay another vocal track over the first and double up on parts that were not as clear (Hodge 2005).

The verbal part of the music connects the person to the whole song itself. Nettl states:

> Music has much in common with language, and the two are almost inseparable as ingredients of the activity perhaps most centrally observed by ethnomusicologist—singing. The relationship of language and music is an important aspect of ethnomusicological literature, extending from comparative studies of two systems at large and parallel characterizations of music and language in one society, on to many other specialized kinds of study (1983:23).

---

[5] See Burnim and Maultbsy ed. (2005) as they edit a book, which discusses a history of Black music. Tupac was part of that history and tradition of the oral

Tupac provided verbal[6] allegories from his perspective and makes sure that his point was made while you were being educated in a non-traditional form. Language remains a large part of Hip Hop culture, and culture in general.[7]

Merriam argues that through behavior, music sound is produced and that without it, there can be no sound. I would agree. These were key tenets to Tupac's music. Further, nommo is also a large part of the behavior in which the verbal aspect of the music gives even more power to the message of the song.

### *Three Intersecting Areas in Tupac's Music*

Tupac had three major intersecting areas of his music that helped make him who he was. Bruno Nettle states, "The task of ethnomusicology is not so much to probe the essential nature of musical creation…it is a task, however, to examine the ways in which various societies conceive of and evaluate musical creation and to derive an analytical system that will permit them to be compared" (Nettl 1983: 27). This is important in understanding Tupac's music as a discipline. This concept was adapted from Bruno Nettl who argues there are 3 intersecting continuums in music, in general. He argues that (1) Music is inspired, (2) improvisations and compositions are not separate, and (3) there are different courses of events that lead in the creation of a piece of music (1964 26-35).

The three major intersecting areas within Tupac's music are (1) inspiration, (2) improvisation and composition, and (3) life events. These three will make up his overall

---

[6] Rap music is largely based on verbal communication and some kind of text that is either spoken or read.

[7] Edward Sapir states, "Language is a purely human and non-instinctive method of communicating ideas, emotions, and desires by means of a system of voluntarily produced symbols" (1949: 7). Language in rap music is fundamental and of paramount importance. It is the means in which the message of the song is conveyed to the audience. Rap music communicates ideas, emotions, and desires by means of the Hip Hop system.

musical output. Moreover, these three areas help shape Tupac's music and help us, the listeners, better understand why his music was such an inspiration to so many.

**Inspiration**

The first area is inspiration. Tupac was inspired by many different things when he wrote his music (Shakur et al. 2003). Tupac's influences, though great, came mainly from his childhood and life situations. Tupac used these to inspire his musical creations and give his songs deeper meaning to everyday life. For Tupac, his every aspect of life became his inspiration. This is another reason why his music is so powerful, and still reaches a generation today: the authenticity of his life, permeated through his music.

Tupac connected with a deeper sense of living while he questioned the very reason for his existence. The inspiration of Tupac's music was drawn from the life around him. For Tupac, his song texts have three major parts:

1. *Allegory and Fable*: a story about what had happened to him, a friend, or a fictional character.

2. *The participant*: He was personally involved in the event of the song and was telling you about it.

3. *The observer*: He had observed a scene or event and was now telling his audience about it.

For Tupac, inspiration was derived from these three areas. There were also many connections in his music to metaphors and hyper-explicit language. For example, in the song "Me Against The World," Tupac was not literally "against the world" but he felt as though the "world" was against him due to the harsh situations he was finding himself in. Those situations actually became an inspiration and in 1995 the title song track went to number one on the Billboard charts.[8]

---

[8] Source: http://www.allmusic.com/cg/amg.dll last accessed on May 31, 2006.

Nettl also suggests that this inspiration is sometimes "divine" (1983:27). This was the case for many of Tupac's songs. His ability to relate scripture with the street and then back into a theological message for the 'hood, was extraordinary.

For example, in the song "Blasphemy," Tupac raises questions about the pastor, sin, and salvation:

> We probably in Hell already, our dumb asses not knowin
> Everybody kissin ass to go to heaven ain't goin
> Put my soul on it, I'm fightin devil niggaz daily
> Plus the media be crucifying brothers severly
> Tell me I ain't God's son, nigga mom a virgin
> We got addicted had to leave the burbs, back in the ghetto
> doin wild shit, lookin at the sun don't pay
> Criminal mind all the time, wait for Judgment Day
> They say Moses split the Red Sea
> I split the blunt and rolled the fat one, I'm deadly -- Babylon beware

This particular track, recorded during Tupac's "Outlaw" era, reflects the inspirations of the time in which Tupac was living. Tupac was never really accepted by the mainstream church, and this song was a reflection of that rejection.

## Improvisation and Composition

The second area is improvisation and composition. For Hip Hoppers, including Tupac, this is connected with free style—the art of rapping a song completely based on improvisation. The final outcome of this is the composition itself.

So many rap artists start songs with improvisation act sublimating with a song that is full and rich. Tupac was no different. For him, improvisation was part of the inspiration. When something "hit" him, he needed to compose a song thereby putting that story into action so that someone else benefited from it.

Tupac was music. Nettle argues that music carries out certain functions in society (1983:147-148). Tupac's music did just that, it inspired others to spontaneously take action. In other words, Tupac's own improvisation would evoke a deeper chain reaction that would cause those listening to take certain actions and change—even if that change was as small as feeling better, knowing that someone else was going through similar things. This is another connection to the spiritual side of music. Donald Hustad argues that God gives us music to inspire, change, and help our lives (1981: 1-13). He says that music can give us meaning and that it is inspired. I would take this theoretical framework a step further and say that music in general, particularly Hip Hop, is God-given, and that God works through both the obvious and incognito to reach people. Further, Rod Gruver contends that Blues is a secular religion that people are able to connect to (1992: 55-67). Gruver presents an interesting argument that also connects to rap being and extension of the "secular religion."

This improvisation was such a large part of Tupac's music, that he carried a pad and pen with him everywhere he went. Moreover, as ideas came to him, he composed different songs.[9]

## Life Events

Life events are fundamental for any Hip Hop artist creating a song. Tupac's entire life became an album, essentially. As seen in Figure 7, we can begin to see how the two other areas intersect, meet, and connect to the larger picture: the song. There were many different life events that helped in forming Tupac's overall musical career. Ultimately, Tupac's songs were one of his most important assets in his life legacy.

For Tupac, the song was the final output of the inspiration, improvisation and composition, and life events; the song was extremely important. Tupac was known for his work ethic in Hip Hop. Trech, from the group Naughty By Nature, called Tupac the

---

[9] It is interesting to note that while he was in prison in 1995, he said that his inspiration was killed. This was evident because he did not record another album until after his release later that year.

"hardest working man in Hip Hop" (Trech in Spirer 2002). For example, many artists recorded a song every two to three hours; give or take a few hours in between the time they were drinking and smoking weed. Tupac, could record three to five tracks in two hours.

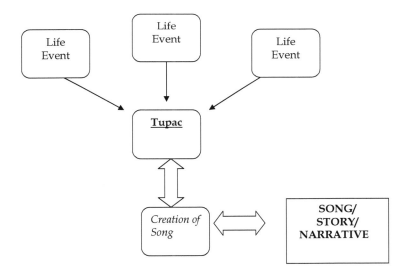

**FIGURE 6**

**FLOW OF EVENTS TOWARDS A SONG**

In Figure 6, we see how different life events influenced Tupac. As inspiration occurred, Tupac turned inspiration into the creation of a song, and ultimately the final product was the song that originated from multiple (sometimes-single) life events.

For the postmodernist [10] Tupac is able to give them that connection to the narrative of life, while assigning meaning to different life events. Whilst putting all that into a nice artist's piece known as a song. In the song, "Something to Die 4" Tupac connects the listener with his own life, and how people around him have been backstabbers and hypocrites. At the same time, the listener hears a deep call for action, where they themselves have been done the same way.[11]

These different courses of events affect the way the song is then produced, promoted, and published. For the album The Don Killuminati: The 7 Day Theory, Tupac recorded the album in seven days, after feeling inspired to put something out that connected with the real niggas around him. These are key systems of belief within postmodern music: connecting people to the larger story, the reduction of the grand Meta-narrative, and the connection to the micro narrative we all live in (c.f. Lochhead and Auner ed. 2002).

Merriam suggests that certain song texts reveal literary behavior that can only be analyzed in terms of both structure and content, and that song text language tends to be a "secret" language to that particular culture (1964: 46-47). While I would agree that there are certain idioms and innuendos that only certain cultures are aware of or knowledgeable of, Tupac crosses the cultural lines and connected with many—particularly Whites and Asians—through connecting life stories into his songs (see Figure 6). For Tupac, the universal human need of acceptance was made clear in all his music. This was a unique

---

[10] I use this term loosely here, knowing that while I argue that the urban context is the heart of postmodern, most within the urban context would not be able to identify or articulate that. Tupac, in an indirect way, inspired much of what is known as urban postmodern music (Clendinning 2002).

[11] See Appendix C for an overview of the Black Panther ten point program and platform.

phenomenon that few other rap artists are able to do. There are different Asian countries that do not speak a word of English, but can recite Tupac's songs word for word.[12]

### *Connecting Tupac's Music for Study*

In Figure 7, we see the beginning to the intersecting areas. However, now, with all three combined, we are able to observe a greater picture of how Tupac's music came about.

When the inspiration, improvisation and composition, and life events all meet, a song is formed that ultimately produces behaviors within the listener as well as the songwriter themselves (Nettl 1983; Merriam 1964). Through this process, Tupac's music took shape. His inspiration, the urban context, gave him much of the lyrical tones for his music.

---

[12] As seen in Tupac's fan letters (Sims 1999). While it is presumptuous to draw conclusions on the meanings Asians in these countries make of Tupac's music, it is assumed that they use Tupac's music to create their own meaning and assign new meaning to different social issues derived from his music that exist in their culture.

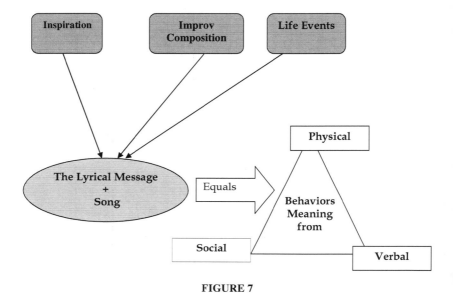

**FIGURE 7**

**TUPAC'S MUSICAL AREAS CONNECTION**

This then raises the issue of language and "cursing." If the contexts shape and form a person's worldview, then their language is a byproduct of that environment (Ting-Toomey and Chung 2005; Cox 1965). As a result, the language that Tupac used in his music was manufactured from the environment and reflected the course of events from that environment. There is also the issue of using the word "Fuck" in lyrics. Edward Sapir (1949) argues that language is merely a reflection of the environment, and that the language we use, to some extent, determines the way in which we view and think about the world around us. Therefore, using the word Fuck in an urban context is not really a curse word, but an average word used daily by its inhabitants. I argue that we as humans put labels and definitions on words, and each culture defines what is vulgar, profane, and just down right ugly in terms of language. Tupac used the word Fuck quite often, but there were many uses for it and not just as a curse word, as we would normally expect it to be used as. A large part of this issue ties into whether or not "cursing" and broken English is a part of what is called "African American Vernacular English" (Smitherman 1998: 203-224; Dillard 1972: 3-38). While the word Fuck is not relegated merely to Black English, Tupac, being Black himself, did use the word and made it a part of his everyday language. However, I am not suggesting that foul language and broken English are solely Black English. I am merely contending, as Smitherman (1998) and Dillard (1972) argue, that foul and profane language is part of the African American Vernacular English system.

Other Scholars such as Arthur Spears suggest that instead of using the term "obscene" language as a term used to describe such words as Fuck, Spears would prefer the term "uncensored speech in order not to prejudge the actions of the users of such speech" (1998: 226). Spears further contends that such words are merely a reflection of context, timing of gestures, and syntax within a particular group of people—in his study, Blacks also supports this notion regarding words (1998: 231-248).

Tupac's language was in large part a result of the third continuum course of events in the creation of a song. Nettl (1983: 44-51) also discusses the different languages of music within a culture. Culture as a whole, influences music, and consequently influenced Tupac to produce more music for the culture he was a part of (Nettl 1983:141-146; c.f. Kaplan and Manners 1972:45)

This is not to say that anyone can speak as they wish and that there should not be a limitation to what one says. I am merely suggesting that language is a direct result of the person's environment. I would also argue, that a person can "curse" another person out without ever using a four-letter word; particularly one who has a grasp of the language they are using and who is educated.

In addition, Tupac's music is a worthy study because of three major notions. First, Tupac's music is a product of the cultural environment he lived in. "Music in or as culture implies a relationship, and what we are about is the examination of views of this relationship" (Nettl 1983: 136). The culture in which Tupac lived was both urban and Hip Hop.[13] That environment shaped and formed him, especially during his early life. Television and music were all Tupac had in terms of his early environment. The music he listened to shaped his worldview.

Second, Tupac largely contributed to mainstream pop culture. His music surpassed the typical borders of Hip Hop culture even invading the suburban home. Tupac greatly influenced those outside of the Hip Hop community (e.g. Nettl 1983:137-138). For example, Tony Danza—well known actor and star of the television series *Who's The Boss?*— was a unlikely Tupac fan. Tony was not known to love rap music, but loved Tupac because of his authenticity (Hodge 2005). Moreover, Tupac remains an American cultural icon. His music still carries much weight in both the urban and suburban world.[14]

Third, Tupac's music is a reflection of the struggles of Blacks throughout history. In other words, there is a connection to the slave narrative within his lyrics. Regarding the historical urban context of Black music in general Mark Anthony Neal states, "It is in this context that Black musical and cultural forms also began to blatantly address Black social and political conditions, both in terms of lyrics and production styles" (2006: 625).

---

[13] While some may confuse the two as being the same. The two are separate. Not everyone in the urban context listens to rap music and is within the Hip Hop cultural scope. There are many different levels to the urban matrix and the word is typically synonymous with Black and Latino; i.e. rap music (c.f. Cox 1965 and 1984).

[14] It is worth mentioning here that the rural environment is also a fan of Tupac, however not as much as the suburban and urban.

Tupac's music and lyrics reflected both a generation and culture that needed a lot of help and attention. Tupac's music was connected to the culture and therefore regurgitated the needs, hurts, desires, pain, love, misery, anger, hate, and sexuality that emerged from both the historical roots of oppression in the urban context (Cox 1984), and the current situation of urbanites.

Thus, we enter into the study of lyrical messages within the music of Tupac. Few other artists have influenced society the way he has. Tupac is a reflection of the culture and a connection to the culture. Tupac helped make sense of life to many people. This is a study I want to enter into and will argue, that as missiologist—and foremost agents of our Lord Jesus, the Christ—we must understand elements of culture, especially the ones that stand out and are not "pretty" to look at.

*Summary*

In this chapter, I have discussed the reason why Tupac's music was important from an ethnomusicological point of view. Tupac's music affected three major behaviors: the physical, social and verbal. He himself was a product of these behaviors, but his music influenced the behavior of others as well. Within Tupac's music three intersecting areas shaped those behaviors as well: inspiration, improvisation and composition, and life events. These came together in the creation of a song. These three areas, shaped Tupac's music as a whole. In that intersecting place, Tupac's songs were formed and given out to the public with a message attached to each of his songs. Lastly, Tupac's music is worthy of study because he himself was influenced by his culture, he influenced not only Hip Hop culture, but mainstream pop culture, and his music is a reflection of the Black struggle in general.

This sets up the following parts and chapters of this book. In the next part I will focus on Tupac's context. When combined with this chapter, I will demonstrate how and where Tupac gained his inspiration for music and where his foundational elements were for music and ultimately, his missiological message.

## PART II:

## HIP HOP CULTURE AND THE 'HOOD: THE CONTEXT FOR TUPAC

In this section, I will discuss the macro and micro context in which Tupac operated and lived. I will discuss Hip Hop culture and the 'hood, and will reveal what Tupac was living in. More importantly, it will reveal the significance and thrust of many of his songs and why he reacted to certain things in certain ways.

The first two chapters deal with the macro context in which Tupac operated. The last chapter deals with Tupac's relationship to Hip Hop culture and the 'hood. This will be seen in the study of Black popular culture and Tupac's relationship to that culture. Tupac is not separated from Black popular culture, Hip Hop culture, and the 'hood. However, each culture has its distinct areas in which they operate. This section will illustrate those.

This section is necessary in order to understand the next section, Tupac's life. In order to truly understand Tupac's theological message in the last section of this book, the next sections will be an interaction and discussion with the literature and research findings that were gathered for this book. Each chapter will have its own set of literature that sets it up and makes it distinct.

The last part of this section will begin to connect Tupac to the macro world listed above, and set the "stage" for part three, his life. Figure 8 illustrates that this section will focus on Hip Hop, the 'hood, and Black popular culture.

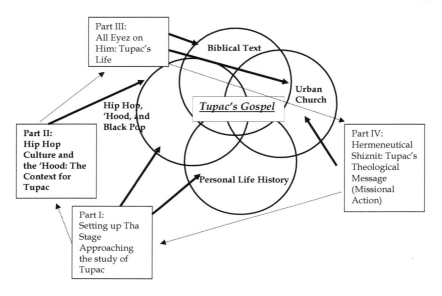

**FIGURE 8**

**FLOW OF BOOK PART TWO**

## CHAPTER 5

## THE CONTEXT OF TUPAC
## HIP HOP CULTURE

As I entered the student lounge at Pasadena City College, I noticed that the room was filled with young students under the age of twenty. They embodied a sense of unity that one could only understand if experienced personally. It was extremely hard to find a seat in the midst of all these young, eager students. The students did not even notice my entrance. Most were so captivated by the speaker, that no one really took notice of my tardiness. It was as if the students had silently welcomed me in, and were actually happy to see someone perceived as "older" within their midst.

I could hardly believe that all these young people— mostly from an urban background— were sitting and listening so attentively to the speaker. More importantly, they were respectful and were actually tracking with what he had to say. I was impressed that this was coming from a generation that most adults would say, "Don't listen or care for older folk." But, this day was different. These young students were captured by the speaker's message. The speaker was none other than KRS-One. KRS-One is one of the founding fathers of Hip Hop culture. He was one of the original MC's out of the Bronx during the late 1970's and early 1980's. KRS-One, whose real name is Kris Parker, is also a renowned scholar and teacher of and for Hip Hop "Kulture."[1] KRS-One had everyone in that room clinging to each word he spoke. More importantly, KRS-One's message was a message of love and peace like that found in the Bible; particularly the

---

[1] "Kulture" as opposed to culture are how KRS-One and The Temple of Hip Hop define themselves, and use the letter K as opposed to C, because the K is more unique.

New Testament. KRS-One could have taken an alter call, and at the very least, would have had 80 percent of 400 students come to know Christ better.[2]

KRS-One spoke about many culturally and socially relevant issues. He spoke about pain, suffering, economic injustice, the war in Iraq, political injustices, and God. The crowd devoured every word of it.

KRS-One ended his time with a call to growth and critical thinking among this next generation of youth; particularly as it pertained to Hip Hop culture. At the end of his time, he was engulfed by requests for autographs and pictures. To the crowd's delight he gladly accepted most of their requests.

Here was a Hip Hop king that had been around when the culture was birthed in the Bronx. Here was a man who was a popular radio personality during the time when I was in junior high (the mid 1980's), but is still captivating a younger generation. Here was a man that encapsulated a new generation of young people, and did not even "perform."

How did all of these young people identify so well with KRS-One? How was it that KRS-One (who is incidentally over forty years old) could connect so well with a new generation of youth? How was it that KRS-One's persona continues to connect with Hip Hop culture? What is this Hip Hop culture that attracts so many young people? Is it evil?

The main reason for such a strong identification with KRS-One and these young people can be summed up in one word: authenticity. This word's meaning is also closely related to Wade's definition of the word, "Authenticity is also thought of as residing in a

---

[2] That being said, KRS-One is a Five Percenter. Five Percenter's contend that the Black masses need to be educated by the five percent that understand the culture, socio-economics, and society for Black America. Five Percenter's are, "an idiosyncratic mix of black nationalist rhetoric, Kemetic (ancient Egyptian) symbolism, Gnosticism, Masonic mysticism, and esoteric numerology" (Miyakawa 2005:23). I am not weary or afraid of the Five Percent nation. They have a lot to offer and I agree with a lot of what they say, while KRS-One is part of that nation and ensuing theology (Miyakawa 2005: 23-37), the image of Jesus does get skewed in juxtaposition to Christian values. However, I still hold that there are numerous ways to Christ, and Christianity is merely only one way.

person who has acquired the knowledge that permits him or her to perform authentically" (2004: 142). KRS-One is someone who not only acquired the knowledge to be authentic, he is also keenly aware of the traditions of Hip Hop culture (Wade 2004: 143), he also produces music in such a way that there is consensus and bears meaning around which a group can form meaning (Wade 2004: 145). Hip Hoppers that can do this process according to Wade (2004), are considered authentic. Hip Hop culture is founded on this word's meaning. The meaning of this word is vast, however the Oxford English Dictionary defines it, "as being in accordance with fact, as being true in substance; as being real, actual; reality". KRS-One's persona emanated this definition. Young people intuitively know and understand this. It is part of the culture. You either have it or you do not. KRS-One had it. And, it did not matter whether he was forty-two or twenty-four. Authenticity is timeless and ageless. In other words, being who you are is not something you acquire when you are young only to loose it when you are older. It simply is who you are.

### *So, What is Hip Hop Culture?*

The Temple of Hip Hop, run by KRS-One and his team, give a basic definition of Hip Hop culture[3]:

> Hip hop, commonly spelled "Hip-Hop," "hip-hop,' "Hip-hop," and "Hip hop," is the name of our collective consciousness and inner-city strategy toward self-improvement. In its spiritual essence, Hiphop cannot be (and should not be) interpreted or described in words. It is a feeling. An awareness. A state of mind. Intellectually, it is an alternative behavior that

---

[3] A good and updated definition of culture is by Ting-Toomey and Chung; they define culture as, "A learned meaning system that consists of patterns of traditions, beliefs, values, norms, meanings, and symbols that are passed on from one generation to the next and are shared to varying degrees by interacting members of a community" (2005: 376). Within a culture there are norms, values, shared traditions, shared beliefs, and identity (Lustig and Koester 1996: 32-38).

enables one to transform subjects and objects in an attempt to describe and/or change the character and desires of ones' inner being (2004).

In this definition[4], we can begin to see exactly what some in the culture are describing when they say that they "feel" the music or that they "Are Hip Hop." Hip Hop culture is about being true to one's self and to ones basic lifestyle, whether that be rich or poor (Dyson 1996; Rose 1994a 1994b; Perkins 1996).

To see this another way, let us begin to break apart the culture. There are some who argue that Rap and Hip Hop are one and the same (e.g. Alper 2000 and Blair 1993), but the two are separate and can be seen better in the Table 1:

**TABLE 1:**

**THE DIFFERENCES BETWEEN RAP AND HIP HOP**

| Rap | Hip Hop |
|---|---|
| • The music and genre of music that drives the culture.<br>• The verbal part of the music, derived from the 1970's slang term meaning: to talk to (Perkins 1996: 1-4).<br>• Anyone can do it and still not be apart of Hip Hop culture; for example, the differences between a Vanilla Ice and an Ice Cube.<br>• Can be made into a fad. | • The culture as a whole which, at times, reflects the music and musical genre.<br>• The personalities, clothing, language, and ensuing attitude that derives itself out of the music while still recycling itself within the culture. In other words, the two are separate yet symbiotically connected.<br>• Authentic and real; no fakes or commercialization of the genre.<br>• Is a lifestyle NOT a fad. |

---

[4] Please note that this section is a "snap-shot" of the culture. For a broader definition see Tricia Rose (1994 a: 1-20); Nelson George (1998: 1-33); and (Kitwana 2003).

Rap can be seen as part of the music while the culture that emerges is Hip Hop.[5] Hip Hop is the lifestyle while rap reflects that culture,[6] or at least "should" reflect that culture. Figure 9 gives us the sub-genres of Hip Hop culture. Each area has its own norms and different set of values. Each area can at any time, be in the forefront. Currently we are in a "party-rap" mode. It takes a revolution or death of some sort—which was the case when Tupac and Biggie Smalls were murdered— to move the sub-genres.[7] Each area in Figure 9 represents a strong sub-culture of Hip Hop. Each sub-genre has its own language, beliefs, customs, traditions, and norms. The sub-genres keep growing, and I would predict that in ten years, this wheel will be twice as large. William Perkins states:

> When the genre first appeared in the late 1970's, culture and music critics falsely predicted a quick demise, but rap music grew and flourished, simultaneously reshaping the entire terrain of American popular culture. Even rap music's hyped commercialization cannot dampen its tough, raw, hard-core street essence. Rap music's most powerful safeguard has been its uncanny ability to reenergize itself, to remain 'true to the game,' in the words of one of Ice Cube's most important rhymes (1996: 1).

---

[5] See Figure 9

[6] See Mclean (1997) in her ethnographic analysis of urban youth.

[7] I have developed this scheme after studying the culture of Hip Hop for over 10 years.

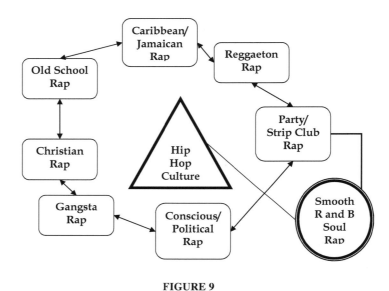

**FIGURE 9**

**THE SUB-GENRE'S OF HIP HOP CULTURE**

Hip Hop culture has engulfed most of Western American culture at some level (Rose 1994 a 1994b; Dyson 2001; Perry 2004; Reed 2003; Kitwana 2002). KRS-One had something larger than a "rap song" in him that attracted so many young people from this Hip Hop generation. Once again, The Hip Hop generation is used here as opposed to using Gen X. Gen X tends to refer primarily to White Suburban males. Hip Hoppers need their own definition of their unique culture (Kitwana 2002; Clay 2003). That "something" transcends age, political status, socioeconomic status, social standings, and even gender.[8]

Hip Hop is a voice and a community for many that do not nor have not had either one of those prior (c.f. Dyson 1996; Kitwana 2002; Clay 2003; KRS-One 2003; Master P 1997). Hip Hop culture has provided many, including myself, a safe, productive alternative to the streets (Stephens 1991: 25-40). We will return to this point.

Trice Rose states that Hip Hop culture emerged as a source for young people of alternative identity formation[9] and social status in a community, to have that social status and identity within a system that had abandoned them (1994 a: 34). Moreover, Hip Hop culture provides an outlet and a voice for many young people in the inner city, as well as the middle class today. In addition, Angela Nelson states, "The racial oppression of black people in many ways has fueled and shaped black musical forms in America" (1991: 51). Rap music is one of those forms. "Contemporary rappers, like early bluespeople, are responding to the 'burden of freedom,' in part by relaying portrayals of reality to their audiences through their personal experiences" (Nelson 1991: 56).

Hip Hop culture has ten foundational elements[10] to it:[11] The first is, DJing and Turntablism:[12] The study and application of rap music production and radio broadcasting.

---

[8] This is what Hip Hop culture is made up of. See Spirer Peter (1997) *Rhyme and Reason*. In this documentary about Hip Hop, rap artist tell the story of Hip Hop and explain the realness and the lifestyle they live in called Hip Hop.

[9] Alternative to main stream American society—which tended to view Hip Hop, and still does to larger extents, as "other" and outsiders.

[10] Some of these images might include a turntable, a person break dancing over a cardboard of linoleum floor, and/or a person with a microphone close to their mouth doing what is called MCing.

[11] While I am aware the scholars such as Pinn (1995: 125-132) and KRS-One (2003: 211-263) give alternate and longer definitions of Hip Hop culture, I have condensed these down into the traditional nine foundational elements. Definitions adapted from www.templeofhiphop.com (Accessed May 21, 2005).

[12] Also see Juliana Snapper (2004) in which she discusses the culture and art behind Turntablism; a mentality and culture that is unique to Hip Hop culture.

Commonly refers to the work of a disc jockey. However, Hip Hop's disc jockey does not just play vinyl records, tapes, and compact discs. Hip Hop's Deejay interacts artistically with the performance of a recorded song by cutting, mixing, and scratching the song in all of its recorded formats. Its practitioners are known as turntablists, deejays, mixologists, grandmasters, mixmasters, jammasters, and funkmasters. Popularized by Kool DJ Herc, Afrika Bambaataa, Jazzy Jay, Grand Master Flash, Grand Wizard Theodore, Kool DJ Red Alert, DJ Cash Money, Marley Marl, Brucie B, Chuck Chillout, Kid Capri, Afrika Islam, and Jam Master Jay.

The second foundational element is Breaking: The study and application of street dance forms commonly called break dancing, or B-Boying. It now includes the once independent dance forms, up-rockin, poppin and locking, jailhouse or slap boxing', Double Dutch, Electric Boogie, and Capoiera[13] martial arts. It is also commonly referred to as Freestyle Street dancing. The practitioners of traditional breaking are called B-Boys, B-Girls, and Breakers. Breaking moves are commonly used in aerobics and other exercises that refine the body. Break-dancing is an acrobatic style of street dancing. Popularized by James Brown, the Nigga Twins, Dennis Vasquez – the Rubber Band Man, Rock Steady Crew, Pee Wee Dance, The N.Y.C. Breakers, the Breeze Team, and Michael Jackson.

Third is Graffiti: The study and application of color, light and handwriting. Other forms of this art include Bombin' and Taggin'[14]. Its practitioners are known as Writers, Graffiti writers, Graffitist, and Graffiti artists. Graffiti is commonly referred to as Aerosol Art, Life Art, Pieces, Burners, Graf, and Urban Murals. Other forms of this art include Bombin and Taggin. Its practitioners are known as writers, graffiti writers, graffitist, and

---

[13] Also derived from Brazil in street dancing.

[14] Another form of graffiti art that involves placing a name or logo on a wall for representation of your gang, neighborhood, community, or self.

graffiti artists. Today, graffiti artists seek to be masters of handwriting and art. Graffiti artists rate themselves on their ability to write, and/or draw a good story. Many have become graphic artists, fashion designers, photographers, and motion picture directors. Graffiti – writing or drawing that is scribbled, scratched, or sprayed on a surface. Popularized by Taki 183, Phase 2, Kase 2, Cope 2, Tat's Cru, Presweet, Iz the Wiz, Seen, Quik, O.E., Revolt, Dondi, Zephyr, and Futura 2000.

Fourth is Break Beats: This is both the study and application of body music which commonly refers to the act of creating rhythmic sounds with various parts of the body, particularly the throat, mouth, and hands. Its practitioners are known as human beat boxes or human orchestras. Philosophically, Beatboxin' is about using the body as an instrument. Earlier versions of this expression included handbone or hambone. However, modern Beatboxin' originates from the act of imitating early electronic drum machines. The early electronic drum machines were some of the original beat boxes; and to skillfully imitate them was called Beatboxin. Popularized by Doug E. Fresh, Biz Markie, The Fat Boyz, DMX, Greg Nice, Bobby McFarrin, Emanon, Click the Super Latin, K-Love, and Razell.

Fifth is Emceeing: The study and application of rap, poetry, and divine speech. Commonly referred to as rappin' or Rap. Its practitioners are known as Emcees or Rappers. The Emcee is a Hip Hop poet who directs and moves the crowd by rhythmically rhyming in spoken word. The word Emcee comes from the abbreviated form of Master of Ceremonies (McWhorter 2003). In its traditional sense, (McWhorter 2003) refers to the hosting of an event – the master of a ceremony or event. Early Hip Hoppers transformed the traditional character of the MC to include crowd participation routines and poetry. Today, the Emcee seeks to be a master of the spoken word, not just the best Rapper. Emcees also deliver lectures and other forms of public instruction. Most Emcees rate themselves on their ability to rock the party, speak clearly, and tell a good story. Emceeing was popularized by Cab Calloway, Coke La Rock, Busy Bee Starsky, Cowboy, Melle Mel, Grandmaster Caz, Kool Moe Dee, Rakim, Big Daddy Kane, and Muhammad Ali.

The sixth foundational element is Street Knowledge: The study and application of life, society, culture, religion, theology, spirituality, and the self. In Hip Hop's inception, knowledge was a fundamental system which distinguishes it from other pop culture forms of art. Knowledge, and the ability to "spit" knowledge in the rhymes, is imperative in understanding where an MC or rapper was coming from. Understanding your historical roots as an artist was also fundamental. If an artist is not knowledgeable about their history, their self, society, and presenting that in a creative way, they would not be seen as original and could potentially be seen as "phony" or "fake." Knowledge is a corner stone of Hip Hop culture and remains so the current trend to sound like every one else.

Seventh is Street Language: With any cultural form comes its own structure of language. Street language is a part of Hip Hop culture that makes it distinguishable from other musical genres and cultures. Geneva Smitherman (1994) gives a dictionary myriad of street language examples: "Busta," "mamma jamma," "marinate," "nine," and "whassaup" to name a few. These words are derivatives from common English words (Smitherman 1994: 5-11) and do follow a structure. Smitherman suggests nine patterns that street language, or as she states "African American Language" (1994: 1-10), follows: 1) the "r" sound at the end of a word or after a vowel is not heard (1994: 12), 2) certain words, such as "cold," get reduced to a vowel sound of single consonant sound to "coal" (1994:12), 3) there is stress on the first syllable of words such as "PO-leece" for "police" (1994:12-13), 4) there are vowel sounds in words that rhyme with "think" and "ring," these words thus change to "thank" and "rang" (1994:13), 5) there is an indicate tense (time) by context, not with an "s" or "ed" such as "Mary do anythang she want to" (1994: 13), 6) "Be" and "Bees" to indicate continuous action or in frequently recurring activity, 7) Intial "th" sound for words phrases such as "Di da bomb!" (1994: 13), 8) final "th" sound that can morph into "f" as in "Def Comedy" or "Def Jam" (1994: 13), and 9) "Is" and "are" in sentences such as "Whats up?" and "Whad up?" (1994:13-14).

Eighth is Street Fashion: Baggy pants, loose fitting clothing, long silver necklaces, and baseball caps slightly turned to one side are just a few of the examples that Hip Hop street fashion is about. These fashions are not just relegated to the "streets" major department stores such as Macy's, The Gap, and Old Navy have also bought into street fashion and market it as well. Street fashion can be almost anything, but typically follows a loose fit, jean style, boot or sneaker worn look.

The final element is Street Entrepreneurialism: Hip Hop's roots are in entrepreneurialism. This is how the culture started. Rap artists such as Sean Puffy Combs (aka: P Diddy), and Jay Z, both have their own clothing label, record company, and recording studios. The sprit of Hip Hop is to be self-reliant, but within a community that can also support you in that endeavor.

The tenth and final element of Hip Hop culture is Knowledge of God & of Self: If you have not already guessed it, Hip Hop is spiritual—another reason why Tupac flourish so well in it. Hip Hop is rooted in spirituality: feeling the beat, moving your mind to a higher elevation in God, connecting with the community in song and dance, building up on another, and even growing deeper in a relationship with God. Through this spirituality, the Hip Hopper is able to gain a stronger and deeper knowledge of both God and the self—key in the journey of consciousness. Hip Hop gains a higher spirituality by embracing other elements of Hip Hop such as breaking, MCing, and the use of street knowledge. Understanding of God and of the self are the most important elements of Hip

Hop. Some have even argued that the reason Hip Hop is in the state it is in is because it has left its spiritual roots.

These ten areas combine to form what we know now as Hip Hop culture.[15] Any one of these areas may interact or overlap with each other. For example, an MC can also be a beat-boxer that keeps the show moving while others are break dancing.

### *Identity of Hip Hop Culture Among Hip Hop Youth*

Peters argues that, "Within music there is a chance to connect with people on a basic level, either to give meaning to suffering, or a reason for being" (2001). Rap music is just that: music. Music is a powerful medium in which many derive meaning, uniqueness, and identity. Larry Starr and Christopher Waterman discuss that music aides people in understanding their world; particularly Americans with pop music (2003: 454-455).[16]

Urban youth are able to identify with many of the issues, concepts, and social particulars that rap music raises. Further, Abercrombie and Longhurst (1998) propose that individuals' or a group's involvement with media content or a particular celebrity and related cultural trappings, could range from consumer, through fan, cultist, enthusiast, to petty producer. In other words, this supports the important reflexive relationship between identity formations, measured as identification, and media use (Abercrombie and Longhurst 1998: 55-60). Accordingly, Ting-Toomey and Chung state, "Through music, some find a common identity, expression and connection with others—

---

[15]Tupac operated within these foundational elements of Hip Hop culture. Tupac embodied all nine elements of Hip Hop culture and elevated them to a new level in his music; yet another reason why people loved and respected him so much.

[16] More importantly, they also discuss the importance of music to this generation and the impact of music on American mainstream culture; particularly Rap music.

especially because music expresses exactly what they might be feeling. Music inspires trends, fashion, and alternative ways of expression…" (2005: 324).

Being able to identify oneself amidst a sea of others is extremely important to Hip Hoppers. "The search for personal identity that intensifies in adolescence can involve several dimensions of an adolescent's life: vocational plans, religious beliefs, values and preferences, political affiliations and beliefs, gender roles, and ethnic identities" (Tatum 1999:53). Identity is fundamental for a true Hip Hopper. To be unique, distinctive, and distinguishing is of paramount importance for a true Hip Hopper.

According to psychologist William Cross (1991)[17] there are five stages of racial identity that exist for young people. These five stages also exist within Hip Hop culture: Pre-encounter, Encounter, Immersion and Emersion, Internalization, and Internalization-Commitment (See Appendix I for details).

Each of these stages represents another step into Hip Hop culture. By the time an individual reaches stage five, they are engulfed in the culture and have embodied, internalized, and personified the culture. For many, this area represents the lifestyle of Hip Hop. While each stage can also exhibit different verbal codes and sub-stages, stage five is the deepest level of commitment to the culture. This is what music does. For people, who are poor and socially downtrodden, music represents an entire sub-system of identity. Being able to have an artist on the radio identify with your problems and issues draws that person to the artist and the artist to that person (c.f. Southern 1983: 400).

There is also the use of identity, among urban teens involved in Hip Hop culture, as a cultural capital. By the term "cultural capital" I am using a concept first developed by John Hall (1992) and later used by Andrea Clay (2003) in determining if Hip Hop

---

[17] According to Cross, this is a stage that many youth take delight within Hip Hop culture. The youth are being exposed to new and creative ideas that are typically not matched within their lives; this stage, for most Hip Hoppers, happens at a very young age (1991:140-149).

culture was a part of this capital. Using Clay's definition, because it fits the best for this context, she states, "Cultural capital is used to position people in a particular status hierarchy among their peers. Furthermore, it acts as a criterion for setting up boundaries and determining who is legitimate or authentic in a setting, excluding those that lack legitimacy" (2003:1349). Many urban youth tend to use Hip Hop culture as a means to see who has the better clothes or "flyer" gear. This capital can be used as a means of peer pressure, as seen in Clay's study of inner city youth in East Oakland (2003: 1351-1356). This capital is a basis for exclusion from the social group. Young people, in Clay's study, used Hip Hop culture as a means to stereotype and label other youth that did not fall into Hip Hop culture's categories. Moreover, in this study, most of the youth sampled, said that "beats"[18] or the "music" was the main part of Hip Hop for them (Clay 2003: 1356). This study is an example of how diverse Hip Hop culture can be in young people's identification factors (e.g. Annegret 2005). This is not the norm for most involved in Hip Hop culture, however it deserves further research.[19]

Further, Imani Perry also contends that, "Good music often has a beauty identifiable across the boundaries of nation and culture. And yet a musical composition, and musical forms in general, have identities rooted in community" (2004: 11). Community helps to form meaning and cultural identity within Hip Hop culture. Perry further states, "To know that community means that the critic possesses both a historic and an aesthetic body of information relevant for understanding the music's original context" (2004: 11). This is one reason why White youth can identify with rap music (c.f. Perry 2004: 38-57). It brings identity to their world and adds culture to White youth who

---

[18] See the glossary for complete definition of the word.

[19] Tupac himself has been called a Hip Hop cultural capital in that he was a figure, icon, and image of Hip Hop culture that does sell and generate money (Neal 2002; Long 2001).

tend to not have a set "culture" (e.g. Perry 2004). For many White youth, Hip Hop is a place where they can express their own thoughts in a space they can be accepted as "one of us" rather than just being White.

For many involved in Hip Hop culture, identifying one another means that the individuals are able to recognize another fellow Hip Hopper. To recognize another Hip Hopper does not necessarily need to take place cognitively, this can happen very subliminally; in other words, you just know another Hip Hopper (August et. al. 2001; Anderson 2003). These means of reorganization can be broken down into several categories: Relevance, respectful and authentic.

Relevance: The person must be relevant and up to date with different issues currently facing the generation. This does not always manifest itself within fashion or knowledge of who is who in Rap music, but more often manifests itself with the person being "knowledgeable" about current debates. KRS-One is a prime example of this. He may not be up to date with all of the current fashions, but can articulate and argue current debates while remaining true to himself and the culture as a whole.

Respectful, Equal and Non-Judgmental: The perfect balance of these is a level well worth striving for. Most people see Hip Hoppers as disrespectful, loud, mean, arrogant, and extremely judgmental. But, when we take away the commercialization of Rap music then we begin to see that individuals involved in Hip Hop culture will posses these attributes, not necessarily all the time, or in order. However, this is a staple mark of true Hip Hoppers: to respect and honor those that respect and honor you; to reserve judgment until all the facts have been researched and sought after. Elizabeth Blair (1993) discusses how Rap music has been commercialized and treated as a commodity. She also gives insight into the deeper issue of rap music being stolen from Blacks by Whites; an issue that Greg Tate (2003), Carl Rux (2003), and Robin Kelley (2003) all discuss in the book, "Everything But the Burden: What White People are Taking from Black Culture."

Authentic: Once again we find ourselves looking into the word "authentic." Being "authentic" simply means to be who you are when you present yourself to the world. Urban youth, and youth in general, can sniff out a "rat" very quickly. If you are not who you say you are, you stand to loose credibility in all three of these areas very quickly. Entry back in is extremely difficult.[20] Moreover, urban youth tend to have an overdeveloped sense of justice and injustice is quickly spotted—having almost become experts of injustice due to their geographic location. Tupac was keen at this process of spotting injustice and calling out the "rats" of a group.

Identification also begins to seep into fashion. For those that are ignorant of the culture, they believe that all "rappers" wear baggy clothing and loud jewelry. While that may be true for some, Hip Hop culture identification does not mean you have to have those fashion statements. Fashion is who you are, if that means you wear a cowboy hat, some Adidas shoes, Wrangler jeans, and a lime green jacket—if that is who you are—then you are Hip Hop. You are not relegated to just wear F.U.B.U[21] or Roca Wear.[22] Fashion is open to the interpretation of the individual. Edward Armstrong describes how the White Rapper Eminem has constructed his own authenticity by being who he is and has constructed his own fashion for poor Whites by his look. This is authentic because no

---

[20] For example, artists such as Vanilla Ice and MC Hammer have had a difficult time regaining credibility because of their "sell-out" labels they attained during the mid 1990's. Their albums and voices are not heard by many in Hip Hop culture.

[21] The clothing line name For Us By Us.

[22] Short for Roca Fella Records, Jay Z's line of clothing.

one has "set-up" Eminem to do this, he was that way before he had a CD out (2004: 336-337).

Regardless, when commercialization meets Hip Hop, you begin to see some of the more stereotypical styles of Hip Hoppers (Blair 1993: 27-29). When the large corporations take over, the public is witness to the commercialization of the style, language, and culture as a whole. Therefore, you have rappers that fit the stereotypical image of Hip Hop culture. This is one of the major debates between the true authentic Hip Hopper and the fake (inauthentic) Hip Hopper (KRS-One 2003; Kitwana 2003; La Point 2003).

There are four areas that Hip Hop youth use to identify each other within Hip Hop culture.[23] However, for Hip Hop culture identification, these four are the most prolific. The four areas are 1) rhythm and audio, 2) language and the verbal, 3) spatial, and 4) written.

## Rhythm and Audio

The rhythm, or the actual music that rappers rap over, is one of the first elements that most urban youth can identify with when they first hear a song. The rhythm is part of the audio component of the culture. The rhythm is what drives the lyrics for some rappers. For other rappers, they desire a rhythm beat that compliments their lyrics. For artists such as Tupac, they choose rhythms that will fit the lyrics they are using for that particular mood or context. For artists such as Ice-T, his rhythms were very simple (a kick drum, snare, melody, and bell), because his lyrics were the dominant force in the

---

[23] These four areas are extrinsically tied into part of the twelve signal systems of Donald Smith (1992). His 12 signal systems are verbal, written, numeric, pictorial, artifactual, audio, kinesic, optical, tactile, spatial, temporal, and olfactory (1992: 146). These 12 systems are active in any culture, according to Smith.

song. For other artists such as Dr. Dre, the rhythm is very complex (major variations of percussion, multilayered keyboards, and voice overs), and his lyrics are not always as intricate.

Further, the rhythm and sampling is part of a larger study that deserves research as well. For example, the use of sampling in Hip Hop is not only creative, but postmodern as well (e.g. Potter 1995; Lash 1990: 45-61). The fact that artists take rhythm and sounds from other albums and use them in such a creative and artistic way for a "new sound" and a "new creation" of sound, is a capitulation to the postmodern way and make Hip Hop culture a postmodern phenomena (c.f. Keyes 2002: 123-131). Jazz and Blues were no different, John Leland states, "Workers in southern cotton fields mixed all these flavors, adding also elements of the Irish ballad, the hymnal and other European influences" (2004: 34). New rhythms for both the Blues and Hip Hop were then formed and a new form of music was structured.

Rhythms are a vital part of Hip Hop culture. For many, it is what makes or breaks a rap song. If the rhythm is "hittin," then the album is worth listening to. However, an artist can have the best lyrics, greatest relevance, and be authentic but have "weak" "beats,"[24] and most consumers today will not listen to their album. Jay Z stated that he "dumbs" his lyrics down to get paid, while his beats remain "tight."[25] So there is still more debate as to whether or not a person is being authentic to Hip Hop culture. The question remains: do lyrics really matter that much?[26]

---

24 See the glossary for the definition of the word "Beat."

25 The Source Magazine (August 2002).

26 An interesting debate that has carried on over the years, according to Gruber and Thau (2003), rap lyrics are responsible for violet acts among inner city Black males.

Within the rhythm, urban youth are able to distinguish which song is actually Hip Hop and which song is not. For example, many house rhythms share a common link with Rap music. However, house rhythms are very rapid and tend to have a BPM[27] of one hundred and ten and higher, and the base drum drives the song. Most rap songs contain a variety of rhythms.

Historically, for many enslaved Blacks, it was the rhythm that gave them hope through the lyrics (Odum 1968:60-65). Through the rhythm, slaves were able to remember the lyrics and connect with God while in the fields. Moreover, there was a social connection between the beats and identifying a good encouraging song; Hip Hop culture and Rap music are no different for this generation (Odum 1968: 168-171). John Leland also contends that like "Gumbo," music was all "mixed-up" and made into a new form for new listening and pleasure for enslaved Blacks (2004: 17-38).

### Language and the Verbal

This section deals with language and verbal issues. These two concepts are part of a larger body of work that cannot be discussed in this book. J.L. Dillard (1972), Cheryl Keyes (2002: 122-156), Salikoko Mufwene (et al.1998), and Geneva Smitherman (1977, 1994, 2000) all discuss African American Vernacular English at length. This book makes mention of language and verbal to build into the study of Tupac.

Every generation has their own style of language. The Hip Hop generation is no different in their patternization of language. The lyrics speak to many within Hip Hop culture. True Hip Hoppers will identify an artist by their lyrics. [28] Smith (1992) discusses how this is the most commonly recognized signal system in many cultures (146). The

---

[27] Beats Per Minute
[28] For more on Hip Hop language, see the Hip Hop Dictionary online at: http://www.anthonyvitti.com/hiphopdictionary.html

language of many urban youth, originated from "broken English," which has a history from diverse nations and linguistic history (Dillard 1972: 73-138), and was modeled (not given) by early Hip Hop artists such as Run DMC and Cool Herc. However, "Black English" and the issue of "Ebonics" are also tied into the language of Hip Hop culture (Alim 2006). Further, the concept of "Nommo," the power of the word (Smitherman 1998: 208), is once again seen here. Smitherman states, "the word is believed to be the force of life itself. To speak is to make something come into being" (1998: 208).

Nommo is a powerful concept within Hip Hop culture—though rarely articulated from its participants. Words are powerful and give meaning to everyday life. This is yet another reason why Tupac was so popular: his words meant something in a world where much else did not. Tupac was a powerful communicator and was able to articulate words in such a way as to create a space of meaning and identity for many.

Many urban young people can identify with other urban people by how they talk. If too much "correct" English is used, then the person might not be too authentic, however if broken English is used, and a few words are mispronounced, then the person might be legitimate (Black 2003 and North 2005). This raises the question of, "what if the authentic self only speaks proper English?" This is an issue for many urbanites who do speak proper English and not broken English (commonly referred to as Ebonics), and their "realness" within the community. This area deserves further research as many young people I have encountered feel as though they may be seen as too "White" or "soft" if they speak proper English; something that each of the television shows studied in this project dealt with but never quite came to a solution. Social face—your social status and credibility— is extremely important within urban and Hip Hop culture (Morgan 1998: 252-254; Keyes 2002: 123-126), and language remains a part of the social face ritual.

Additionally, Elijah Anderson discusses how the code of the street is predominantly a spoken trait (1999: 35-36). This code brings with it the rules and norms for street living; for many urban youth, this is reality and Hip Hop culture is the vehicle to make sense of it all (Rose 1996 and Kitwana 2003). Within the first seconds of speech,[29] a young person is able to distinguish if you understand where they are coming from or not.

Language, within Hip Hop and urban culture, can also take on an "insulting" form. This is called "Playing the Dozens" or, as a more contemporary way to phrase it "Baggin." Baggin is part of the verbal styles of Hip Hop and urban culture in which the participants use words in a creative and rhythmic way to insult and verbally abuse each other. Richard Majors and Janet Bilson state, "Playing the dozens…represents a way to act and be cool with astonishingly intricate verbal play" (1992: 91). For Tupac, this was a part of daily life and a form of being "cool," as discussed by Majors and Bilson (1992: 100-102).

## Spatial

Nowhere is space more an issue than in the inner city. Gangs set their territory by space. Families relegate themselves to a certain square mile and never leave that space. Urban neighborhoods are "sectioned" off by city officials, and Rap artists identify themselves with the "space" they are from (or the 'hood they are from) (Baldwin 2004: 160).

This is one of the reasons why you hear Rap artists yell out their area code. In the film *8 Mile*, the characters were distinguished and categorized by which area code they were from. For many urban youth, this is one of only a few self identification factors they

---

[29] In some sub cultures of Hip Hop, speech could also be seen as "rapping."

have; therefore area codes become a large identification factor for the inner city, i.e. Hip Hop culture.

Many within the inner city use streets, area codes, zip codes, and even street numbers to identify themselves with their hood. Hip Hop culture embraces that and gives the young person identity through the music and culture as a whole. Space is very important in the inner city. For Hip Hoppers; it represents who you are as a person. Space can also determine how much of a woman or man you are as well (Anderson 1999). As a whole, Hip Hop culture allows for the individual (as well as the group) to identify themselves with whatever part makes them feel comfortable. We can begin to see the postmodern in this concept.[30]

Space[31] can also take on different locations within cities too. In 1992 West Coast Rap artist DJ Quick, recorded "Jus Lyke Compton." This track made Compton identifiable for many youth who were living in the city, as well as many who were not. Compton was further made popular in earlier years by the famed group N.W.A.[32] who joyously claimed to be from Compton (c.f. Forman 2002: 193-198).

Furthermore, Anderson further contends that respect, a strong part of the code of the streets, has a role in the identity formation of teens within their space. Anderson states, "Typically in the inner-city poor neighborhood, by the age of ten, children from decent and street oriented families alike are mingling on the neighborhood streets and figuring out their identities. Here they try out roles and scripts in a process that challenges

---

[30] Murray Forman discusses that spatial discourse coheres around the concept of the hood; this concept is manifested in what is called "Gangsta Rap" or "West Coast" rap. This is an important special element that Forman argues is a pivotal point for Hip Hoppers (2002: 191-192).

[31] For Tupac space was extremely important, he was known for his upbringing in Marin City, California. This was important because of Marin City's reputation for being "hard" and "mean."

[32] Niggas With Attitude

their talents..." (1999: 68). Street corners then in turn become spatial corners in which not only identity formation is taking place, but also socialization skills (Anderson 1999: 69-72). Tupac was a direct product of this being raised in his teen years by street hustlers, pimps, and prostitutes.

## Written

Graffiti art is more than just "vandalism" on a wall. It is a means of identifying who the other artists are. In the film Wyld Style, graffiti artists are known by how well they can use a spray paint can, and how well they can tag up[33] subway lines. For many in the inner city, graffiti art is another form of identification. Hip Hop has its roots in graffiti art. Many of the concerts that were put on in the early years were marketed by flyers that were designed and printed by graffiti[34] artists.[35]

Moreover, these same artists were also part of the act and left their mark in the park, club, studio, or street corner of the performance. The written aspect of identification is an important one for Hip Hop culture. It is how many are able to let others know who they are. For some, talking is too overwhelming, but in their creative mind, they are able to express their identity through the art of written graffiti.[36]

Gangs also use written mediums to identify each other. Each gang is known by their tag or mark that is written on a wall. If another gang or person marks over that tag,

---

[33] Also known as marking ones territory. Hip Hoppers, and gang members, will mark up a territory with their name to serve two purposes. The first is to allow others to know their "tag" (or graffiti name) name. And the second is to be identified in the community (Tiersma 1999: 200-208).

[34] Pictorial, which is another one of Smith's (1992) signal systems, is also involved in graffiti.

[35] Even the way Tupac spelled his name was connected to the written.

[36] Douglas Kellner makes mention of the radical discourse through a combination of the written and the verbal (1995: 174-177). Kellner argues that Rap music is the medium and voice for angry Black males (1995: 180).

then it is a sign of extreme disrespect, and typically, a death ensues (e.g. Anderson 1999 ; Mahiri and Sablo 1996).

All four of these areas are important for urban youth to identify themselves within Hip Hop culture. All of these areas interact with each other and overlap, as seen by Figure 10.

The four areas can converge or be separate at any given time. For many urban youth, they are unaware that they are operating within this ideology. For many Hip Hoppers they know, but cannot put the words to the feeling.

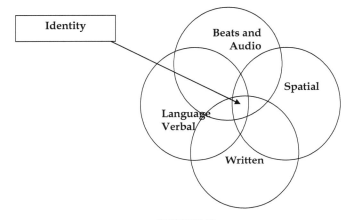

**FIGURE 10**

**THE INTERCONNECTION OF THE FOUR IDENTIFICATION FACTORS WITHIN HIP HOP CULTURE**

### *Hip Hop's Rootz*

To understand why Hip Hop culture is attractive to youth, we must first begin by reviewing some basic history of the culture. In doing so, we are able to see the big picture of why urban youth are attracted to rap music and Hip Hop culture. It is interesting to note that Odum (1968) begins to unpack this oral African tradition that had been passed down for many generations. This connects with jazz and the emergence of Black Gospel music (Southern 1983), which gives rise to Rap music during the early 1970's. Both of these authors give a generous history to the musical genres of jazz, blues, Black Gospel music, and the music of the slaves.

Tricia Rose states that, "Hip hop culture emerged as a source for youth of alternative identity formation and social status in a community whose older local support institutions had been all but demolished along with large sectors of its built environment. Alternate local identities were forged in fashions and language, street names, and most important, in establishing neighborhood crews or possee's" (1994 a: 34). These postindustrial conditions were a part of the argument that Daniel Bell makes about the shifting from an industrial to a post-industrial society (1973: 47-118). This "shift" caused the middle economic section of urban communities to fall out, displacing many, and un-employing thousands. Within this rubble, rap was formed.[37]

Michael Eric Dyson contends that Hip Hoppers were able to conjure up a certain type of capital from the misery and pain of inner city living. Dyson states, "Hip-hoppers joined pleasure and rage while turning the details of their difficult lives into craft and capital. This is the world Hip Hop would come to represent: privileged persons speaking for less visible or vocal peers" (Dyson 1996: 177). This was the humble beginning of what is known today as Hip Hop. To understand any culture or people, one must first understand its history. [38]

Hip Hop developed in the early 70´s in the South Bronx (Bennet 2000:134; Chang 2005: 3). Its initial practitioners were DJs (often playing disco, funk, or reggae dub records), assisted by a "master of ceremonies," who would handle the verbal interchange with the crowd. DJs such as Kool DJ Herc and Pete Jones began to draw huge crowds at clubs and block parties. As DJs started to develop the rhythm and breaks of Hip Hop, some of the focus was transferred from the turntables to other things such as MCing and B-Boying. These artists were speaking to Gen X'ers—The Hip Hop generation (Kitwana

---

[37] Also see Rose (1994 b) where she also describes the post industrial living conditions in which Hip Hop culture was formed.

[38] For a look at basic Hip Hop terminology, see http://www.anthonyvitti.com/hiphopdictionary.html

2002)—, a generation that was clearly under-represented and needed a voice in the public sphere.

The live atmosphere and the ability of the DJs to continuously keep the "beat" flowing between records created B-Boys. B-Boys were fanatical followers of the music who battled on the floor with dance moves. This became known as "break dancing." Hip Hop also created its own visual art: graffiti. Graffiti has existed in some form for centuries, but the colors, design, and attitude of Hip Hop graffiti have given Hip Hop an accompanying aesthetic presence that has survived the years virtually in tact.

Despite an impressive urban following and an expanding live circuit, many of these acts never put out a commercial record. "Until 1979 rap was a key component of a flourishing underground culture in the Bronx and upper Manhattan, where parties went on all night in seedy nightclubs or the music was played in schoolyards and small public parks" (Perkins 1996:9). Of the groups that did, most never enjoyed significant commercial success on the airwaves, since rapping was seen as a musical novelty. At the time, it was not as much of a concern, because so much of their efforts were focused on live performance, many of which were known as "battles," because the MCs were competing with each other for prize money. Although difficult to find through conventional retailers, live recordings of these jams do exist, they are known as "battle tapes" (Guevara 1996:55).

The localized scene of rap music became a national phenomena. Additionally, the live atmosphere of Hip Hop became secondary to the recordings (and subsequently, music videos) (Rose 1994 a; Alper 2000; Evelyn 2000).[39]

---

[39] All four of these authors agree that Run DMC "club scene" is what launched a large part of Hip Hop culture.

The term "Old School" is an all-around marketing term, often applied to Hip Hop performers of the mid-to-late 80s, such as Eazy-E, EPMD[40,] and Eric B and Rakim. It is absurd to try and definitively delineate what is and what is not "old school", but it should be noted that all of these rappers benefited from rising to the top during a period of time when Hip Hop was rapidly growing in terms of mainstream accessibility and commercial success. The ground was laid for a new culture; a culture that spoke to people; more importantly, young inner city youth (Rose 1994 b 73-75).

The term "Representin" was used extensively in the eighties. This term simply means: to show who you are; or better yet, let the world know what you are about (Perkins 1996; Dyson 1996; Rose 1994 a; Forman 2002). Hip Hop was about representation in the public sphere, a sphere that most inner city youth were denied access to; the denial of representation and voice. In its initial commencement, Hip Hop was about history. It was about past, present, and future telling a story. Even rap's largest controversies are about representing. Hip Hop's attitudes toward women and gays continually jolt in the unvarnished malevolence they reveal. The sharp responses to rap's misogyny and homophobia signify its central role in battles over the cultural representation of other harassed groups (Dyson 1996: 177-178).

Craig Watkins discusses the marriage between MTV and Hip Hop during the late 1980's and early 1990's. This was one of the first notations of the emergence of the profane through Hip Hop culture (1998: 169-180); Tupac had a part in this as well. Watkins (1998), Neal (1999 and 2002), Dyson (2001), and Rose (1994 a) all agree that Tupac's influence on television and MTV gave voice and rise to Black popular culture (more on this later in the book).With the rise of videos and MTV, Hip Hop spread as though it were set ablaze with gasoline. "As high culture became distanced from the lives

---

[40] Eric and Parish Making Dollars.

of most people, the new electronic-based entertainment forms with distinctly contemporary features were appropriated as living and vital art, especially by younger generations" (Romanowski 1996:199).

Hip Hop set the stage for public voices and a new form of music. It was the music for the postmodern generation. The Music became the philosophical base for Hip Hop artists. Modern social theory sought a universal, a historical, and a rational foundation for its analysis and critique of society. "For Marx, that foundation was species-being, while for Habermas it was communicative reason" (Ritzer 2000: 604). Postmodern thinking rejects this "Foundationalism" and tends to be relativistic, irrational, and nihilistic, post moderns have come to question foundations believing that they tend to favor some groups and downgrade the significance of others, give some groups power and render other groups powerless (Ritzer 2000: 610; White 2002:200).

N.W.A was the pioneer of Gangsta rap in 1985 (c.f. Blake 1997: 32-34), and among the first Hip Hop groups to question such foundations (educational, political, social). Dr. Dre, Ice Cube, MC Ren, and Tupac (not directly involved, but connected) emerged from this group. This group's peak came when the United States saw the brutal beating of motorist Rodney King. After the Los Angeles riots, the mood was set for a new era of Hip Hop: Gangstas and Thugs. Dr. Dre dropped[41] the album, setting the precedent for what we see today in Hip Hop. His album, "The Chronic", was the number one album for four weeks in 1993.[42] The culture was being represented and talked to. The numbers proved it. Even more amazing, we began to see youth (other than Black) buying the album and going to concerts (Forman 2002: 252-255).

---

[41] Or, released his album.

[42] Rolling Stone Top 10 lists 1993.

What N.W.A did was groundbreaking. They brought what everyone in the inner city was thinking, doing, and saying into the public sphere. In other words, they introduced the good, the bad, and the ugly of the "hood" into mainstream culture. This situation makes it difficult for Blacks to "affirm" the value of nontraditional or transgressive artistic expression. Many Blacks, and other conservatives, tend to simply dismiss such works with hypercritical disdain (Dyson 1996: 199; Dyson 2001). Most people did not know how to react to this; in addition, it brought fear into the minds of countless adults, as many young Whites flocked to the record stores to buy these albums by the millions. For one of the first times in Hip Hop history, White youth were beginning to see a new element arise from the 'hood: rap music that they could not only identify with because of its dealings with marginalization, but also enjoy the musings—from afar—of rappers like Eazy E and Ice Cube.

The ground was now set for an explosion of Hip Hop culture into mainstream United States. At that point, we begin to see "hints" of the profane seeping into every area of American pop culture. "Hip-hop was saturating the media spaces of the mainstream press and, of greater consequence, television, gaining unprecedented attention throughout North America" (Forman 2002: 214). Urban youth joined pleasures with suburban youth, and the attraction to Hip Hop culture was unanimous: it is the voice of a multiethnic generation (Hodge 2003; Kitwana 2003; Watkins 1998).

Because Hip Hop emerged from the inner city,[43] its attraction to those particular youth residing in these traverse locations in cities, is a natural appeal. Hip Hop culture speaks for those who cannot. Moreover, it speaks for those who need a voice in the public

---

[43] Let us not get the elements of the inner city "twisted." The inner city is not all about guns, ho's, drugs, and gang violence. Elijah Anderson discusses the differences and the unique qualities between "street families" and "decent families" (1999:35-65). These two entities of urban community life represent the urban community, both the good and the bad.

sphere. Many urban youth do not have this "voice." Rap music and Hip Hop culture provide that outlet and medium in which to argue, love, hate, yell, whisper, chill[44], eat, sleep, walk, talk, confide, and build community.

In this attraction, we begin to see the rise of three personas of Black males[45] in mainstream American pop culture[46] as it relates to Hip Hop culture. They are The Race man, The New Black Aesthetic and The Nigga.

The Race Man: this is a bourgeois sentiment that locates itself in the politics and power of cultivating the advancement of the race of Black people—primarily, but not exclusively. This race man symbolizes positive representations of Black people—both the individual and the ethnicity as a whole. There is a strong critique of the negative images of the inner city, and a strong desire to do "what is right." Bill Cosby is the representative of this particular image. His role has been to serve as the "race man" and be the spokesperson for Blacks during cultural debates. Todd Boyd states, "The concept of the race man was applicable to African American cultural producers as well. Musicians, artists, and entertainers were celebrated or criticized for their ability to provide positive images…" (1997: 19). The race man is an image carried over from the Civil Rights era: a person who can lead out; typically one individual. This denotes a very modern ideology in the manner in which this unravels within the Black culture. The death of the race man came during the mid-1980's after the rise of Gangsta rap and its realness and authenticity. Todd Boyd further argues that there have been no major world wars,

---

[44] See the glossary for complete definition of the word.

[45] The Black male image and Black youth are the foundational piece to Hip Hop culture when it emerged within the inner city. Hip Hop has embraced many different ethnicities, but overall, the Black image, particularly the Black male persona, is still referred to when Hip Hop culture is discussed (e.g. Dyson 1996 and 2001; Kitwana 2003; Clay 2003; Hodge 2003).

[46] These concepts are derived from Todd Boyd (1997: 13-37).

cultural events, or even movements for the Black race in the last twenty five years; the concept of the race man is dead (1997: 20).[47]

The New Black Aesthetic: this represents a more political person who is more into community and the reality of injustice within the inner city. This rise takes place during the late 1980's and early 1990's. The death of the race man sees the rise of civil justice leaders like film maker Spike Lee. Todd Boyd states, "Lee is the perfect example of this new generation, having attended Morehouse, the citadel of the Black male bourgeois, and the highly regarded New York University film school" (1997: 25). Spike was the spokesperson for this aesthetic. Characteristics of this model[48] included speaking up about injustices, going to college, attaining an education in a known university, getting ahead, and doing your best to represent the Black race. Still, this suggests a notion of middle to upper middle class socioeconomics (Boyd 1997: 26). You need to have some money to go to college, and most in the inner city do not have that type of money. This persona fit a more "cultured" or "civilized" Black; one that was not necessarily from the ghetto, but was more shaped and refined. This image lasted for several years.[49]

The Nigga[50]: "The concept of the nigga is a return to an older form of Black masculinity in popular culture, but rejuvenated relative to the circumstances of contemporary culture" (Boyd 1997: 30). This is the image we are currently dealing with.

---

[47] Rap groups such as De La Soul, Tribe Called Quest, and Arrested Development would come near this concept, but do not represent the entire concept entirely.

[48] This image is not totally gone, Pearl Stewart's study on Black Universities reveals that many feel that Hip Hop is a negative influence on many Black students, and some are arguing to ban the music and fashions (2004).

[49] Rap groups such as Public Enemy, X-Clan, and Professor X are representative of this image, but do not encompass all of the attributes.

[50] The term nigga also takes on a class-conscious state as argued by Kelley (1994: 183-227). I will be discussing Kelley's use of the word "nigga" as I feel it has a significant relationship to how Tupac used it too, later in the book.

The film *Menace II Society* captured this image well, "Old Dogg was America's worst nightmare: Young Black and don't give a Fuck!" This is the "in your face," restless, rebel that many urban youth identify with. This image is about the reality of the streets. The reality that, even though a person desires to go to college, he or she may not be able to attend because of their living situation; more importantly, their hood and identity is more important than a "formal" education. "Gangsta rap, with its origins on the West Coast, specifically addresses the worldview of the truly disadvantaged" (Boyd 1997: 34). Many older Boomers have issues with this image; they see it as troublesome and negative. Tupac emerged from this, and with him came the emergence of the profane during the mid 1990's. Tupac was and still is the spokesperson for this image: one that embodies the positive and the negative, while embracing education, injustice, and social activism—a contradiction for many, but a reality for people like Tupac.[51]

Still another reason many urban youth are attracted to Rap music is the arrival, through the music, of postmodernity (Alper 2000; Anderson 2003; Forman 1995). Rap music embraces three crucial elements of postmodernism term "The Three Negations" by Dick Hebdige (1998: 374-381). The three areas are:

1. *Against Totalisation*: Hip Hop culture is not in favor of one grand story, or in postmodern terms "meta-narrative." Rap music calls out the faults and errors of the previous and current generation's dogma on success, life, theology, love, hate, women, men, and sex. Hip Hop culture begins to dismantle this point of view by word and prose and questions its substances. This is attractive to many urban youth, as they have been questioning this ideology ever since they were born. The belief that was given to many in the Hip Hop generation—just work hard and you will succeed in America—is bullshit, and the chickens are coming home to roost in the passionate lyrics of artists such as Tupac and Eve. There is not a total story for all, we are each created uniquely and individually, yet we require the community of others while engaging in their stories; this is a large part of Hip Hop culture and its ensuing attraction to many urban youth.

---

[51] This is what Richard Middleton calls "Locating the People from within the music." The Nigga image, Gangsta and political rap genres (See Figure 9), speak to and for the people (2003: 251-254).

2. *Against Teleology*: Hip Hop culture is against the "final word" from scholars and professionals that explain the origins and existence of the earth, humanity, God, religion, and humanity. Rap music calls out the monopoly of rich White males that have dominated most of Western Culture to this day (e.g. Neal 1997; Gottdiener 1985). Rap music and Hip Hop culture begin to dismantle the grand stories that we all came from one source: apes. Hip Hop culture increases the span of knowledge and brings back the mystery of Christ and creation. For many urban youth, it is a relief to know that they do not have to follow in the former generation's footsteps to be successful; this is one reason why so many urban youth are entrepreneurs and are seeking alternative employment (c.f. North 2005; Murch 2003).

3. *Against Utopia*: This particular area should be familiar. However, for many urban youth, the reality of a utopia is not within reach. The harsh realties of the inner city surround their daily lives and force them to question whether there really is a God that allows such despair. This has been the belief of many urbanites for many years. However, many political officials continue to argue that people must just work harder and faster to succeed, or attend another program for happiness. Hip Hop culture calls the lie out and ushers in the reality of ghetto living. This is attractive for many young people. It is their daily life.

I discuss postmodernity here for several reasons. First, postmodernity gives Tupac a context—philosophically and pedagogically—in which to operate. His understanding of the 'hood, urban youth, Hip Hop culture, and God had postmodern qualities to them.

Second, Tupac was a postmodernist. He himself did not like the norms of society. He questioned absolute truths, absolute authority, and believed deeply in community, which are all tenets of postmodernity as argued by Lash (1990), Lyotard (1984), Kuçuradi (2004), and Kirk (2000).Tupac's life was about "going against the grain" and living as an outlaw. More importantly, Tupac's understanding of Jesus was an unorthodox attempt to understand Christ—a Jesus that walks like us[52], talks like us, smokes like us, and drinks like us. One of the aspects of postmodernity is that it allows for a wider, newer, and unorthodox way of coming to Christ. This was Tupac's goal for the Gospel.

---

[52] "Us" being the urban community, to be more consice, Black and Brown youth (Shakur 2003).

Lastly, Tupac was and still is a product of Hip Hop culture. To ignore the culture, is to ignore Tupac's very life. "Hip Hop is our CNN,"[53] (D 1997) is now a common phrase coined by Chuck D of the rap group Public Enemy. Tupac was a substation (a large one) of that news network.

## *Summary*

This chapter dealt with identity to Rap music and Hip Hop culture among urban youth, and the attraction of Rap music and Hip Hop culture. Music is a type of language for many; especially young people. Rap music begins to fill voids in young people's lives and they are able to identify with the music in many different ways. Beats and audio, language and the verbal, spatial, and written are all elements of identity within the music and culture, which urban youth are able to identify with.

Six foundational elements of Hip Hop culture are DJing and Turntablism, breaking, graffiti, break beats, Emceeing, and knowledge. These six elements combine to make up Hip Hop culture. They are neither exclusive nor static. Authenticity and being real are the overriding philosophies of Hip Hop culture.

For many, the attraction to Hip Hop culture is simple: it speaks to their everyday lives and everyday madness. Hip Hop culture embraces a variety of ethnicities and is quickly becoming global.

In this chapter, I have begun to lay out the basic reasons for the significance of Hip Hop culture, how it relates and interrelates to urban youth, and we are able to begin to see Tupac's connection (broadly) to the culture. This chapter is important as we now move into the urban context—the 'hood. These chapters have given a brief historical treatment of the culture and allows the reader to better understand why so many young

---

[53] Cable Network News.

people in general, are so attracted to Hip Hop culture and why and how Tupac was involved in it.

In the next chapter I will examine the context in which Tupac grew up. That context was the urban environment, or better stated, the 'hood. I will demonstrate how the urban context operates and give a clear picture of the atmosphere of Tupac's environment.

## CHAPTER 6

## THE 'HOOD COMES FIRST:
## THE URBAN CONTEXT

The urban context was a large part of Tupac's life and worldview. The 'hood shaped much of Tupac's poetry, theology, and lyrical points. This chapter will focus on the 'hood context in which Tupac operated. This will give a broad overview of the context in which Tupac was born, operated, and lived in.

### *The Rootz of The 'Hood*

At the turn of the 20$^{th}$ century, the growing population coming to the cities was a result of the rise of the machine age and the industrial revolution (Le Gates, Stout 2000: 143). People steadily flowed into cities, and the population of cities like San Francisco went up by 50 percent[1]. At the turn of the century, cities began to grow at an alarming rate. In fact, in 1900, 14 percent of the world's population lived in cities, and in the year 2000 over 55 percent live in the world's cities[2]. There was, and is, no doubt that cities are a "hot-spot." However, with the rise in population, decrease in job security, and racial tensions mounting, cities began to experience issues that most did not know how to deal with. Compounding the situation even further, the church looked at the city, (with its problems like prostitution, gangs, violent crimes, and theft), with the eyes of an angry and vengeful Jesus. Carter Heyward states:

---

[1] Taken from the U.S. Census Bureau of San Francisco 1901.

[2] U.S. Census Bureau World City Population, 2001.

> ...among right-thinking Christians, at least four images of Jesus have been forged historically: Jesus Christ as authoritarian Lord, Jesus Christ as moralist, Jesus Christ as adversary and against his enemies, and Jesus Christ as obedient son of his father. These four theological portraits of Jesus no doubt have represented the real faith of countless Christians over the centuries (1999:19).

Therefore, the churches began to take this message, ideology, and methods to the cities to "win" souls (Banks 1972: 128).

This attitude appeared to get the church somewhere by way of its "hell-is-hot" evangelism. Ultimately, it has only alienated a culture of young people, and made the others feel guilty for watching television. It was the beginning of sustained modern thought of the urban church and of urban Christian culture[3]. The urbanite has accepted this line of thought and viewed Jesus as an authoritarian that would dislike you if you sinned. Churches and ministries, particularly charismatic venues, bought into this belief as well and have widely used guilt tactics to evangelize the city.

After the Civil War, the nation was in disarray. Most of the country was still split, in two. The South, whose pride was damaged more than its lives and families lost, wanted revenge. Also the South's focus on "holiness" fostered a culture of traditionalism (Hood 1980). Yet the nation had passed laws that made it illegal for anyone to practice slavery. Nevertheless, ethnic relations grew worse (Myra 1999: 22).

In the beginning of the 1900's the automobile, new inventions such as the airplane, ships that could carry one across the Atlantic without a sail, and the telegraph were all "sudden" concepts that enraptured American culture. Blacks were beginning to gain notoriety as well. They were noted as solid musicians and good artists.[4] Blacks, for

---

[3] For a deeper view of this see: David Harvey, Social Justice and the City (Oxford: Basil Blackwell, 1988).

[4] As noted by *Slavery and The Making of America*, (Loeterman and Kalin 2004) and West (1988).

one of the first times in the public sphere, began to have a piece of American culture. For years, enslaved Blacks served their masters with music that they had written (As noted by *Slavery and The Making of America*, Loeterman and Kalin 2004). Eileen Southern states:

> As during the colonial period, slave musicians continued to serve their masters by providing music for entertainment and dancing. Among themselves the slaves sang their own folksongs about their work, their places of abode, their loves, their frolics and jubilees, their religion, political events—about what ever was closest to their hearts and minds. Early in the nineteenth century, some free black men began to establish themselves as professional musicians. It was no easy thing to do. As we have noted, European musicians were in firm control of music making in America: they filled the important posts in theatres and churches; they gave the concerts and directed the musical institutions, which they, for the most part, had organized. Native-born white musicians, who had achieved recognition in the eighteenth century for the psalms, hymns, and anthems, added popular music to the list in the nineteenth century (1983: 98).[5]

Music was one of the only creative outlets for many Blacks. Within music, Blacks were able to discuss and talk about the searing pain that existed and had existed in their lives for so many years. The industrial revolution, with its influx of population growth in the cities, helped Blacks gain notoriety and fame. "At the beginning of the nineteenth century, about 10 percent of the black population of the United States lived in urban communities" (Southern 1983: 97). By the early 20th century, that number almost tripled.[6]

Southern notes that Blacks took an active part in the industrial revolution because of its high work demand and pay. This also helped many Blacks to have access to the nightclub scene after work was over (Southern 1993: 221-223). Jazz was forming in the

---

[5] It is also interesting to note that Spike Lee in his film, *Do The Right Thing (1989)*, discusses how Blacks, for years, have entertained Whites with their music. In fact it makes them less a "nigger" when a White man can laugh or be entertained by the Negro.

[6] This was taken from U.S. Census Bureau World City Population, 1900.

womb of urban pop culture. Jazz paved the way for popular music such as the blues, funk, rhythm and blues, and ultimately Hip Hop (Starr and Waterman 2003: 86-87).[7]

Additionally, Eugene Perkins states, "When institutions fail, the gang will prevail" (1987: 54). He states that there are five major appeals to these gangs: 1) sense of identity, 2) sense of belonging, 3) sense of power, 4) sense of security, and 5) sense of discipline (Perkins 1987: 54). Gangs are a part of any town, city, or county in which systems have failed the people they are supposed to serve (Anderson 1999; Perkins 1987:54-60). In opposition, Tupac provided a secondary source of security, discipline, belonging, power, and security for young people through his life and music. The Thug Life mantra was supposed to be that "fill in" for urban youth.

## Jazz Music

Aside from Hip Hop and blues, no other genre of popular music has had the influence, soul grabbing, and multiethnic response like jazz music. Jazz music embodies the pain, suffering, anger, love, hate, religion, and moral codes of a people all within five notes. Jon M. Spencer notes that jazz music had its roots in slave protest and slave praise from Blacks on plantations. He intrinsically disassembles the slaves "protest" musical structure, to better understand its imposing values:[8]

- The Cries of the Slave: To God and to man.
- The Slave Comforted: With the consolation of religion and with the hope of deliverance.
- The Slave Exhorted to Patience and Hope

---

[7] Please note that Raymond Betts discusses at length the cultural significance of WWII; the rise of images, the self, consumerism, and a higher sexuality. For the purpose of this paper WWII will not be covered at a broad length (Betts 2004: Chapter 2).

[8] Adapted from Jon M. Spencer (1990: 53-54).

- The Rights of the Slave

- Appeals on Behalf of the Slave: To their masters, to rulers, to freedom, to women, and to Christians.

- Slaveholders Admonished

- The Friends of the Slave Encouraged: To Act and to Pray

- The Friends of the Slave Assembled: To pray, for consolation, on the fourth of July, on the first of August, and on a fast-day

- Emancipation: At hand and Accomplished

- Thanksgiving and Praise

- Dismissions: Getting the people ready for the song to end.

- Doxologies

Spencer argues that this type of music structure found its way into jazz music, and that jazz music has a theological progression (1990: 53). This type of flow, if you will, continually morphs into different aspects of Black music throughout history. Jazz was a monumental musical genre that began to ask the question "why?" "From the fusion of blues and ragtime with brass-band music, and syncopated dance music came jazz, a music that developed its own characteristics" (Southern 1983: 361).[9]

Music became one of the focal points of the industrial revolution for many Blacks. Music was their outlet and creative expression to the world. Blacks, which helped develop the inner city socially, would not be set up for years of musical genres including blues, gospel infused with jazz and blues, rhythm and blues, disco, and the funk era. Blacks were on the forefront of these musical revolutions, that when combined, set the stage for a postmodern philosophy; in which the grand meta-narrative[10] was questioned,

---

[9] For a detailed look into the "Jazz Age," see Southern (1983: Chapter 10).

[10] This merely means the "Grand Story" or the "Absolute History of Mankind." These were rational mindsets that evolved during the modern era to explain the universe and world around us (Lyotard 1984 and West 1993).

traditions were broken, and worldviews were affected and changed. Music led the way (c.f. Keyes 2002: 186-209).

## The Rise of Black Popular Culture

In his work, *A History of Popular Culture*, Raymond Betts gives great historical insight into the rise of pop culture, as we know it today. He entreats the affect of WWII, the rise of media, and the rise of trans-global corporations. However, Betts does not cover one of the most significant pop culture trends in America today: Black popular culture.

Betts overlooks this significant historical piece in pop culture. Throughout the 1930's the rise of "Black music" was apparent. Many Whites enjoyed listening to jazz, blues, and during the late 1950's rhythm and blues (Southern 1983: 470-471). Black pop culture greats like Louie Armstrong, Ella Fitzgerald, Billie Holiday, and gospel great Mahalia Jackson, all gave voice and "steam" to a cultural phenomena termed "Black popular culture."

Initially, Black popular culture was relegated to slave quarters (Southern 1983 and Spencer 1990). However, after the Great Depression, the Zoot Suite Riots, WWII, and the dawn of The Civil Rights Movement, Black popular culture was set up for success in the public sphere. Blacks were becoming popular and their music became their cultural signature in a culture of oppression.

Stuart Hall attempts to define what Black popular culture is:

> By definition, black popular culture is a contradictory space. It is a sight of strategic contestation. But it can never be simplified or explained in terms of the simple binary oppositions that are still habitually used to map it out: high and low; resistance versus incorporation; authentic versus inauthentic; experiential versus formal; opposition versus homogenization. There are always positions to be won in popular culture, but no struggle can capture popular culture itself for our side or theirs (1992: 26-27).

Hall deals with Black popular culture, but leaves the reader wondering how this can then be defined. This is still another quality of postmodernity: not answering all the questions with neat answers. Black popular culture had its birth between the years of 1949-1964 (Southern 1983: 489-490).

Black popular culture, which gained momentum in the late 1970's and early 1980's, began to "turn-out" American popular culture. Though it was very difficult in the beginning for many Black artists to gain fame and notoriety, Blacks persisted, and paved the way for the explosion of urban culture in the 1990's.[11]

Ray Charles did more for Black culture than most others in his generation. Ray combined and infused the musical structure of gospel, jazz, and ragtime blues into a unique musical score that grabbed the soul and would not let go. Charles was one of the first Blacks to enter the homes of Whites, without Whites feeling uncomfortable and awkward. Charles began to carve out another niche in Black popular culture. Charles led the way during the late 1960's and forced racist minds to ask the question, "Can people of color be that bad?"[12] Charles also enraged Black Christians when he merged Gospel music with jazz and blues.[13]

## The Civil Rights Movement

All of these historical events culminated to form one huge event in American history called The Civil Rights Movement. All of the anger, acrimony, hate, marginalization, and mistreatment boiled over into the streets of America during the

---

[11] I am discussing Black popular culture here. This is not to say that other ethnicities did not have a strong influence in American popular culture. However, I would argue that Blacks have a significant driving force in the shaping of urban America, popular culture as we know it today, and hip-hop music; others have followed and joined in, but it commenced with Blacks.

[12] Taken from, *Ray (2005)*, DVD.

[13] See the film *Ray* (2005) DVD, chapter 22.

1960's. The Civil Rights Movement (CRM), when combined with the rise of the United States power, the industrial revolution, and the politically charged lyrics in music, began to set a tone of dissent, pessimism, and the ability to question Mommy and Daddy to attain answers to injustices that had gone on far too long in America. Larry Neal notes the new space and the growth of Black consciousness in the 1960's that helped shape and form the CRM (1970: 9-30).

The CRM marked the beginning of a voice for the underprivileged, the marginalized, and the voiceless. The 1950's era of "Father knows best" had ended, Father, America, or Uncle Sam did not know best. The grand narrative that assumed that everyone was "created equal" and had the "same opportunity" was bullshit in the eyes of minorities. The CRM gave voice to that desire and movement. For many, the CRM developed a social order that is still with us today: protests and marches. The CRM began to reinvent their own philosophy on life, social order, and more importantly, a better place for individuals to live.

Todd Boyd notes that the CRM was an activist voice embodied in a community (2003). The CRM gave that voice fire and the establishment, that was a majority of White men, did not understand, nor have the know how, in order to understand the social and political significance of the CRM.

The single spokesman for an entire race began during this era (Bynoe 2004: 3-4). Martin Luther King became the spokesperson for all Black people. For many Blacks, this was ok. Did he speak for all? How were people like Malcolm X dealt with? Bynoe argues that this was (and still is) a problem when you have a spokesperson speaking for "everyone." Nevertheless, this figure emerged during the CRM.

The CRM paved the way for Malcolm X, Martin Luther King, and Caesar Chavez. The CRM, with its use of technology, the media, and the press, opened up a valley of opportunities for individuals like those just mentioned. Men and women alike were beginning to realize that they had a voice in the public sphere, and no one was going to take that voice away from them.

The music reflected the social order of the 1960's protest. Musical artists such as Janis Joplin, The Beatles, and James Brown began to shake the very foundations of American fundamentalism. Other social groups such as the Black Panther Party took matters into their own hands and began to fight violence with violence. The CRM made it possible for people to protest, complain, gripe, object, and reject the standard that had been laid before them by the United States of America.

## Malcolm X

Malcolm X represented the anger and pessimism of the day. His love combined with rage, profane mixed with sacred, and activist merged with militant resonated in the hearts and minds of so many young people of that day and age. Malcolm spoke to the heart of the issues, lighting a bon fire within the soul of the individual. Malcolm was able to articulate and execute the vision of independence, justice, and equal rights for Black America.[14]

This moral questioning that Malcolm encompassed, parallels what Adam Seligman discusses on the loss of difference and from mediation to representation with a postmodern world (1992: 123-127). Here Seligman argues that within a postmodern culture, differences become lost in the vast chasm of universal individualism, and the individual then becomes part of a larger community (1992: 123). Malcolm was part of the larger Nation of Islam community, which represented many Black American's sentiment. Malcolm also moved beyond individualism and mediation to representing the Black community as whole, not just one person (c.f. Best and Kellner 1991: 29).

---

[14] Taken from *The American Experience: The Making of Malcolm* (2004) VHS.

Malcolm's role within Black America was to establish a voice and a savior figure (Little 1966: 191-210). Malcolm's vision was that Black Americans begin to think critically about what was happening socially around them. Malcolm also wanted to bring some type of unity, or communal aspect to the ghetto, which encompassed many Black's views; (still another aspect of the postmodern).[15]

Dyson writes:

> For many adherents, Malcolm remained until his death a revolutionary black nationalist whose exclusive interest was to combat white supremacy while fostering black unity. Although near the end of his life Malcolm displayed a broadened humanity and moral awareness—qualities over looked by his unprincipled critics and often denied but his true believers— his revolutionary cohorts contended that Malcolm's late-life changes were cosmetic and confused, the painful evidence of ideological vertigo brought on by paranoia and exhaustion (1995:29).

Controversy surrounded Malcolm. He even knew it and wrote about it in his autobiography (Little 1966: 236-265). Even today, many still can not agree with who Malcolm really was.[16] Yet, within this controversy, emerges another postmodern value: different opinions that matter and have validity despite their vast opposition. In other words, the individual, in postmodernity, is valued and considered as opposed to a more modern approach which states that the larger, meta-narrative truth is what is right; regardless of how correct the individual may be (c.f. Best and Kellner 1991: 215-224).

Malcolm X[17] embodied one of the first militant approaches to dealing with injustice, poverty, inequality, discrimination, bigotry, racism, and prejudice. Malcolm gave voice to a new generation in the 1970's which said, "We're not going to take it anymore!" Others, who followed, such as Cesar Chavez, followed the lead and began to

---

[15] Ibid.

[16] Bagwell (1994) *Malcolm X: Make it Plain,* DVD.

[17] Malcolm was considered the "Prophet of Rage" for the Black community; a name that would carry on to Tupac as well.

embrace the community and the individual. Chavez and others embraced the postmodern culture Malcolm embodied, and began to question the grand meta-narrative; new micro narratives were established, and a new world order of postmodernism with the urban community was being formed. Further, "Malcolm X articulated black rage in a manner unprecedented in American History. His style of communicating this rage bespoke a boiling urgency and an audacious sincerity" (West 1993: 135).

The urban world now had feet to stand on with a person such as Malcolm X. Latinos, Asians, Blacks, and poor people in general, embodied that vigilant attitude and took it to the streets. Malcolm paved the way and set the stage for this, even in his death. Malcolm even helped to set a new cultural code within Hip Hop culture as rappers consistently discussed and embraced the activist side of who Malcolm was (Dyson 1995: 87). Afeni (Tupac's mother) was witness to all of this firsthand and shaped a lot of Tupac's philosophical worldview from Malcolm's worldview (c.f. Guy 2004: 58-60).

## Martin Luther King Jr.

With the rise of media, consumerism, and the shrinking of time and space within American culture, post WWII, Martin Luther King (MLK) had a stage set before him where people were ready and willing to listen within the urban community (c.f. Betts 2004: Chapter 3). MLK took an opposite approach to the CRM. While Malcolm advocated, at times, violence if necessary, MLK was dedicated to the idea of non-violence and peacemaking while dealing with the realties at hand, i.e. racism and bigotry in America.

MLK[18] entered the scene at a time when people in the urban community needed a voice in the public sphere. MLK gave them that voice along with hope, sanguinity,

---

[18] MLK gave rise to many current activists such as Ras Baraka, Thabiti Bruce Boone, and Tamara Jones; his vision of a non-violent protest still carries on for many (Kitwana 2002: 156-174).

anticipation, and optimism. MLK had to deal with Black Nationalism at a very early stage in his career (Dyson 2000: 105). MLK also had to deal with the rise of Black power and Black radicals. Still, MLK, despite his adversaries, overcame and began to build up the next generation activist.

MLK represented a voice for not only the Black community, but for the urban community as a whole: Black, Latino, and White. MLK embraced a Jesus that was, as James Cone describes, Black, powerful, and for the family (Cone 1997 a: 38-43). MLK began to live out the suffering Christ in his own daily life. For the urban community, this was authentic and transparent. MLK began to open doors for many who were trying to deal with the new fast and furious world they were living in. MLK gave them shelter.

Speaking from a postmodern perspective, MLK discussed openly the negative and positive aspects of consumerism. This was not the cultural norm for his context. After WWII, capitalism was considered to be the "best" way of life for the world. MLK did not see it that way. While he did not support communism, MLK saw the weaknesses of capitalism, especially at the expense of urban and Black community. He questioned the norm and the standard that had been set by the larger cultural White hegemony (Gottdiener 1985:993-996); people followed his lead. Still, with all of his movements forward, some felt as though MLK might not have been a positive model for the CRM (Dyson 2000: 298-299). A hundred years prior, any Black person who had achieved the status of MLK would have been praised regardless of their shortcomings, but during MLK's era and the 1960's, people within the urban context, began to think more critically about their leaders and how their leaders represented them, yet another postmodern quality.

## *The 1970's and The Rise of 'Hood Culture*

During the 1970's (1971 being the year of Tupac's birth), there was an emergence of "Blackness," or an emergence of the Afrocentric values that governed a Black nation years ago (Peters 2001). With that, came the rise of Black popular culture; however, at this time it was not termed "Black popular culture." And American pop culture did not know how to handle such an uprise.

After the urban revolt of the early seventies, the Watts riots, and the upheaval of traditional family values that had been set forth from White conservative Christians, came the tumultuous 1970's. The 1970's had a significant impact on the lives and social culture of the inner city, particularly the younger generation that came to be known as "Gen X."

The 1970's made it "ok" to go against the tide of popular culture and the incoming wave of the sound bite society. This decade can be broken down into three significant categories that gave rise to postmodernity.

First was the emergence of Black cinema. With its stereotypical roles, male driven plots, and comical story lines, the Black male appeared on the silver screen. He was in charge and in control with women adoring him and Whites afraid of him. Black cinema began to give mainstream American popular culture a view of inner city life, the Black male, urban sexuality, and ghetto values (Donalson 2003: 45-47). Black cinema paved the way for many actors including Curtis Mayfield, Gordon Parks Jr., Richard Roundtree, Sidney S Poitier, and Eddy Murphy. Each of these actors embodied what James Cone describes as, "Black and urban comedic energy; a wry sense of humor" (1997 b: 22-27). American popular culture now had its new cinema.

The second area that the 1970's influenced was morality. The envelope was pushed, so to speak, with films, music, and art that depicted the deep hurts, desires, and sexual energy of the artists. The body and the self image were seen as a sexually driven individual (Donalson 2003). The sacred was beginning to be trampled over and even questioned as to how the "sacred" was even termed the "sacred." The profane gave rise in the 1970's and morality was redefined (e.g. Foucault 1990: 14-24). Young directors, artists, and musicians led the way.[19]

The 1970's began to question Black religion and if it had true meaning the Black community (Joseph 1970: 69-84). Further, studies such as Eric Lincoln and Lawrence Mamiya contend the relevancy for the Black church in contemporary times too. Lincoln and Mamiya state, "many young African Americans, teenagers, and young adults, have increasingly questioned the need for God and relevancy of the Black Church to their own lives in the world as they have come to see it" (1990: 309). The way they "see it" was vastly shaped during the 1970's and has grown into a cultural norm in the Black and urban community to question the relevance for the church.

The third and final area of significant cultural importance during the 1970's was in the area of language and linguistics. A new language was emerging from the inner city! A language we now "nicely" term, (because we cannot figure it out and need to), Ebonics. At the time, most people would say that broken English signified ignorance and a lack of knowledge. Still, broken English, slang, or "hood" talk made it possible for inner city dwellers to communicate with each other, in their own language and in their own terms. "Ebonics" would later make it into the popular mainstream, but during the 1970's, it was mainly relegated to the inner city. Still, there was an emergence to say it was ok to write and say "ain't," especially if it angered someone else.

The worldview that says "what is right for me is not always right for you" began to emerge as well (c.f. West 1993: 16-20). Nelson George states "The '70s would spawn

---

[19] It is also interesting to note the church took a "Christ against culture" stance during the 1970's which had it lose a lot of its credibility in mainstream culture. Because of its sharp criticism of popular culture, the church has not recovered since.

the first graduating class of affirmative action babies" (1998: 1). Tupac was raised in this type of environment, and he was aware that the overall message of "well-being" that was being told to United State citizens was not the same for urban dwellers.[20]

## Postmodernity and Hip Hop Language

I am limiting this study to brief overview of Hip Hop history. I will not detail the history of Hip Hop, other authors such as Tricia Rose (1994 a; 1994 b), Nelson George (1998), and the edited book by Jared Green (2003) exhaustively discuss the history of Hip Hop. For this project, I am merely discussing the cultural significance.

Broken vernacular (Dillard 1972) saw the materialization of Hip Hop culture. Hip Hop is a culture that embodies the irreverent, the profane, the sacred, along with the ghettoness of life, and combines them into a transposed culture known as Hip Hop. Hip Hop is rough, rugged, and raw. It reflects the life the inner city people know all too well.[21] Hip Hop culture began during the late 1970's on the East Coast in the city known as the Bronx. "Like any generation, much of the Hip Hop generation's group identity has been shaped by the major sociopolitical forces of our formative years" (Kitwana 2002: 9). Hip Hop rose during much turmoil and angst in the nation. The language was a direct reflection of that. Russell Potter writes:

> Finally, hip-hop's coherence and continuity are a result of its practice of its improvisations upon language itself, which form the verbal corollary of musical samples, repeating with a difference, troping dopes, and serving as a crucible for reformation and deformation of language (1995:54).

Further, Nelson George states, "Hip-hop is, as we'll see, the spawn of many things. But, most profoundly, it is a product of schizophrenic, post-civil rights movement

---

[20] This is seen in Tupac's first album "2Pacalypse Now."

[21] Taken from *Wild Style* (1982).

in America" (1998: xiv; also c.f. Boyd 2003). Hip Hop culture had humble beginnings; until the early 1970's the recording industry was not truly apart or viewed as corporate America (George 1998: 3). More so, rap music was considered, at the time, a passing fad; a "fad" that was only relegated to the inner city and Black youth. After a brief stint at the top, Disco music found its way into the archival halls of record heaven. The Funk era began, and with it, came a generation of young people that wanted some representation in the public sphere that truly represented them as a whole. Rap music did just that.[22]

Scott Lash (1990), Russell Potter (1995), Steven Best (1993), and Douglas Kellner (Best Steven 1991) all argue that the postmodern era has disrupted, fragmented, and rebuilt a new "language for its culture; Potter (1995) would argue that Hip Hop was postmodern's first language (55-79). Best and Kellner (1991), argue that Karl Marx's theory of the underclass revolting and taking over, is apparent in the postmodern (56-58). Hip Hop culture and rap music accomplished just that; they began a social revolution with the psyche of the urbanite.

By the mid 1980's, groups such as N.W.A[23], Public Enemy, and X-Clan, gave a voice, like MLK and Malcolm, to the marginalized and disenfranchised young person living in the hood. Tupac's message and outlook on life was being formed in a social hive of broken promises, corrupted social and governmental structures, and the much hated Reagan era in the 'hood.[24] Rap music spoke of the hard realities of street living, and the brutalities of the police with songs like "Fuck the Police" (1989) and "Fight the Power"

---

[22] See the film *Wild Style* (1982) to better understand how hip-hop culture came into its own from urban beginnings. Also listen to the director's commentary on the DVD for more on this.

[23] Niggas With Attitude.

[24] In the film *Letter to the President* (2005), one is able to grasp at a birds eye view, the magnitude and the struggle of urbanites during the 1980's.

(1990), urban youth gained a voice. Chuck D states, "Rap music has been a refrigerator for today's musical culture without any payback" (1997: 105).

Chuck D suggests that Hip Hop culture is an unorganized form of music with no real set boundaries, much like that of the 1960's era of rock music; people are doing the music, rather than doing the job for the money and the music comes second (1997: 103-104). This holds true for much of what postmoderns hold to be sacred: the unknown and searching for the answers. Tricia Rose states, "Many hip hop fans, artists, musicians, and dancers continue to belong to an elaborate system of crews or possee's" (1994 a: 34).

The mere fact that turntables were used to "steal" break beats and other artists drum lines so that rappers could transpose music that had already been written into their own art form was an enormous and noteworthy cultural change. Most, at the time, did not know how to deal with this "jacking"[25] of beats and music (Potter 1995). This tearing away from traditional music forms, gave rap music its own unique identity. Moreover, Tupac capitalized off it in his music.

### The Niggarization of a Nation

Cornel West, noted scholar in the field of urban postmodernism, writes about this phenomena:

> The Afro-Americanization of white youth—given the disproportionate black role in popular music and athletics—has put white kids in closer contact with their own bodies and facilitated more human interaction with black people. Listening to Motown records in the sixties or dancing to hip-hop music in the nineties may not lead one to question the sexual myths of black women and men, but when white and black kids buy the same billboard hits and laud the same athletic heroes the result is often a shared cultural space where some human interaction takes place (1993: 121).

---

[25] Liberally, openly, and at times violently taking someone else's materials

Cornel West (1993), Bakari Kitwana (2003), and Nelson George (1998) all comment on the Blackening of a nation through popular culture. They seemingly agree that Black and urban youth culture, has gained much momentum in the public sphere, a noteworthy accomplishment (The results of this are yet to be seen) that was not available to youth of this culture even ten years prior. Cornel West adds that Black popular culture is the, "thermometer of the nation as well as the projector of possibility for prophetic thought and action…" (1993: 67).

During the early 1990's, White America and mainstream popular culture were exposed to Black and urban popular culture. Television shows such as The Fresh Prince, The Cosby Show, A Different World, Martin, Def Comedy Jam, and New York Undercover, gave mainstream America a "peak" into the lives, social conditions, and social structure of urban and Black America. These phenomena gave birth to the traverse (and at times), profane humor of the ghetto. Comedians such as Eddie Murphy, Richard Prior, Red Foxx, and Martin Lawrence were admired and adored by White and Black fans alike. The profane began to creep in. "Sacred" and wholesome shows like "Mr. Rodgers Neighborhood," were seemingly defiled when Eddy Murphy spoofed the show on Saturday Night Live with his impersonation of "Mr. Robinson's Neighborhood." The show was a running series with Murphy playing a man from the ghetto that broke into homes each week. The sacred, nice, and neat suburban world was now being taken over by urban ghetto youth; and America was enjoying every minute of it (c.f. Neal 2002). This is what Craig Watkins discusses as "Remixing of American Pop" in which the "niceties" of mainstream American pop culture, get a ghetto face lift and twisted it into a new rhythm for a new day (2005: 33-54).

Nineteen hundred ninety three marked the first year that Hip Hop albums were sold primarily to a suburban audience. With the release of Dr. Dre's "Chronic" album, millions of White youth now peered into the world of Snoop Dogg, Dr. Dre, and the G-

Funk era.[26] American popular culture, which was once governed by The Beach Boys and Apple Pie, now had to contend with weed, Snoop Dogg, Crips and Bloods, "pimps," "ho's," and "baby daddies."[27] Postmodernism was beginning to gain more momentum, and ghetto values were its fingerprint on American popular culture. Mel Donalson's book also has a chapter on Black cinema with a Hip Hop twist. There he analyzes and critiques the social structure of the rise of Black comedy infused with Hip Hop culture (2003: 252-277).

Bakari Kitwana suggests six major phenomena that emerged in the 1980's and 1990's. These aided in the Niggarizing of American popular culture. The following is adapted from Bakari Kitwana (2002: 9-24):

1. Popular culture and the visibility of Black youth within it.
2. The rise of globalization and transnational corporations (particularly those that took advantage of Blacks).
3. The worldview of the Hip Hop generation has been influenced by persisting segregation in an America that preaches democracy and inclusion, yet contradicts itself by doing just the opposite.
4. Public policy regarding criminal justice, particularly policy that has clear racial implications.
5. The media's representation of young Blacks; particularly negative images.
6. The deadly disease AIDS that was once thought to strike only gay White men, now took its toll on Blacks and the inner city.

These six areas had a significant affect on popular culture, Black popular culture, and American culture as a whole. Postmodernism within the 'hood, grew out of urban youth culture. Tupac, who was fertilized and grew in these six areas added to the growth of

---

[26] Gangsta Funk Era.

[27] Urban culture, infused with Black popular culture, had begun to Niggarize a nation.

urban postmodern culture in which. This postmodern attitude also gave voice to a new spirituality, spirituality that questioned whether or not Heaven has a ghetto for "rydas."

### *Spirituality in the 'Hood*

The topic of spirituality is a vast undertaking. For the purpose of this section, I will scan over the spirituality of the postmodern urban youth. Scholars such as Anthony Pinn (1995), Eric Lincoln and Lawrence Mamiya (1990), and the edited volume by Anthony Pinn (2003) on spirituality and rap music all deal with spirituality, the 'hood, and rap music at length. Further, the edited volume by Anthony Pinn deals with rap music and its religious traditions; here there is an in depth discussion on the connection to rap music and theological associations (2003: 29-101). Spirituality deserves its own independent research and is an area that deserves further research.

Unconsciously, James Cone began the debate between the sacred and the profane when he questioned the White theology of Jesus (1997 a: 34-37). The ideology that Jesus was White and blonde was passed down from generation to generation to slaves. Cone began to argue, back in the 1970's, that Jesus has African features and power that Whites could not even understand (1997 a: 38-42).

Cone began to shake the fundamental theological understanding about God, the church, and theology. At first, this was considered profane and irreverent, that a Black man would question the moral authority of four hundred plus years of White theology. Now, Cone's theology, while still debatable, is accepted in most Black churches. James also connects the blues with what he terms a "secular spiritual" (1992: 68-97); a true postmodern tenet.

Postmodern urban youth identify with Jesus. However, they identify with a Jesus that can relate to them. Hip Hop culture and music gives them a theologically transcendent outlet. Hip Hop and Tupac's theology encompasses Herbert Edwards' (1975) three tasks every new theological movement must accomplish. Those three areas are:[28]

1. Prove The Inadequacy of Previous and Existing Theologies for The Present Crisis: Hip Hop and Tupac begin to question the moral authority of its modern theological gate keepers. Hip Hop addresses the crisis of urban America and begins to seek answers that are spiritual.
2. Demonstrate its own Adequacy for the Present Moment: Hip Hop prophets such as Tupac establish a new adequacy for this postmodern ear and give a new view of Jesus.
3. Establish its Continuity with Normative Expressions of the Faith: Hip Hop and Tupac takes on a more "relic" and African feel to its spirituality. This is in line with 13$^{th}$ and 14$^{th}$ century African theology.

The irreverent spirituality infused with a sacred element of God in Hip Hop music, has formed, what Jon Spencer (1990) calls, its own theomusicology, "musicology as a theologically informed discipline" (1990: vii). The fact that Hip Hop music is theologically rooted is no coincidence. Hip Hop is about liberation, authenticity, and freedom from the shackles of modernity. Spencer relates Black gospel music as a liberating tone for Blacks; Hip Hop is the postmodern response for this generation of urban youth (1990: 35-59; c.f. Rose 1994 a). Tupac stood for these as well, which infused him even deeper into his ghetto saint image.

Postmodern urban youth are wrapped up with the irreverent. Andres Serrano's The Piss Christ, was a starting point for many urban artists to begin to use the irreverent as the sacred. Serrano urinated into a jar, put a crucifix into it, and then took pictures of Christ to symbolize the scandal of the cross and the fact that Christ took on all "sin," which was symbolized with urine, for humankind—see image below (Fusco 1995: 80-81).

---

[28] I will cover these concepts further in chapter twelve.

Graffiti art, as seen in *Wild Style's* social structure of artists, is another example of that. Once thought of as "vandalism," graffiti has made its impression on contemporary American culture and gives a voice to the artists who use graffiti as their transcendent voice and medium.

## *Summary*

In this chapter I have covered a brief historical reflection on: the 'hood context, the industrial revolution, jazz music and the rise of Black popular culture, the CRM, the cultural significance of both MLK and Malcolm X, the cultural significance of the 1970's and the rise of Hip Hop. Finally, I have discussed how America came to know urban and Black popular culture. Tupac grew out of this context. Tupac's life, pedagogy, and worldview were formed in BPC and during his formative years, 1973-1982.

All of these phenomena, in this chapter have had significant affect on Tupac. These areas, when combined, and critically evaluated, form what we know today as urban postmodern youth culture in which Tupac currently has had a large part in influencing. This gives a solid foundation to see how Tupac's life was influenced positively and negatively. Moreover, now we can see how both Hip Hop culture and the 'hood context affected Tupac and helped shape him into the person he became. This is crucial in understanding the entire context of Tupac's life.

In the next chapter, we will see how Tupac interacted with all of these areas. In that chapter, we will see how Tupac viewed BPC and how he influenced the culture as a whole.

# CHAPTER 7

# TUPAC, BLACK POPULAR CULTURE, AND HIP HOP

Black popular culture (BPC) encompasses a wide variety of areas. For the purpose of this chapter and book, I will follow five criteria that were developed out of the research in this book. Those criteria are:

1. Societal frameworks
2. Class and Socioeconomics
3. Sexuality
4. Cultural Exposition
5. Spirituality

First, societaly speaking, BPC provides many with an expression of anger, truth, love, hate, fear, disgust, hurt, pain, suffering, oppression, freedom, and joy. BPC, due to its roots in slavery, has a fundamental grounding in suffering, pain, love, and angst. Because of this, BPC is a relatable culture for many who are marginalized, hurt, and considered outcasts.[1]

More importantly, as Samuel Floyd suggests, all African societies have a notion of who God is both minimally and fundamentally. (1995:15-16). He states, "Like the Christian God, the African God is known as a High God, a Supreme God, a father king, lord, master, judge, or ruler, depending on the society doing the naming (or in some matriarchal societies, Mother, although the image of God as Father is not limited to

---

[1] Yet another reason why Tupac was such a popular figure among so many different ethnicities. His ability to relate to the downtrodden and hurt was a value that gained him higher credibility much more than most rap artists.

patriarchal societies)" (Floyd 1995:15). This fundamental rooting in God, gives way to a society that deeply understands the spirituality of life. Once again, we are able to have yet another appeal for people in this current postmodern spiritual age (c.f. Cone 1997 a; 1997 b; James 2004, Lewis 2002). This is seen widely in the music of BPC, which recently, is composed largely of R and B and Rap (e.g. Ramsey 2003).

Second, economically speaking, for too long Blacks have not had much wealth. Economics remains a formidable barrier in the advancement of the 'hood (Anderson 1999: 15-32). It is only within the last twenty years that we have seen a rise of the Black middle class (Dyson 2004, McCoy 1999, McWhorter 2003, and Early 1997). With the rise of wealth, we are able to see Blacks as lawyers, doctors, news anchors, sports heroes, and musical demi-gods. While this phenomenon is not without its own troubles, financial resources within BPC are beginning to grow.

With all of its success, BPC still remains largely supported by lower middle to lower class people. BPC, that began in a blue-collar culture, is still largely that way. It is reflected in the media and music as well. Shows such as *Good Times*, *What's Happening Now*!!, and *Different Strokes* are examples of that lower blue collar working class. BPC embraces that work ethic. Tupac did the same. For an interesting view into the arguments between the lower class of BPC and the upper class of BPC, see (Kirkland et al. 2004) as they discuss the comments from Dr. Bill Cosby from several view points.

Third, sexuality is an area that has produced much debate and angst from many in Black society. Sex and Blacks have roots, once again, in slavery. Black males were typically used as breeding machines to produce new slaves, thereby increasing slave owner's property, which equaled more money (Hood 1980:120-190). Sex was used as a means to gain more power. [2] As Dyson states:

---

[2] See the PBS special on "Slavery and the Making of America" (Kalin 2004).

At the beginning of the African presence in the New World, black bodies were viewed in largely clinical and capitalist terms. The value of black slave bodies was determined by their use in furthering the reach of Western colonial rule; expanding the market economics of European and American societies; institutionalizing leisure for white cultural elites; deepening the roots of democracy for white property-owning gentry; and providing labor for the material culture that dominates the American landscape. Interestingly, when Christianity poked its nose in, chattel slavery, already a vile and dehumanizing affair, got even uglier (2004: 223).

Sexuality has not been something easy to define in BPC. Sex, for the church in general, is not something that is easily discussed nor dealt with according to Harvey Cox (1965). Cox states, "we must admit that we have created a set of cultural conditions in which sexual responsibility is made exceedingly difficult" (1965:213). He further argues that for the city, sex is great, fun, and explorative. But, for the church, it is much more sterile and systematic (Cox 1965: 210-216). Tupac made sexuality acceptable for many young people, sex was recreational, not systematic, yet there still remained the issue of adultery and sex outside of marriage, an issue that is still debatable today (c.f. Forman 2002: 173-212; Dyson 2001; Cone 1991: 114-118).

For many, sex is a leisure activity and one that is objectified in the opposite sex. This is seen in its extreme form in the current party rap era. Men—which it typically is—are the ones who get to pick from a wide array of readily available women; some of which are more than eager to "give it up" at any cost. Sexuality within the Black church is not any better (e.g. Dyson 2004). Sex is seen and used, at times, no differently than in a club. We are also seeing this in such films as *Friday*, *The Best Man*, and *Soul Food*. Often, Pastors are no different than a street hustler. Tupac knew and saw this, and spoke about it at great length. Sex continues to be a dominant aspect of BPC.

Sexuality is not easily defined either. Nor is it easily debated.[3] There are many issues on both sides of sex (either to have sex outside of marriage or inside of marriage),

---

[3] See Foucault (1984) for an in depth study into the history of sexuality.

and BPC will continue to struggle with it; we see this in such films as *Brown Sugar*, *8-Mile*, and *Boyz in the Hood*—to name just a few.

Fourth, is cultural exposition. In other words, what are the main cultural points that BPC presents. One such area is the area of language. Nigga, fuck, shit, and bitch are common words for people within BPC. These words can be used in combinations such as, but not limited to: bitch ass, shit, motherfucka, bitch ass nigga, and punk nigga. All of these are common language in BPC, especially among the young (c.f. Hooks 1992; Neal 1999). These verbal cultural expositories are a reflection of not so much the person, but of the context and environment that each person involved in BPC occupies.

Another cultural exposition is cultural elements such as African heritage and being authentic. These are seen in the films, television shows and music that I studied. These particular cultural expositories are ones that arise repeatedly within BPC. Therefore, they are ones worth noting. African heritage, especially, is something that many within BPC, especially Blacks, see as a connection to the "roots" or "motherland" of the culture. African heritage is seen in many ways, from hats, t-shirts, pendants, colors, and jackets. Being "Black" takes on another conversation not allowed in this project. Bell Hooks (1992 b) discussed race, representation, and self-identity. She argues that there are many who are now trying to be Black while acting Black. Her works look into the issue and commonness of being Black in today's society.

Fifth, is spirituality. It should come as no surprise that many Blacks have their foundational roots in the Christian church. Moreover, in my experience, I have not met a single Black person to be ignorant of who Jesus was. While they may have an elementary theological foundation, the person is aware of the Father, Son, and Holy Ghost. This is a staple of BPC. BPC is drenched with religion, and while there are several different types of images of God, Christianity is the dominant theology (Lincoln and Mamiya 1990: 20-46).

Still, BPC remains essentially rooted in Christianity. It is seen repeatedly in the music of such musicians as Ray Charles, Quincy Jones, Aretha Franklin, and now, Tupac. This dates back to slavery when one slave was picked to be the pastor of the slave unit and "evangelize" the rest of the slaves. Slaves learned that God was one who supported slavery, but quickly began to understand a new theology of Christ and of freedom (Cone 1997 b, 1991 and Bennett 1993).

Spirituality takes on diverse forms in BPC. It can be:

- A symbol such as a cross
- A prayer
- Attending church
- The value of community
- The value of brother and sister hood
- Being your sister or brother's keeper
- Overcoming
- Death

- Love for your fellow person
- Social justice
- Social fairness
- Forgiveness
- Grace
- Humility
- Love
- Anger

BPC takes spirituality seriously. Tupac did too. However, it is expressed differently than that of traditional American forms of church, theology, and Christianity; these forms typically refer to a White way of doing things and not contextual at all for the urban and Black context (Cone 1997a; Floyd 1995).

Additionally, Gina Dent's edited volume on BPC discusses at length the cultural significance of spirituality, gender, sexuality, and Black images in popular culture (1992: 95-138). This book project does not allow such a discussion and is limited to these areas.

## *Tupac and Black Popular Culture*

Tupac, in my opinion, is BPC. What follows here is my attempt to connect Tupac to BPC. This will be an ongoing argument.

Tupac embodied all five elements of BPC and gave it a sixth element, the Thug image.[1] This image is not the traditional image of a thug; a hoodlum, street mugger, or rapist. The Thug, for Tupac, was the marginalized, the poor, the downtrodden, the person who needed help and needed someone to care about them. The Thug was the person, who Tupac sought after, which, ironically, is a large portion of BPC's young audience.

Tupac embraced the good, the bad, and the ugly of BPC. More importantly, Tupac was transparent (A character element that many take issue with, both in and outside of BPC). Tupac, in his personhood, was the social, sexual, economical, cultural, and spiritual structure for BPC. He embraced it all, while being able to be a critic of that same culture. Tupac embodied the struggle between positive Black Awareness and Black Pride on the one hand, while on the other he had the Thug, ghetto mindset, and "fuck-you" attitude that manifests itself in so many young Black males. Tupac's ghettocentric values drove him to incredible success with the Hip Hop generation and BPC as a whole.[2]

Derrick Gilbert (aka D-Knowledge) writes:

> Not only was Tupac perceived as being real, he was also viewed as knowing how to overcome pain. In other words, despite everything Tupac had gone through, he could still smile/ he could still dance/ he could still get paid/ he could still get high/ he could still live...Tupac had a presence and a charisma that attracted the attention of even those who disliked him (1997: 67).

Tupac had the keen ability to embrace and deal with pain in such a way that people were attracted to him. BPC has had its share of pain and suffering, but Tupac took that

---

[1] This thug image also connects with Todd Boyd's "Nigga" image (1997).

[2] Or that generation commonly referred to as Gen X. The Hip Hop generation is used here to embody a more urban and Hip Hop feel that can culturally identify someone from this generation.

experience to the next level. As Gilbert (1997) suggests, even people that did not particularly care for rap music or Hip Hop culture, respected what Tupac stood for, while not agreeing with everything he had to say or offer.

Tupac had the ability to deal with the negative elements of capitalism in this country and how a capitalist mindset has, at times, taken advantage of Blacks and BPC. Tupac knew this and was able to articulate this back to BPC. This, in turn, empowered many young Blacks, and made many others aware of certain situations. This did not make Tupac especially popular with mainstream media, including some Blacks. Tupac did not always choose the "correct" language to state his point—yet another characteristic of BPC as well, Black humor has always been known to be on the "raunchy" and crude side.

Tupac lived in the ghetto part of BPC. He was formed and shaped within that atmosphere. Tupac had many strong views and opinions about how to fix the ghetto parts of society. Tupac was strongly criticized for his extreme political views and harsh lyrics. Angelo Williams states:

> Clint Eastwood seems to live in the world Tupac wished for. A world were Eastwood, playing the part of Dirty Harry, can buck down the bad guys with his .44 and still make it home in time to successfully run for mayor of Malibu. Tupac did not live in that world. The world where human beings can be separated from the killers and thieves they play. Anthony Hopkins lives in that world. No one ever asks him if he eats human flesh nor do they mistake him for Hannibal Lector (1997: 57).

Tupac was politically and socially aware of critical issues; an element of BPC. Still, as many in BPC, he was criticized and labeled a Thug and/or "gangsta." This, unfortunately, is the fate of many Blacks who take a stand and speak up against immorality and political regimes in the United States. Tupac was no different. Yet, despite all criticisms, remains one of the most prolific figures of BPC today.

***Themes in Black Popular Culture and Tupac***

Some of the major connections to Tupac's life came from the films I reviewed that deal with BPC. As I reviewed the films, certain themes in the "societal frameworks" section of the content analysis began to emerge. Some of these themes are seen in Table 2. These themes were a culmination of the overall gathered data and are not from a singular source:

# TABLE 2

## BLACK POPULAR CULTURE SOCIETAL THEMES

| Theme | Cultural Value |
|---|---|
| New York and Los Angeles; The West Coast and The East Coast | Two major areas and hubs for BPC. A majority of the fashion, films, and television shows are either set in one of these places or deal with an aspect of these places in regards to BPC |
| Education and Black males | This is a major topic in BPC. While Black women are not to be ignored, the issue of Black men and education is a struggle for many in BPC. For young Blacks, if you are young and smart, then you might be seen as too White, if you are too dumb, then you might be seen as too ghetto and a bum; a paradox indeed. |
| Property valued over Black human life | This is a theme that is seen in several films such as *Do The Right Thing*, *Juice*, and *Scarface*. We see the emergence of commerce over community, business over human value and morals, and personal gain over community well being. |
| Sellouts and Uncle Toms | How authentic are you? In fact, how connected to the community of the 'hood are you that you are in touch with the reality of the streets? These are questions arising within BPC. How real are you? If you move up out of the ghetto, do you remain real? What is real? |
| Fathers | The presence of the male figure, especially the Black male, is a phenomenon unrivaled in other ethnicities. Black men owning their responsibility of being a father is an issue that will not soon go away in BPC. |
| Broken Homes | The home that is shattered from the result of poor communication, lack of education, the vicious culture of poverty, and the effect of having different children with different fathers are all causal effects for a broken home. BPC demonstrates this a lot in television shows such as *Good Times,* |

| Theme | Cultural Value |
|---|---|
| | *Whats Happening Now!!, and The Fresh Prince of Bel Air.* |
| Mother figure | In the Black community mom is next to God (Dyson 2001). She is the counselor, father, doctor, banker, judge, jury, court, and lover for many young Black men; and also for other men of color as well. |
| Culturally appropriate contexts | In all of the media content, there was culturally relevant material for the time period. In other words, Different Strokes has language and themes that were appropriate for 1982. Each of the television and film contents had this aspect in them. |

These themes are not uncommon in BPC and/or the 'hood as a whole. Eugene Perkins discusses at length the issues of street life and Black street gangs in Chicago (1987). Perkins also notes several of the themes above as cultural issues with BPC.

With the film *Do The Right Thing*, you have almost all of the elements of BPC wrapped up nicely into one film. For example, in Lee's film, we see:

- **Mookie**: a self absorbed Black man who does not care for his son; single mother, Tina, has to cope with the results of a sexual experience that resulted in the birth of their child. Mookie further complicates things with his love and passion for getting paid. Still, Mookie remains connected to the community and is the first to "Do the right thing" and throw the garbage can through the window.

- **Sal's Pizzeria**: The *Italian* landowner that drives up in a white Cadillac that does not live in the current community they serve. A disconnect happens, especially with Korean store owners, when business owners do not respect the values and cultural norms of the culture they serve in. Sal, Pino and Vito were no different. Still, Vito was sensitive enough to have the conversation about race with Mookie.

- **Old Black Men on the Corner**: Every hood has this phenomenon. There is not one single urban environment that does not have some men sitting on the corner talking about nothing, people, politics, sex, money, fame, themselves, and the future. Typically, these men are from the Civil Rights generation (The Boomer generation) and are disconnected from the Hip Hop generation (The Gen X generation) and one even further disconnected from the Bling-Bling generation (Gen Y or the Millennial generation).

- **Race and Class Issues**: This remains a signifying theme in BPC. Race will continue to be an issue in America, and events like the ones that transpired after hurricane Katrina in New Orleans, are mere reminders of how far we are behind the race and class mark here in America.

Tupac embraced all these elements mainly because he had elements of these in his life too. Tupac came from:

- A single parent family
- A broken home with different daddies
- A poor ghetto family
- Different hoods
- A Black Panther tradition
- An awareness of social justice for the poor
- The East Coast to the West Coast and knew the dynamics and context of each area.[3]

These are all unique qualities for any individual to have indeed, but Tupac was able to embody much of what BPC was about. While artists such as Nas, Jay Z, and Eve represent BPC, Tupac was almost a "poster child" for the different elements that make up BPC. This was evident in his music and his lifestyle.

## Sex

BPC, whether upper class Blacks wish to admit it or not, encompasses a wide variety of issues. Sex, obviously, being one of them. Sexuality was yet another theme that

---

[3] The phenomenon of being relevant is something not many are able to explain. For most artists, work that is over 2.5 years old, is considered "Old-School." However, Tupac is for many still current. There is no real explanation for this.

arose in all of the media content. However, sexuality took on several different aspects than just sex itself.

First, male and female roles fell into this category. More than 80 percent of the female's roles in all of the media content were traditional homemaker roles. Women cooked, cleaned, knew better than men, and raised children. Women were also erratic and emotional. Women were objectified 25 percent of the time in the films, and 99.8 percent of the time in films such as *Juice*, *Scarface*, and *8-Mile*. Women were seen as the "bitch" or "lesbian" when they would not perform "favors" for men.

Second, language took on a sexual flavor. Men used words such as baby, honey, cutie, sexy thang, baby girl, and even ho to attract women. Men relied on words to cover up faults such as lying, cheating, forgetting an anniversary, or just simply "messing-up." Words seem to be the necessary cure-all for women. Women appeared to respond to words and not men's actions. Women appeared to almost be hypnotized by the right words from men. In Scarface, Tony uses his ghetto tact to entice Elvira into marrying him and dating him, never mind the fact that he never actually *does* anything for her, other than buy her material objects.

Third, men held most of the power and exerted that power through money, cars, other women, and words. In 85 percent of the media seen, men held powerful positions while women held less powerful positions. In the film *Juice*, all the men were in control and women were their subjects. In the film *Boyz In The Hood*, there was a mixture of women doing different things. Brandi was able to go to college to get a good job, while Ricky's mom stayed at home and had no man, but wished for one (Furious). In the hit TV show, Different Strokes, there appeared to be even more sexual tension between Willis and Kimberly—this is an inferred statement based off several sexual interactions between Willis and Kimberly.

Repression is also a form of sexuality that many Black's in general do not wish to discuss or deal with. Rap music simply places the issue out in all light for everyone to see. This, as Jon Spencer suggests, causes, primarily Black Christians and churches, to denounce the music and genre as "sinful" and "of the devil" (1991: 1-5), relegating "everyone" in the culture to "hell" (Spencer 1991: 8-11). While there are several studies on the issue of sexuality, rape, and rap music (Kohl 2004; Armstrong 2004; Mahiri and Sablo 1996), when sexuality is repressed it becomes a serious problem in which many are not ready to deal with. Michael Foucault states, "If sex is repressed, that is, condemned to prohibition, nonexistence, and silence, then the mere fact that one is speaking about it has the appearance of a deliberate transgression...a person somehow anticipates the coming freedom" (1984: 6). Sexuality is a complex subject and further research is needed on this subject as it relates to Hip Hop.

## Economics

Within the television shows, a theme of socioeconomics that arose stood out among the television series that I saw. These themes can be seen in Table 3:

## TABLE 3

## TELEVISION THEMES ON ECONOMICS

| Television Series | Theme |
|---|---|
| Fresh Prince of Bel Air | A Black male butler<br>Privileged kids<br>"Boo-She" Black girls (Hillary)<br>Designer Clothing<br>The character Will assimilates quickly to wealth<br>Name brand autos<br>Prep Schools and the issue of privilege<br>Pay offs (for bully's and others)<br>Pay to have services rendered for them<br>White collar work (high end)<br>Large living environment<br>The suburbs |
| The Jeffersons | A Black Woman maid<br>George lost contact with the ghetto and likes it<br>Blacks own business<br>Differences between "workers" and "owners"<br>Large living environment<br>The suburbs |
| Different Strokes | Rich White man takes in Black kids<br>Large living environment<br>White owned business<br>The suburbs<br>Money is power and power equals more money<br>White men as "Lords"<br>Privilege and power<br>Prep school<br>Blacks on welfare |

Within each of these television series, we are able to see that money plays a large part in the privilege for the children. While Tupac lived in Baltimore, he attended the Baltimore School for Performing Arts. Tupac states:

> I had a few times when I just zoned out and had good luck. When I auditioned for the Baltimore School for the Arts, that was one of my good luck times. I spent three years in Baltimore, my high school years. I loved

my classes, made a lot of friends that I wanted to keep over. We were exposed to everything. Theater, ballet, different people's lifestyles—rich people's lifestyles, royalty from other countries and things, everything (Shakur 2003: 44).

Here Tupac honed his stage presence, polished his natural poetry skills, and developed a deep sense or knowledge through reading voraciously.[4] Tupac began to see that the world was not fair, nor did the world—The United States—truly care for her poor and lower class. This strengthened Tupac's sense of social justice that one can see throughout his life. Still, Afeni had to scrimp and scrape to gather money for him to attend this school, and eventually Tupac had to leave the school due to lack of finances when Afeni lost her job.

Tupac states:

> And I started going, Damn, man, I would have been a totally different person had I not been exposed to these things. Hell n, I was living in the ghetto. We didn't have any lights, no electricity. We was about to get evicted. I thought, we're not being taught to deal with the world as it is. We're being taught to deal with this fairy tale land we're not even living in anymore. Its sad. I mean, more kids are being handed crack than they're being handed diplomas. I think adults should go through school again. I think rich people should live like poor people and poor people should live like rich people and they should change every week.
>
> Growing up in America—I loved my childhood but I hated growing up poor, and it made me very bitter. We live in hell. We live in the gutter, a war zone. They got us stacked up eighty deep in one building. By the time you get out of your house you strap just to protect yourself. The same crime element that white people scared of, black people scared of. The same crime element that white people fear, we fear. So we defend ourselves from the same crime element that they scared of, you know what I'm saying? So while they waiting for legislation to pass, and everything, we next door to the killer. We next door to him cuz we up in the projects with eighty niggaz in a building. All them killers that they letting out, they right there in that building. But its better? Just cuz we're black we get along with the killers or something? We get along with the rapist's cuz we

---

[4] The School for Performing Arts affected Tupac a lot. He loved that school and saw it as a turning point in his life. The school gave him opportunities that many urbanites did not or could not have at the time. Tupac excelled in this school. It is interesting to note that Tupac never finished high school because he wanted to pursue his career.

black and we from the same hood? What is that? We need protection too (Shakur 2003)!

The issue of economics is a strong one within BPC, and each of the films, television shows, and musicians address that topic in different ways. 90 percent of the time it is addressed from a blue collar perspective—i.e. moving on up, coming from the gutter to the suburbs, and "making it"—and for a blue collar context, i.e. the working class Black.

### *Cultural Values*

Cultural values are shared ideas of what is right and wrong, fair and unfair, and important and unimportant within a society (Ting-Toomey and Chung 2005:54). While cultural values are pervasive in any society, this project focuses in on two: values on language, and the value of authenticity.

Once again, we find ourselves in a myriad of meanings, definitions, and issues within BPC on cultural values. One of the main themes that arose within all the content studied was the issue of language and how values were placed on language. We see in Table 4 the top words that were used:

## TABLE 4

## LANGUAGE USED

| Words Used |
|---|
| *Fuck* <br> A common word used in many areas of BPC. It can be used as a noun, verb, adjective and adverb. Very common in all of the films, and while not mentioned in the television content, it was hinted towards. |
| *Nigga*[5] <br> A term of endearment for a brother hood or sister hood, punk, fool, and/or best friend. This is a term that is not the typical negative form of the word classically known as "nigger." The Hip Hop generation (Gen X) has made this term popular. Tupac used this word continually. |
| *Bitch* <br> A term used to describe women, men, a situation, person or persons, and/or a place. This term is a popular word within BPC and most comedians use it. |
| *Ebonics* <br> While this is an ambiguous term, I use it here to mean the use of broken English. Words such as ain't, yo, fo, yeah, they be, and fo sho—to name just a few—are normally characterized as non-common English words, i.e. Ebonics. |
| *Cool* <br> A word that transcends ages. This word continues to be used to calm people down, describe people who are good, and used as a signifier (Are you cool? Yeah? Ok, Cool!). |

### The Value of Words

Language plays a large role in any culture. Language, in whatever form (be it verbal or non-verbal) is a fundamental part of any culture and has a significant role to play as culture develops (Sapir 1949: 205-208). While rap music does not necessarily follow a standard grammatical structure, as outlined by Edward Sapir (1949: 92-93), it does present a fragmented grammatical structure of language in which the artists morph broken English into a new language that fits the context in which it is being played

---

[5] It is also noted that Boyd (2002) and Kelley (1994 and 1997) argue that the term "Nigga" is related to class. It is argued that Tupac also used the term in that way as well; to illustrate the working lower middle class Black person; the Blue collar worker.

(Smitherman 1994; Dillard 1972). Within BPC, language has developed into something significant. The language of the streets now becomes everyday language. For example, there is currently an ad that states, "Pimp Your Glove Box: Buy the new Thompson's City Map." The word "pimp" is a throw back to the 1970's which meant the literal definition of a person who was the CEO (of sorts) of illegal sex operations. Most from the Civil Rights generation are appalled at such a word, while individuals from the Hip Hop generation understand it to have several different meanings; yet another example of BPC penetrating American mainstream culture and being commercialized (c.f. Turner 2004; Baldwin 2004; Bell 1975; Cook 1999).

Tupac chose his language carefully. As a poet first, then rap artist, Tupac knew that words are crucial in making an impact on society at large, let alone BPC. Tupac knew that he needed to use words to critically engage society. This is what he did. Artists that followed, such as Snoop and Master P, have developed a language all their own that is now being used in everyday language. [6]

In Table 4 we see just a few of the common words used today in BPC. Tupac used each of those words as well. Still, as a whole, BPC is not just about using language that is considered vulgar or profane. BPC encompasses a large vocabulary of words and word phrases. In *The Fresh Prince of Bel Air*, Will uses words such as "love ya," "my boyz," and "much love," in seemingly positive contexts. BPC can, at times, be seen as largely vulgar and profane, but this is simply not the truth. Elements of love, community, brother hood, sisterhood, and the common wellness of human kind are all elements that are present in BPC.

---

[6] Words such as Fo- Sheezy, Fo-Shizzel, Skins, Chronic, and Homie are all derived from Hip Hop culture. These words have infused themselves within BPC as a whole.

## The Value of Being Real

Another cultural value present in BPC that relates to Tupac is the issue of authenticity. What is real? Are you still real if you leave the ghetto? In season two, episode eight of *The Fresh Prince of Bel Air* Will is faced with the dilemma of going to the prom. Will knows the prom costs at least two hundred dollars, but also knows that he does not have the money. Therefore, he begs Uncle Phil to give him the money. He does. Later, Will finds out that his friends are working their way to the prom—his friends that do not go to a private school. Will's friends begin to mock him because of his privilege. Will tears up the check Uncle Phil gave him, and begins to work for his payment to the prom. In the end, Uncle Phil confronts Will about his decision to take on a second job. Will confesses that he felt as though taking the money, and having privilege, made him less authentic and real. Uncle Phil lets him know that he worked hard to get where he is so that his kids, i.e. Will, could have those privileges. As a result, Will and the audience is confronted with a conundrum.

Does moving up (out of the ghetto) make you less authentic? This is a question that remains central to Hip Hop culture as a whole. Imai Perry contends that the "outlaw" image within Hip Hop is celebrated and glorified as being authentic and "real" (2004: 102-116). Being real and establishing your "rep" is a large part of rap music (Keyes 2002: 122-123). Further, authenticity appears to fade as the individual is more privileged and/or appears to be "acting White" (Rux 2003).

In Figure 11 we see the break down between perceived reality and perceived fakes from the media content:

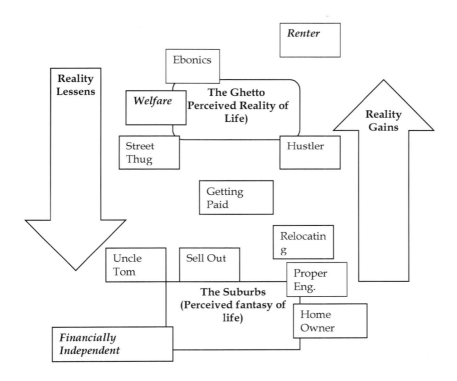

**FIGURE 11**

**PERCEIVED REALITY AND FANTASY WITHIN THE MEDIA**

In Figure 11, we gather from the data that the closer you move to the suburbs the further you are away from the reality of life, i.e. the streets. The more financially independent you are, the less you have a grasp on life. For example, in season two episode eleven of *The Jeffersons*, George meets Louise's cousin. George perceives him to be an Uncle Tom because of his proper English, his relocation status and education; never mind the fact that George has done the same, minus the proper English. Still George is convinced that he is a "sellout" and has lost touch with the realness of Black people.

In the end, George and his son are challenged by Louise's cousin to really think about the term "Uncle Tom" and "sell-out." They make the connection that just because you move out of the ghetto, does not mean that you have lost touch with Black people.

Additionally, this remains a factor throughout the media content. An interesting note is in the film *Scarface*, Tony moves out of his apartment into the suburbs and into a mansion. He remains himself, although he becomes obsessed with money and drugs, which eventually kill him. Still, he was considered "real" and "authentic" because he remained himself.

It is also interesting to note that many rappers today, including Tupac,[7] move out of the ghetto to a better place. As rapper MC-Eiht once said, "Man, I needed to get the hell out of the hood. I got kids, and now things are completely different. I can't have them growing up in that shit." Therefore the question remains, who is real? Who makes the mark and who is authentic? Is it a self-identity issue? Why does the media content not support the suburbs as equally being real? We are left with these questions, as further research into BPC is needed.

The issue of reality is furthered when the term nigga is brought into the spectrum. Tupac used the term frequently. Most from his generation—the Hip Hop generation—use the term freely without its historical negative connotation. The term itself is still surrounded by a mixture of total disgust and a term that is endearing.

Robin D.G. Kelley offers up another perspective worth investigating. He states:

> More common, however, is the use of "Nigga" to describe a condition rather than skin color or culture. Above all, Nigga speaks to a collective identity shaped by class consciousness, the character of inner-city space,

---

[7] Tupac was strongly criticized by people during his life, for moving out of the hood. Some, in Marin City CA, felt as though he had changed because he had moved away; that he was too "Hollywood" and was different because of the fame. This remains to be a central issue for BPC as a whole.

police repression, poverty, and the constant threat of interracial violence. Part of NWA's "Niggaz4Life," for instance, uses "Nigga" almost as a synonym for oppressed (Kelley 1994: 210).

The term "nigga" has taken on a broader definition, and now, as it would seem, takes on a representative term.[8] For Tupac, being real meant being a nigga. Someone who is from the ghetto, from the streets, from a difficult situation, and someone who understands other niggas. "To be a 'real nigga' is to be a product of the ghetto" (Kelley 1994: 210). This was part of Tupac's mantra for the term.

Another aspect of the term for Tupac was his acronym for it. For Tupac, nigga[9] meant: Never Ignorant Getting Goals Accomplished. Tupac could relate to real niggas and people who associated themselves with real niggas. In a 1994 interview, he stated, "niggas, spelt N I double G A. Niggers are the ones with ropes around their necks. Niggas, are the ones with gold ropes around their necks gettin paid, there's a difference" (Lazin 2003). This image and definition of "nigga" is a more common one now.

For example, many Blacks in blue-collar working class would see themselves as a nigga. I have even heard Latinos calling themselves "niggas" because they could identify with the fact that they and Blacks were all in the same "class" and economic brackets (c.f. Kelley 1994: 31-34). However, for educated, correct English speaking, well mannered Blacks, they would have lost the "nigga" status, and would just be Black (Kelley 1994; hooks 1992; and Neal 2005). That type of Black person's "realism" would not be as valued to a Hip Hopper, or blue-collar worker. This issue is not easily approached, but worth mentioning here. Tupac has similar issues with the "educated" and "well-off." A

---

[8] This raises the very important debate. Can, by Kelley's definition, a White person be a "Nigga" too? This is an issue that is raised in the book by Greg Tate ed. (2003).

[9] Another aspect to the word nigga for Tupac was that he applied the letter "z" to the end of it: niggaz. This term applied to the working, blue-collar, lower class person; particularly someone who was Black or Brown. This little letter communicated a powerful meaning of class and social position as opposed to its most common meaning which refers to a person's race and ethnicity for Tupac.

question that Tupac posed to God in several of his songs was, " Do real niggas get to go to Heaven?"

Conversely, there is a growin body of literature that suggests rap music is violent, misogynistic, and promotes gang violence. Jeanita Richardson and Kim Scott report on their 2002 study:

> There is a symbiosis between violent reactions in rap music and a culture that rewards violent expressions. Writers, researchers, and scholars continue to be incensed by the counter hegemonic dimensions of this new art form, elated that the music is a cultural elixir for Black communities, or intellectually engaged in dismantling the lyrics in the name of scholarship. Meanwhile the youth culture continues to create a music trajectory replete with money, popularity, and fame. Dialogue with an emphasis on self-evaluation seems conspicuously absent. It is precisely this point-this failure to facilitate a dialectical approach to the evolution of and reaction to rap music and hip-hop-that allows our youth to prioritize economic gain and fame over self-reflection and critical thinking. It is the adultist society's rejection of anything related to African American youth culture that allows youngsters to remain culturally insulated (2002: 173).

Further, James Johnson, Lee Jackson, and Leslie Gatto contend that there is a greater acceptance to violence when the individuals, who were studied, were subjected to violent rap music (1995: 27-41). These are serious issues in which further research is needed.

## *Summary*

In this chapter, I began to uncover some of the connections between Tupac, BPC, and Hip Hop culture. Language is a large part of BPC and Hip Hop, and it is used in many different ways, including both positive and negative elements. Sexuality is seen in several different ways including gender roles and how language is used for sex. Social class and economics are issues within BPC as well. Does being from the ghetto mean that you are real? What exactly is "being real?" Can someone who is Black with a PhD still be a nigga? These are all questions we are left with as Tupac himself had different opinions on each of these areas himself.

We now move onto Tupac's ethnolifehistory and begin to uncover what it was that made him into the ghetto saint. In the next chapter I will focus on his major life eras, how those eras shaped both his ethos and worldview, and we will begin to see what it was that made him stand out in a sea of rappers within Hip Hop culture.

# PART III:

## TUPAC'S ETHNOLIFEHISTORY

In part three, we now begin to focus on Tupac himself. In part three, we move from a world context into a more biblical context as we look at the narrative of Tupac's life, and how his life connected to the story of Christ (See Figure 12). In part three, I will focus just on Tupac's life, how his spirituality was developed, and what his spirituality was, derived from my data.

Figure 12 illustrates that this part deals with Tupac's biblical and church context. In other words, the formation of Tupac's worldview and life is dealt with in part three.

Part 3 will then set up part four, where I will focus on Tupac's missiological message from the data gathered from within his music and poetry.

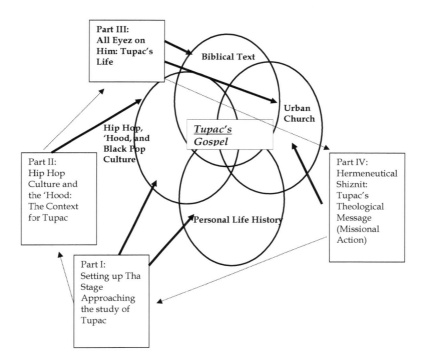

**FIGURE 12**

**FLOW OF BOOK PART THREE**

# CHAPTER 8

# TUPAC'S LIFE ERAS

This chapter focuses on the ethnolifehistory of Tupac. This chapter takes a closer look into the being, way of life, standard of living, and existence of Tupac. Each era is broken down and I demonstrate how each era connected to the other.

## *Military Mind (1971-1980)*

Where did it all Begin? On June 16, 1971 in the Bronx, New York, Lesane Parish Crooks was born to Afeni Shakur. Tupac's original name was Lesane Parish Crooks, but Afeni later changed his name to Tupac Amaru Shakur. The name was derived from an Incan Chief who was torn apart by Spaniards meaning, "Shining serpent, thankful to God" (Peters 2001). Afeni had been involved in The Black Panther Movement for quite some time. Tupac's father remains a bit of a mystery. William Garland is thought to be his biological father, while Jeral Williams or Dr. Mutulu Shakur is his stepfather and mentor (Spirer 2002).

Afeni was a revolutionary. She had been actively involved with the Black Panther movement and vigorously stood for their principles and platform.[1] Afeni threw herself into the Panther 21 (Their name at the time) in 1968. She was at rallies, gave speechs, and protested the racist attitude of American White Culture of the time. In 1969, she was arrested for allegedly trying to bomb several buildings in Manhattan, New York. In February of 1971, she was sent to the Women's Detention Center in Greenwich Village

---

[1] See Appendix C for a copy of the Black Panther's 10-point platform and program.

where in June of that same year, Tupac was born. To his own admission, he was cultivated in prison. Tupac said, "My mom was pregnant with me in prison, and after she got out (a month before her due date) she gave birth to me. I was cultivated in prison; my embryo was made in prison" (Peters 2001).

Being pregnant with Tupac in prison, Afeni helped to shape some of the love and hate that many urban youth deal with in regards to prison. Tupac did not want to go jail, but it gave him more street credibility—more on this in his outlaw era.

Afeni defended herself in court, and through hard work, persistence, and her knowledge of the law, she was found not guilty of attempting to bomb a government building. She was free to go. This set a precedent for Tupac that lasted his whole life: never give up!

## The Black Panther Party

The Black Panther Party's vision of Black Unity, Black Power, Black independence, and self-sustaining power was an intricate part of Afeni's life. This in turn transferred directly into Tupac's life.

The Black Panther party was about helping Black people. They took the message of Civil Rights and Equal Rights, spoken of by Martin Luther King Jr., which stated that we are no longer taking the "crap" we took in the 1960's; we are no longer taking the dysfunction that America calls racism; we are no longer capitulating, no longer surrendering to the will of White America, we are standing up for ourselves and we have a platform to do that. It was a return to the Blackness of the soul, and a building up of Black people. This was a theme in the 1970's.[2]

---

[2] As also seen in many of the films and songs of that time. "Superfly," "Shaft," and "Foxy Brown" are just a few of the many Black pride films of the 1970's.

The Black Panther Party educated themselves and began to understand the law of the land. They knew the law and understood how to interact with it and deal with it. Afeni was a large part of that faction. She was an avid reader and a devoted student of the law. Armond White states:

> Although the seventies had been relatively complacent, Black America found itself confronting new social challenges that threatened to reignite the activism and rage that had exploded in the sixties. Young Tupac's dream of revolution stood out—a rare raised fist amongst the millions of kiddie hands clutching Pac-Man joysticks. His answer to Rev. Daughtry reflects Afeni's experience and her soberly-adjusted attitude toward social change—his mothers son's loyalty mixed with an early sense of inherited mission (1997: 3).

Tupac was raised with the mentality of helping each one and reaching each one. For many Blacks during this era, this too was their mantra. A young man states, "my mother always taught me that if I wasn't doing or living for Black people, what was I living for" (Tan 1998)? The Black Panther Party stood for helping the next generation, the young people. Afeni embraced this idea, especially after Tupac was born.

Afeni instilled a sense of civil duty for Blacks, particularly ghetto Blacks, in Tupac. The Black Panther Party wanted to help end ghetto poverty and build up the communities that were torn down. Tupac's response to Reverend Daughtry's question of life goals was, "I want to be a revolutionary" (White 1997: 3)! This statement was at age ten.

Tupac, even at age five and eight, was continually trying to help out young Blacks. Even in church, he would want to be a part of the marches and speeches that helped the community he lived in. By age nine, he had memorized the Panther's ten point platform and program and desired to put those issues to use in the Black community (Tan 1998).

Tupac was raised to believe that he was a soldier bred to fight a war. This is seen early in some of his lyrics:

> As real as it seems the American Dream
> Ain't nothing but another calculated scheme
> To get us locked up shot up back in chains
> To deny us of the future rob our names
> Kept my history of mystery but now I see
> The American Dream wasn't meant for me[3]

The reality was that Tupac had both revolutionary and thug in him.

Tupac was partly raised by men in the streets considered by many to be pimps, hustlers, junkies, and common criminals. These are some of the minds that influenced him in his early work. The streets were his classroom and he was an A student, but not just in the violence and crime that occurs on the streets, but in how to overcome those issues. Tupac states:

> My father was a panther. I never knew where my father was or who my father was for sure. The times that I came up, was the late sixties. They were still having free love, they was just hittin' what they was hittin'. My mother wasn't married, and she got pregnant and had me, and I didn't have a father.
>
> My stepfather was a gangsta. A straight up street hustler. He loved the fact that the Panthers would go to jail and wouldn't snitch. He didn't even care my moms had a kid. He was like, 'Oh, that's my son.' Took care of me, gave me money, but he was like a criminal too. He was a drug dealer out there doing his thing—he only came, brought me money, and then left. I hate saying this cuz white people love hearing black people talking about this. But I know for a fact that had I had a father, I'd have some discipline, I'd have more confidence (Shakur 2003).

Here we see that Tupac was beginning to make distinctions of who was real and who was there for him. Even at a very young age, Tupac had a keen sense about people and wisdom beyond his years.

Throughout this era in Tupac's life, we begin to see the makings of a Hip Hop revolutionary.[4] Throughout Tupac's career, almost all would agree that Tupac was still a

---

[3] Taken from http://www.ohhla.com/YFA_2pac.html last accessed Tuesday September 6, 2005.

[4] Part of that revolutionary came out in Thug Life, which focuses in on helping the thugs, pimps, and people society has looked upon as "trash."

Black Panther in Hip Hop Clothing. All of his music related back to the struggle of ghetto Blacks in one way or another. This era helped to solidify Tupac's hard-core, dedicated, devoted, and enthusiastic vigor for life, the urban community, urban youth, and Black people in general. The Black Panther connection through Afeni and extended family members, helped shape Tupac's social awareness and construct his social identity.

More importantly, The Black Panther Party laid out a social norm that stayed with Tupac for the rest of his life. This belief system—which consisted of being respectful, being unified, having and earning trust and honor, and having a deep social awareness—was manifested in such songs as "Young Black Male," "Brenda's Got A Baby," "Strugglin," and "Black Jesuz" which have inspired many current Hip Hoppers such as Kanye West, The Game, Mike Jones, and Eminem.

## Afeni

Throughout Tupac's early childhood years, Afeni was the centerpiece of his life. She instructed him on his life path. Moreover, her values, philosophy, ideology, and principles were transferred to him orally and through her actions. Tupac states, "My mom was my homie, we went through our stages…really all males period, but males from that ghetto mentality especially, have a deep love for their mamas cuzz they usually raise us by themselves" (Peters 2001). Afeni had endured many hardships and was aware of difficult times (Guy 2004: 51-68). Afeni, through her experience, raised Tupac and gave him one of his first views of the world.

In the ghetto, Mama is next to God (c.f. Dyson 2001). Mammas are the ones typically raising young men, predominantly young Black men. Grandmas and mammas are one in the same, and for many grandparents, while most grandparents are enjoying the "years off from parenting," they are now doing "double duty" as they raise the second and third generations of children. Tupac, being raised by many women, began early in life to understand the complexities of womanhood and to appreciate and respect those complexities. [5]Tupac had many women around his life that helped him appreciate women and helped him better understand women as a whole; particularly Black women and women from the ghetto.

Afeni has always been a solid figure in Tupac's life; this is seen throughout his music and career. Afeni gave up the Panther "Movement" to stay home with her children and raise them (Lazin 2003). Initially Afeni was still actively involved in the movement, but after several talks with her children, particularly Tupac, she decided to stay home and get a regular job to take care of her children. Tupac states about Afeni:

> My mother was a Black Panther and she was really involved in the movement. Just Black people bettering themselves and things like that. She was high in position in the party which was unheard of because there was sexism, even in the Panthers. All my roots to the struggle are real deep.
>
> There's racism, so when the Panthers hit, the government panicked and they felt like the Panthers were detrimental to American society. So they raided every Panther's house, especially the ones who they felt like, could do damage as an orator (Shakur 2003).

Tupac discussed how he and Afeni went through their stages. They struggled to communicate since both of their personalities were so strong. Tupac was allowed to speak his mind, so long as he respected his mother. Respect was a fundamental issue for Tupac: respect infused with knowledge. Tupac states, "My mother, she's totally brilliant. Totally understanding and caring. And she's human—I mean, she'll be wrong a lot but we can talk about it. My mother taught me three things: respect, knowledge, and search for knowledge. It's an eternal journey" (Shakur 2003).

---

[5] This is something that many do not know about Tupac. They hear the word "bitch" in one of his songs, and most will assume that he is refereeing to all women. For Pac, that is not the case. Bitch can be broken down into many aspects of womanhood. It can mean a tramp, someone who is a knucklehead, someone who is scared, and/or a woman who is a gold-digger and only dates me for their money. However, in most cases it is used negatively. For Tupac though, he knew the differences between a woman and a bitch; within Hip Hop culture as a whole, there is a difference.

> Let knowledge drop
> Why should I be forced to play dumb?
> I know where I came from so I'm going to claim some
> But rocking to the top where the cream of the crop
> Suckers calling the cops but they can come and get dropped[6]

In this early piece, we are able to see his construction of neo-political rap music. This was ahead of its time. For most Hip Hoppers in the late 1970's and early 1980's, the theme was about partying and having fun, while proving to others you are the man and/or woman. For Tupac, however, this was certainly not the case. He saw a deplorable plaited theme in the different ghetto's he lived in: poverty. Tupac hated poverty. He wanted to do something about it. Afeni instilled in him that he had the power to do so.

Afeni also knew that Tupac needed a man's role in his life. Tupac even states, "Your mother cannot calm you down the way a man can. Your mother can't reassure you the way a man can. My mother couldn't show me where my manhood was. You need a man to teach you how to be a man" (Shakur 2003). Afeni took Tupac to church. Reverend Daughtry was introduced to Tupac through Afeni while they lived in New York. At a young age Tupac was introduced to Christ and the Black church. He writes:

> God
> When I was alone and had nothing I asked 4 a friend 2 help me bear the pain no one came except…GOD
> When I needed a breath 2 rise from my sleep no one could help me except…GOD
> When all I saw was sadness and I needed answers no one heard me except…GOD
> So when I am asked who I give my unconditional love 2 look for no other name except…GOD[7]

---

[6] Taken from http://www.ohhla.com/YFA_2pac.html last accessed Tuesday September 6, 2005.

[7] The poem "God" taken from: http://www.ohhla.com/anonymous/2_pac/the_rose/god.2pc.txt Last accessed on Monday October 23, 2006.

In this poem we begin to see the deep love that Tupac had for God. Tupac was affected by deep and complex issues at a very young age. For many young people, childhood years are filled with fun, games, trips to grandma's home in another state, or simply "being a kid." However, many inner city youth, especially Tupac, deal with adult issues and are burdened with crime, murder, and violent acts; these years resemble those of a forty five year old. Issues such as money, crime, jobs, and the welfare of the family are all areas Tupac had to deal with on a daily basis. Tupac states that when he was a kid, he remembers one moment of calm and peace, and three minutes after that, it was on (Shakur 2003)! Afeni tried to shield him as much as she could, but poverty is a harsh mistress. Armond White states, "Probably the only child who understands the relation between pleasure and struggle is an artistic child" (1997: 5).[8]

Tupac hated poverty because he felt he and his family missed out on a lot. Afeni wanted to give her kids more, but could not. When Tupac did finally become a Rap superstar, he bought each of his family members houses, cars, and paid most of their bills. [9]

### The Music and Arts

Tupac had an eclectic taste in music. Hip Hop culture during this time was in its early stages. Rap music could only be heard on underground mix tapes and at DJ parties. Rap groups such as Run DMC, and LL Cool J were some of the more famous ones that

---

[8] Further, Armond White goes on to discusses how some parents try to shield their young from the harsh realities of life. But for many it is their natural instinct to learn more about the world in which they live. For Tupac that was no different. He was able to see the death, sexuality, drugs, crime, violence, and hard core life issues such as poverty and homelessness first hand. Armond states that Tupac had to face that reality while others were able to simply ignore it. Afeni did her best to shield him from it, and to instill hope, but Tupac was introduced to the harsh realism of this world first hand (White 1997:4-6).

[9] Because of his mother's prominent role in his life, songs such as "Brenda's Got A Baby," "Dear Momma," and "Keep Ya Head Up" came from her significant influence in his life.

made it onto the public scene. Hip Hop culture was in its most infant form during this time. Still, Tupac loved rap music whenever he could listen to it.

The beginning of Tupac's stage presence began at the age of twelve when Afeni enrolled him in a Harlem theatre group called The 127$^{th}$ Street Ensemble. This was a key time period in Tupac's life. At age twelve he had his first performance at the famous Apollo Theatre. It was at this time that Tupac realized that the stage and being in front of people, was where he wanted to be (Shakur 2003).

> When I was young I was quiet, withdrawn. I read a lot, wrote poetry, kept a diary. I watched TV all day. I stayed in front of the television. It was when I was in front of the TV by myself, being alone in the house by myself, having to cook dinner by myself, eat by myself. Just being by myself and looking at TV, at families and all these people out there in this pretend world. I knew I could be part of it if I pretended too, so early on I just watched and emulated…and I just thirsted for that. I thought if I could be and act like those characters, act like those people, I could have some of their joy. If I could act like I had a big family I wouldn't feel as lonely (Shakur 2003).

Tupac had a natural stage presence, and many around him could see that he was different and was going somewhere in life. Still, the issue of poverty was an intensifying one, and Afeni needed to move the family to Baltimore after she lost her job and the family had nowhere to stay (Dyson 2001 33-34).

Baltimore produced more of the same for Tupac: poverty and isolation. Still in the midst of all of this, Tupac was able to enroll in The School For Performing Arts, and became a top-notch student. More importantly, it was in this school that he was able to develop some of his keen skills on the stage as well as his acting skills.

Rap songs such as LL Cool J's "I'm Bad" and Run DMC's album "Raising Hell" helped to soothe Tupac's harsh reality of life in the inner city. Music was a way out and a way to deal with difficult issues that arose each day living in the ghetto. We begin to see the toll in his early writings as well.

> Life through my bloodshot eyes
> Would scare a square 2 death
> Poverty, murder, violence,
> And never a moment 2 rest
> Fun and games R few
> But treasured like gold 2 me
> Cuz I realize that I must return
> 2 my spot in poverty
> But mock my words when I say
> My heart will not exist
> Unless my destiny comes through
> And puts an end 2 all of this (Shakur 1999:11)

We are able to see the passion and zeal that Tupac has for life, all the while that passion is slowly being extinguished by the realities that exist in the ghetto. The Arts and music were a way for Tupac to express himself. They helped him through those dark nights, as a therapist would have done with a client.

These are the beginnings of Tupac's musical career. At an early age he was able to develop deep lyrics that shaped his entire life. In each of his songs during this era there is some type of message: an admonition to change, to learn from his mistakes, to gain a broader vision on life, and/or to gain some knowledge on the realities of life around us. This was one of the many reasons why so many young people still love Tupac today and still view him as a cultural icon. Tupac was beginning to place his mark on the culture. The Apollo theatre's performance was the first of many that would inspire him to continue with this passion to perform.

The era fades into the next, criminal grind (1981-1988) when Tupac and his mother Afeni change locations in the country. Tupac was now aware that the world was not as he thought it was and that Black people were being "dogged" out all over the country and not just on the East Coast (Shakur 2003).

## *Criminal Grind (1981-1988)*

Tupac's criminal grind era does not mean that Tupac was involved with crime, but that his daily life was surrounded with crime. Therefore, that crime element gave him much meaning, identity, perspective, and outlook on the world at large.

### Growing Up in Different Hoods

In this particular era of Tupac's life, we begin to see the hardness, despair, and gut wrenching realities of the ghetto. Tupac moved from The Bronx, to Baltimore after Afeni lost her job and needed a change for the family. Tupac had different feelings about that move, he states:

> ...and we moved to Baltimore which was total ignorance town to me. It gets me upset to talk about it...Baltimore has the highest rate of teen pregnancy, the highest rate of AIDS within the Black community, the highest rate of teens killing teens, the highest rate of teen suicide, and the highest rate of Blacks killing Blacks. And this is where we chose to live (Shakur 2003: 34).

In this era, Tupac begins to develop his natural skills to rap. Moreover, in this era, Tupac begins to realize that ghetto poverty is not just in one ghetto, it expands into many.

Here, we can begin to see a strong sense of social justice emerge from Tupac as he sees the differences in each ghetto he is in:

> He's bragging about his new Jordans
> The Baby just ran out of milk
> He's buying gold every 2 weeks
> The baby just ran out of Pampers
> He's buying clothes for his new girl
> and the baby just ran out of medicine
> U ask for money for the Baby
> The Daddy just ran out the Door
> Tears of a Teenage Mother (Shakur 1999: 101)

Tupac's music has roots in this era. Songs such as "Brenda's got a Baby,"[10]"Young Black Male," Crooked Ass Nigga," "Holla If you Hear Me," and "Looking at the World Through my Rearview," to name a few, all connect to this era. All of his albums trace back to these years spending time in different ghettos.

While Tupac was in Baltimore, Afeni enrolled him in The Baltimore School for Performing Arts. He auditioned and made the cut. Tupac's life was now being influenced by other artistic students and by different friends; friends that were not all Black. Tupac was surrounded by Whites, Latinos, and Asians. This helped Tupac to better understand different cultures.

Tupac immersed himself in theatre and began to read voraciously. This was a growing period for Tupac's life; we can see this a little clearer with Figure 13:

---

[10] This particular song deals with the harsh realities of being a single, pregnant, teenage mom. Tupac was heralded for this song, as he presented the "other-side" of sexuality.

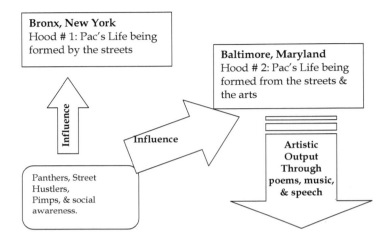

**FIGURE 13**

**TUPAC'S SOCIAL INFLUENCE**

In Figure 13 we see that Tupac's influence mainly came from the ghetto streets being peppered with artistic values and theatre while he was in Baltimore. All of the influence from the streets, hustlers, pimps, and The Panthers were still "in" Tupac's worldview. That element never went away. While some people grow out of their different "eras" Tupac kept a lot of the knowledge and skill gained from each of these eras. This is why he remains one of the most respected rap artists: authenticity. Still, this was a unique time for Tupac. While in Baltimore, he writes:

> I had a few times when I just zoned out and had good luck. When I auditioned for the Baltimore school for the arts, that was one of my good luck times. I spent three years in Baltimore, my high school years. I loved my classes, made a lot of friends that I wanted to keep over. We were exposed to everything. Theater, ballet, different people's lifestyles—rich

people's lifestyles, royalty from other countries and things, everything (Shakur 2003: 44).

Here Tupac honed his stage presence, polished his natural skill of poetry, and developed a deep sense or knowledge through reading.[11] Tupac began to see that the world was not equal and fair, nor did the world—America—truly care for her poor and lower class. This strengthened Tupac's sense of social justice, as witnessed throughout his life.

Tupac's sense of awareness was growing at a rapid rate. This fueled him for his career ahead. More importantly, this attitude of life was imparted to others as well. Tupac did not live in the "Hollywood Bubble" that so many do. His home was—as Big Sike and Quincy Jones recall—a refuge and solace for lost souls. Tupac never forgot his "people" —the downtrodden. Rapper and actor Snoop Dogg states, "Tupac was a magnet for lost souls, lost people just knew he would love them—regardless!"[12]

## Marin City

After a good friend of Tupac's was shot in Baltimore, Afeni decided to move the family once again, to escape that violence. Therefore, in the late 1980's Tupac's family moved to Marin City, California. This was the beginning of a new era in Tupac's life. Tupac hated leaving his beloved school in Maryland. He has been quoted saying, "Leaving that school affected me so much, I see that as the point where I got off track." For Tupac, the ghetto woes did not end on the East Coast, they were just as bad on the West Coast.

---

[11] The School for Performing Arts affected Tupac a lot. He loved that school and saw it as a changing point in his life. The school gave him opportunities that many urbanites did or could not have at the time. Tupac excelled in this school. It is interesting to note that Tupac never finished high school because he wanted to pursue his career.

[12] Taken from Tupac: Resurrection; DVD, audio (2003).

> Come to Marin City and there's skinhead violence. There's racial violence, which I deplore. But don't get the wrong idea; I feel like I'm being gloomy. I don't mean to just be like, 'Damn it's bad out there.' I still try to be positive. I chase girls and want the car and loud music. But I like to think of myself as socially aware. I think there should be a drug class, a sex education class. A real sex education class. A class on police brutality. There should be a class on why people are hungry, but there are not. There are classes on…gym. Physical education. Let's learn volleyball (Shakur 2003: 63).

The streets of Marin City influence Tupac extensively. In a 1992 interview with Davey D, Tupac states:

> Being in Marin City was like a small town so it taught me to be more straightforward with my style. Instead of being so metaphorical with the rhyme, where I might say something like, "I'm the hysterical, lyrical miracle. I'm the hypothetical, incredible," I was encouraged to go straight at it and hit it dead on and not waste time trying to cover things.[13]

Tupac enrolled in public school and he began to realize that they had left nothing in Baltimore, the same element that Tupac despised was present here in Marin City: poverty. To compound the situation, the political economy of crack cocaine was in full swing. More importantly, Afeni the activist was now becoming Afeni the addict. Afeni, Tupac's "Homie" and mom, was now addicted to crack cocaine. And as some have stated, " was now breaking into the republican political régime with crack" (Peters 2001).

### The Political Economy of Crack Cocaine

Crack cocaine became a commodity that many in the ghetto fought for and died for. Both Black and Brown people were vying for this new commodity that manifested itself in a small "tic-tac" like substance called crack. Tupac was first hand witness to this. Michael Dyson states:

> Then what you get in the 80's is the political economy of crack. Crack crimes, addictions, and people began to organize their lives in these terror enclaves called ghettos.

---

[13] Taken from the 1992 "lost interview with Tupac Shakur" by Davey D—renowned Hip Hop DJ and B-Boy.

The reality of it was that the community was drenched with crack. The government turned a deaf ear and eye to what was happening in the ghettos across America. The crack economy created hostility between Black and Brown families…Joseph Marshall states that crack cocaine did what 300 years of slavery could not do. It undermined and subverted the integrity of the black family by virtue of creating a commodity over which black people were literally killing themselves to get access to. And Pac had to watch that contradiction within his own mother of the Black revolution. On the one hand you had the promise to make it and succeed, and on the other hand the capitulation to the worst form of anti-revolutionary there was, that is addiction (Peters 2001).

Moreover, Tupac had to witness his "homie" or best friend—his mother Afeni—became broke down by this addiction. "My mom, she was lost at that particular moment. She wasn't caring for herself. She was addicted to crack. It was a hard time, because she was my hero" (Shakur 2003: 69). For Tupac, to see such a revolutionary person like his mother—who once stood for independence and freedom—now stricken with an addiction, was hardening his soul.

This was a difficult time for Tupac. Many of his friends during this era state that this was the point in which Tupac began to feel depressed and became real hurt and dismayed about life. [14] He was discouraged and began to feel as though the world was just too hard to live in. There were thoughts of suicide and there was much pain in his life at this time. [15]

The travesty of Afeni's addiction was also coupled with the fact that he had to go to a "ghetto" high school. He longed to go back to the performing arts school, but now, he was faced with what so many urban youth are faced with still today: underrepresented and under sourced schools. During this era, Tupac began to develop a corner stone in his

---

[14] E.g. Tan (1998) DVD and personal interviews with friends who stayed with Tupac's family during this era.

[15] The 1980's crime and crack wave was an unrivaled phenomenon. Crime and murders are nothing compared to the crime and violence that existed in urban communities during this decade. As I grew up in this decade, I saw first hand what crack can do to a family member, and how violent the streets really are. That element was even more powerful in cites such as Marin City and East Oakland where Tupac was raised and spent a majority of his years.

mantra, it was the mantra of "Fuck it" and "Fuck the world." Years of pain, misery, hurt, and despair led him to finally begin to feel as though America did not care. In my estimation there was a fundamental shift in Tupac's attitude in late 1987. The once bright eyed and hopeful idealist was now saying "Fuck You" to the whole world—and the ghetto was backing him.

This was a shift in Tupac's worldview once again: from idealistic and hopeful, to a negative and vengeful outlook. Afeni's crack addiction was taking its toll on Tupac (Guy 2004: 125-144). Crack cocaine and its vicious distress on the Black and urban communities were too much for Tupac. In certain poems he wrote, "The only way 2 change me is maybe blow my brains out. Stuck in the middle of the game, come and get the pain out" (Shakur 2003: 71).

### Ghetto Mindset

Around late 1987 early 1988, you begin to see Tupac's life changing. He is fighting a lot more, there is more weed smoking, and there is a lot more frivolous living. Marin City was taking its toll on Tupac. For many, especially those with even less hope and vision than Tupac, they cannot escape this enclave of horror. They simply end up a statistic. However, for Tupac, music was his savior and music helped him through those rough times (c.f. Spirer 2002 DVD).

In Tupac's writings and poems during this time, there is a shift from being positive to a gloomier feel. Tupac was on his own and being taken care of by people who he was used to: the thugs, gang members, pimps, and hustlers of the 'hood. Tupac states:

> All my songs deal with pain. That's what makes me, that's what makes me do what I do. Everything is based on the pain I felt in my childhood. Small pieces of it and harsh pieces of it. My inspiration for writing music is like Don Mclean did when he did 'American Pie' of 'Vincent.' Lorraine Hansberry with A Raisin in the Sun. Like Shakespeare

when he does his thing, like deep stories, like raw human needs (Shakur 2003: 70).

Part of the Ghetto mindset is rooted in Black nationalism where on one side of the table you have the ideology of "how to get paid" using American capitalism while on the other side you have the struggle of identifying and helping your fellow Black people. For Tupac, he was now consumed with trying to rise above his current situations and gain knowledge at any cost. He was inspired to get out of the lifestyle he and his family was living. The only means he saw to do that was music. While others around him were just giving in to the pressure of ghetto life, Tupac used his experiences to inspire him to write magnificent songs that would later become hits for the Hip Hop Community and would change the Hip Hop Cultural continuum forever. For Tupac, he now begins to take on one of the three roles in his music (as seen in Table 5)[16]

## TABLE 5

### TUPAC'S MUSICAL POSITIONS

| Observer | When Pac is involved in the story he is telling, he is typically telling it as a 1st person: involved in what is going on. The song "How Long Will They Mourn Me?" is an example. |
|---|---|
| Participant | Pac is telling the story from a $2^{nd}$ or even $3^{rd}$ person point of view. He is merely observing what is going on in the culture or in a particular context. Songs like "Dear Momma" are a good example of Pac observing reality as he sees it. |
| Messenger | Here Pac is telling you a message about what is going to happen, what has happened, or what is happening. This is where Pac is considered to be a Prophet. Songs like "If I Die Tonight" (which actually predict his death over some real dumb stuff) is an example. |

Here we are able to gain more insight into how Tupac's music is broken down. For Tupac, there was never a time to make a song that did not have some type of meaning

---

[16] Taken directly from Dan Hodge, http://www.cyfm.net/article.php?article=tupacs_insights.html, last accessed September 9, 2005.

in it. Even songs like "I Get Around" and "How do You Want it" had a message inside of them. They went beyond the typical gangsta, party rap style that so many Rappers are stuck in today.

Tupac's musical influence originated from several key elements seen in Figure 14. First, he was the child of a passionate revolutionary. Second, he was raised poor. That in itself is an entire book, album, or book. Growing up poor makes the individual either rise to magnificent heights, or breaks the person down so much that the only hope they have is a government check and twenty dollar ride. Third, Afeni had been on crack. Crack cocaine demoralizes the person. And while all of us are held accountable for our decisions, Afeni's situation might have been different had she had different opportunities and outlets in her life. More importantly, one must ask the question, "What if she had been living in a better neighborhood, stronger community, and had a different socioeconomic background, would she have not been an addict?" Fourth, Tupac had a father that was steeped in the thug traditions of the ghetto. The values, cares, and concerns of the street were etched into Tupac's mind, social construct, and soul. These would never leave him. As he put it, "the thugs shown me love, so until you all [speaking to a crowd of Black adults] begin to step up and help raise us, I don't want to hear fuck about it" (Shakur and Lazin 2003). All four of these areas shaped Tupac's life in this era, and are the cornerstone of his musical and acting career until his death in 1996.

At the end of this era Tupac is rising to popularity with the rap group Digital Underground. Tupac is now touring and rapping with this group and gaining some fame. This era ends when Tupac begins to see the media as a source for helping the 'hood through rap videos. This was a shift that led to his next era: the ghetto is destiny (1989-1992).

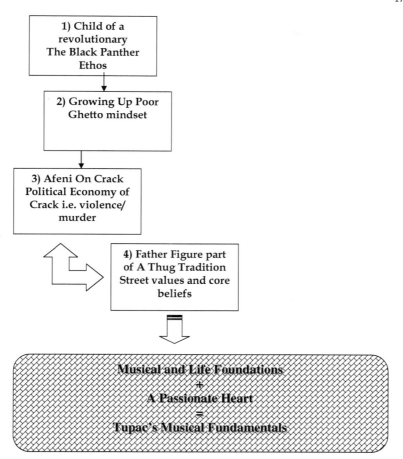

**FIGURE 14**

**TUPAC'S MUSICAL FOUNDATION**

## The Ghetto Is Destiny (1989-1992)

This era saw Tupac glamorizing the ghetto within his music. Tupac felt as though the advent of music videos was a poster board of sorts, to help effect change in the ghetto. For Tupac, the ghetto was his destiny, and he wanted to tell the world about it.

### The Era: Sources of Tupac's Passion and Vision

Tupac makes an amazing statement about this era in his life:

> It's like, you've got the Vietnam War, and because you had reporters showing us pictures of the war at home, that's what made the war end, or that shit would have lasted longer. If no one knew what was going on we would have thought they were just dying valiantly in some beautiful way. But because we saw the horror, that's what made us stop the war. So I thought, that's what I'm going to do as an artist, as a rapper I'm gonna show the most graphic details of what I see in my community and hopefully they'll stop it quick. I've seen all of that—the crack babies, what we had to go through, losing everything, being poor, and getting beat down. All of that. Being the person I am, I said no no no no. I'm changing this (Shakur 2003).

This era in Tupac's life begins with him being introduced to a community leader named Leila Stenberg. Leila—another woman—was a significant influence in Tupac's life. She was married, had kids, and was living a steady life in Marin County. Tupac, while he was homeless and living from house to house, came to live with Leila and her family for quite some time. Leila first spotted Tupac rapping at a community show, and from then on she had him come to her poetry night for the young people.

Tupac was on fire at this point. He used all of his past experiences to infuse his lyrics with a combination of social justice, comedy, and theology. Tupac was on the road to a great rap career. He continued to grow in his lyrical skills as well.

Dyson states that the ghetto was the source and major metaphor of Tupac's music and life (Peters 2001). For Tupac, the ghetto was a wide-open storybook that needed to be told. Tupac felt that the story needed to be ushered into the living rooms of White America. It is from this notion that White Americans began to get its first taste of what

Black life was all about. This is the reason why so many suburban Whites idolize Tupac just as much as urban youth do. Quincy Jones said that you cannot sell forty million records without someone who is White buying them (Spirer 2002). White youth today know Tupac well because of the reality that he spoke, the authenticity he brings, and the universal sentiment of being caged—whether in the terrenes of the ghetto or behind the pristine gates of suburbia—White youth know an authentic person when they see one.

Ester Iverem writes:

> ...affinity for Tupac mixes what is potentially a positive attitude toward self determination with the worst definitions of that over used- phrase: Keep it Real. At its most meaningful, the phrase urges those in the hip hop nation to remain true to their beliefs and rooted in reality. At its worst, it implies that only those things ghetto centric and hard are real in black culture. It endorses the use of street ethics to settle disputes, like the willingness to bust a cap in someone, usually another African-American, if necessary (1997: 41).

Tupac embodied the struggle between, the positive Black Awareness and Black Pride on the one hand, while on the other he had the thug, ghetto mindset, and "fuck-you" attitude that manifests itself in so many young, Black males. Tupac's ghettocentric values drove him to great success with the Hip Hop generation.

Tupac's lyrics were beginning to take shape in early works such as "Panther Power:"

> As real as it seems the American Dream
> Ain't nothing but another calculated schemes
> To get us locked up shot up back in chains
> To deny us of the future rob our names
> Kept my history of mystery but now I see
> The American Dream wasn't meant for me
> Cause lady liberty is a hypocrite she lied to me
> Promised me freedom, education, equality
> Never gave me nothing but slavery
> And now look at how dangerous you made me
> Calling me a mad man cause I'm strong and bold

In this particular piece, performed at a Black Panther rally in East Oakland, Tupac's passion and knowledge begins to take shape in his music. All of the pent up anger and pain was beginning to come through in his music. James Cone argues that through Black Power, a Black person is able to develop a sense of contextualized theology (1997 a: 5-30). As much as many older Blacks do not want to admit it—especially those born prior to 1970—Tupac reflected Black Theology. A Theology that says that Black people have a place too, at the throne of God. More importantly we must assert that position and fight to keep it. Tupac knew the Bible inside out; he had grown up with it and was raised in the ways of the Lord. He was simply vocalizing a cry, which had gone unheard for too long. Dyson writes, "Tupac was obsessed with God. His lyrics drip with a sense of the divine…Tupac's spiritual matters never left him, although its form and function in his later life may have become almost unrecognizable by earlier standards" (2001: 202 and 207).

## Death

There is an admiration in the 'hood with regards to death. It is valued, feared at times, and also glamorized in the ghetto. Dyson writes

> The sheer repetition of death has caused black youth to execute funeral plans. In its response to death, black youth have reversed perhaps the emblematic expression of self-aware black morality. Martin Luther King Jr.'s cry that 'every now and then I think about my own death.' They think about it constantly and creatively. With astonishing clinical detachment, black youth enliven King's claim that he didn't contemplate his death 'in a morbid sense.' They accept the bleak inevitability of death's imminent swoop—which, in truth, is a rejection of the arbitrariness we all face, since death to these youth is viewed as the condition, not the culmination, of their existence. Black youth tell funeral directors to portray their dead bodies with a style that may defeat their being forgotten and that distinguish them from the next corpse (2001: 227).

For Tupac, death was on every corner. In his song "Death on Every Corner," Tupac depicts death as an event that is on every ghetto corner:

> I see death around the corner, gotta stay high while I survive
> In the city where the skinny niggas die
> If they bury me, bury me as a G nigga, no need to worry
> I expect retaliation in a hurry
> I see death around the - corner, any day
> Tryin to keep it together, no one lives forever anyway
> Strugglin and strivin, my destiny's to die
> Keep my finger on the trigger, no mercy in my eyes

Tupac continued to rap about the horrors and pleasures of death. On one track you might have him rapping about the horrible death of a friend, while on the other he is rapping about the joy of finally being free.

For most urban youth, death is a time to rest. Death is a time to finally be out of the hell called the ghetto. Regardless, Tupac wanted to help provide a way out of that. In this era of his life, he did not know how though, when a lot of his friends were dying everyday. Tupac states, "Don't feel bad for the people that died, Feel bad for the folk that gotta stay behind. They the ones still in hell. The person who's dead is now at peace, and in joy, finally resting" (Shakur 2003: 80).

### Digital Underground

Around the late 1980's, Tupac was introduced to the famed Rap group Digital Underground. This was the start of Tupac's professional career as a Rap artist. He started very humbly. It was a time where he developed a rigorous work ethic. For many in Hip Hop culture, they referred to Tupac as the hardest working man in Hip Hop. He was not married, had no kids, and did not have the typical responsibilities of a married man. This has also been referred to as a parallel between Tupac and the Apostle Paul.

Leila introduced Tupac to the manager of Digital Underground. Tupac states:

> This lady named Leila introduced me to Atron Gregory who was managing Digital Underground. He was like, 'Ima send you to Digital Underground, they in the studio. You just rap for Shock G on the spot. If he likes you, I'ma pick you up.' I just walked in and rapped for him. He's like, 'Ok, good, you're in, boom-boom-boom, I'll see you later.' I just

walked out of there like, dang! I look back with the greatest fondness. Those were like some of the best times in my life. It's all funny to me, it's all good. The silly part is like me running around in zebra print underwears, and making simulated sex. We had like the funniest, craziest show. Think hip-hop needs another Digital Underground right now. As soon as I got a chance to say what was on my mind, I said what was on my mind and we have a platinum record now. So I went from dancing naked with dolls, being unknown, to having a platinum record (Shakur 2003: 73).

Tupac was on the road to success. Digital Underground paved the way. Tupac was able to meet a lot of important people in the industry and began to be well known. For Tupac, this was another opportunity to help his people and his family. Tupac began to send checks home to his family. He paid their bills, their rent, helped his mom get off crack, and bought homes for them. While many rappers would have taken the money and spent it on frivolous things, Tupac saved and spent it on "the people." Tupac helped many in need with his new found fame, strengthening his authenticity within the urban and Hip Hop communities.

Shock G, of Digital Underground, said, "Tupac didn't care about the mundane things in life like new rugs, gold, and new things in general. He was like, man check this new beat out, or shit, this new rhyme is dope right? Tupac was on another level; something we can't even comprehend" (Spirer 2002).

Tupac got a track on the song "Same Song." After which, he dropped his first solo album 2Pacalypse Now. This album laid out much of his early childhood struggles, and Digital Underground helped produce most of the album

## 2Pacalypse Now

In a 1992 interview with Davey D, Tupac talks about this new album. Tupac sated that this album was for the nigga, the real niggas, and that he wanted to give insight into the life of a Black man. Tupac dedicated this album to the working class Black person. Tupac remained who he was. In fact it brought him no better pleasure than to have people see him at a club or house party the same night he was in concert. Tupac and The Black Panther Party's mantra of "being for the people" was manifesting itself in the way Tupac lived his life.

Further, with this new album, young people in the Hip Hop community began to see Tupac as the ghetto prophet. 2Pacalypse Now sparked many conversations such as these. With songs such as "Young Black Male," "Brenda's Got A Baby," and "Trapped" Tupac began to be seen as the irreverent theologian. This irreverence, or the profane, is no mystery to Blacks. In fact, most early Black gospel music was considered profane and indecent in comparison to White gospel music (Cone 1997 b). For many Blacks, they had to have church without any set "ordained" pastor, because some denominations would not ordain a Black minister. Tupac faced the same dilemma, except this time it was not a White audience condemning Tupac's music, it was a Black audience.

## T.H.U.G. L.I.F.E

It is around this time that Tupac, after seeing violence erupt in his home town (Marin City) and different concerts, developed the code for THUG LIFE. THUG LIFE for Tupac stood for: The Hate U Give Little Infants Fucks Everyone. It was a code for the streets. It was a way to organize the different hoods and get thugs on one accord.[17] Tupac knew that no one else had a heart for the ghetto, so he decided to take matters into his own hands and deal with the ghetto problems straight on. He states:

> There was no spot for Tupac. Its not like there was somebody like me before and I moved into the spot so I can ask him how he did it. There was no spot here. Nobody wanted to be the person the thugs and the street people could rally around nobody wanted to be that. So when I was that, I couldn't handle it. I *could* handle it, but not right away.
> 
> I'm twenty two. I was havin' concerts, they was sold out—white boys, Mexicans, Blacks and they would all do whatever I said. I could tell

---

[17] See Appendix B for the complete code. This code has been implemented by many gangs, hustlers, pimps, and O.G.'s.

all those people in the audience 'Turn around in a circle' and they would do it. I was havin' love, undeniable love, and I was scared. I was so scared that I would come to a town and I would have the leader of the gang there tellin me, 'What you need?'

But that makes me rise to the occasion. Makes me wanna give my whole life to 'em, and I will give my whole life to this plan I have for Thug Life (Shakur 2003:121).

For Tupac, the thug did not mean the criminal, the fool, the person who is robbing old ladies or stealing cars. For Tupac, he meant the underdog. The person who has never had anything. People who knew Tupac intimately agreed with this assessment. Many state that their own family members called them "little hoodlums" and "thugs" so, in turn, they lived up to the label. Tupac wanted to end crime and violence. However, he soon realized that it was not going to just end. Tupac then figured that it could at least be organized; gangs, pimps, hustlers, or people in the "game"[18] could at least give back to the neighborhood they were raping (Peters 2001).[19] Tupac decided there needed to be a street code for the 'hood.[20]

Tupac argued that if the person who has nothing succeeds, then he was a thug because he overcame all the obstacles in life. For Tupac, the word "thug" had nothing to do with the dictionary's definition of "thug."[21] Tupac states, "I know it's not good, violence ain't good. It's just there are certain situations that there is no way out. There is

---

[18] The hustle, drug sales, and/or gang life of the urban environment.

[19] It is also interesting to note here what Dr. Mutulu Shakur (Tupac's stepfather) states on thug life: "The word 'THUG-LIFE' came from the word Thuggie. The British colonized India and it was a group within India who resisted the British and they were known as the "Thuggies". They had a similar tactic like the Mau Mau's in Kenya. The British used the word Thugs to refer to any group of Outlaws defying oppression. Since Tupac was confronted by exploitation and oppression he accepted the principle and evolved his meaning of it amongst the same lines. We built the code THUG-LIFE to respond to street life here in America" (Taken from http://www.allhiphop.com/features/index.asp?ID=644 last accessed on September 9, 2005.

[20] See Appendix B for the THUG LIFE street code.

[21] Thug: a cutthroat ruffian; a hoodlum; an aggressive or violent young criminal (From www.dictionary.com).

a way out, but until we can find that way out, then there is no way to stop talking about this type of lifestyle" (Peters 2001).

Tupac, once again, made the ghetto a stage in this era. He set up the ghetto in a way that other Hip Hop artists had not done in the past. N.W.A.[22] had spoke on police brutality, Ice Cube spoke on the injustices experienced by young Black males, and Ice T constantly warned The United States about the anger and despair boiling over in the ghettos. Tupac took that a step further and made the ghetto into a show. Tupac was able to reach deeper into Middle America and let those people know that there were separate societies that existed in The United States.

Tupac states about thug life and ghetto life:

> You know what gang violence is, I'm gonna tell you, and people don't want you to hear this; someone shoots your family member, then of course you retaliate. Same thing US does, except no one shot they family members. They shoot up some school or something, then the US says we gotta go help them and show them who the real killas are, that's the same mentality these gangsters have. The US is the biggest gang in the world, look what they did to Cuba, they didn't agree with Cuba so they blocked them off. That's what we do on the street (Peters 2001).

For Tupac, thug life set a precedent that would stick with him the rest of his career. His heart beat for thug life. Tupac felt as though America did not have any room to criticize him about this mantra of his. "What makes me saying 'I don't give a fuck' different from Patrick Henry saying 'give me liberty or give me death?' What makes my freedom less worth fighting for than Bosnians…" (Shakur 2003: 122)?

Thug life did not want to "clean-up" any young Black male. Thug life took them as they were: raw, stinking, foul, and open to change (a Christ-like value); yet another reason that Tupac was a ghetto saint. This Christ-like value is still heard in today's Hip Hop culture and Rap music. In 2004 Kanye West recoded "Jesus Walks." In the song he

---

[22] Niggas With Attitude.

makes mention that Jesus still cares for the pimps, the hustlers, and the thugs. Tupac reached deep into the Hip Hop Cultural continuum.

## Exodus 18:11

Finally, we have the scripture of Exodus 18:11 tattooed on the back of Tupac's back. This scripture was a staple for Tupac's mantra. He felt as though God would have His wrath on those who mis-used their power and authority, and urbanites would have justice. Tupac constantly referred to Old Testament images of God; a God that would take revenge and kill His enemies. Dyson writes:

> The gangsta's God—or the thug's theology—is internally linked to his beliefs about how society operates and who is in control. For many thugs, God is the great accomplice to a violent lifestyle…this may ring true for the vengeful deity depicted in the Old Testament, where the principle of a life for a life prevailed. But the last couple of millennia have witnessed a transformation of God's image. To an extent, thug theology is willfully anachronistic or at least staunchly traditional (2001: 211).

Thug life was intrinsically connected back to God and Exodus 18:11. God would take revenge. "He did this to those who treated Israel arrogantly" (NIV) was how Tupac viewed the "promise-land" for young urban youth.

Exodus 18:11 provided hope. And Tupac, as much as he loved the ghetto, searched for a way out of this style of living. He himself said that no one really wants to live there, no one really is talking about "killing each other for fun." This gave many young people hope and vision for a gloomy tomorrow; Tupac was part of that hope and Tupac would continually point to God.

Exodus 18:11 developed around the early 1990's, when political and conscious rap were beginning to take shape in Hip Hop culture. This was a significant event in the making. Several years later Tupac recorded and rapped the song "I Wonder if Heaven got A Ghetto?" In this track Tupac made several references to peace, rest, retribution, and a place for everyone to "chill" and take it easy. The Exodus 18:11 theme stayed with Tupac and the people around him. After seeing the first hand hardships his family and friends faced living in the ghetto, Tupac had to have something to hold on to, this was Exodus 18:11.[23]

It is during the latter part of 1991 that Tupac's life begins to change once again. Tupac had his first major encounter with the law in 1992 with the Oakland Police Department. Tupac, up until this point, had never experienced police brutality firsthand, nor many of the negative interactions with the law, he had rapped about in many of his songs (Shakur 2003: 80). Tupac's life would be changed forever, and it was now, that he was moving into his next life era, outlaw.

## *Outlaw (1992-1995)*

This era finds Tupac in trouble with the law. It seemed between these years that Tupac was in and out of trouble with the criminal justice system. For many years, Tupac had only rapped about being an outlaw, but Tupac's vision became reality between these years.

### The Long Arm of the Law

The talent that Tupac developed in his early years at the school of performing arts in Baltimore was beginning to flourish in American popular culture. Hip Hop culture as a whole was experiencing an influx of suburban Whites that were falling in love with Rap music. Moreover, Tupac was the perfect Black male image that Cornel West describes as being the Black sexual image that many White women want: the hard core rebel that is also the "forbidden" fruit (West 1993: 122-129). Hip Hop culture was also growing and

---

[23] See Appendix D on Tupac's pictorial view of his tattoo's and explanations into those tattoo's.

flowing into suburban homes. As Quincy Jones once said, "You can't sell over ten million records without *somebody* White buying them!"[24] Tupac's "thug" persona was fitting into American popular culture. Moreover, that persona was gaining momentum in an era in American popular culture that saw the rise of Hip Hop culture and Rap music. The "Black-Bad-Boy" image was on the rise in America, and Tupac was leading the way.[25]

Tupac's interaction with the law and criminal justice system only strengthened his street credibility and Hip Hop authenticity. For Tupac, during this era, he felt as though he was the leader of a thug life nation. A nation that was going to rebuild the ghettos and restructure The United States Black communities. For Tupac, this era was a significant milestone to gain his street credibility and to further the thug life cause.[26]

In this particular era of Tupac's life, we begin to see a pattern of "outlawish" activities—while not insinuating that he was a criminal—Tupac had some areas that were causing him problems in his life. During these years, Tupac's life was adversely affected. He felt that he was the spokesperson for Blacks and the ghetto community. During this time, however, he began to receive much criticism from the Black community about his lyrics, lifestyle, thug persona, and his seemingly violent behavior; this was mainly from older Blacks, ages thirty and up – mainly from the Civil Rights Generation.

Tupac's thug life credibility was boosted when he went to jail. Moreover, his vigor and fighting personality made him a spokesperson for thug life and for fighting the law as a whole. His fight against corrupt police was also strengthened during this era.

---

[24] Quincy Jones in *Tupac Shakur: Thug Angel, The Life of an Outlaw* (Spirer 2002).

[25] It was also during this time that many gangsta films such as *Menace II Society (1993), Boyz in the Hood (1991), New Jack City (1991), and Belly (1994)* made a hit on American cinema as well. This also had significant affects to the rise of Tupac's status. His "thug" persona only strengthened many young White's already positive view of him (e.g. Kitwana 2005).

[26] See Appendix K for a complete table of Tupac's interaction with the criminal justice system.

Tupac constantly encouraged young Black males, to take up "arms" against corrupt police. Tupac's legal troubles were also a result of his "big mouth" that he so often admitted he had (Lazin 2003). We see this trend of incidents (that more than likely could have been avoided) emerge from Tupac's life during this particular era of Tupac's life.[27]

It is during this era that the deep rage, anger, and despair that engulfed his life emerged through these incidents. Tupac's life was nothing more than a mirror of the rage, despair, and anger that so many young Black males have and still feel to this day (e.g. White 1997: 100-108).

**Hollywood**

Tupac made his film debut in *Juice* (1992). In this particular film, Tupac played the troubled teen named Bishop. Bishop's life was consumed with making a name for himself and attaining the "juice;" in other words, the respect and admiration that so many young people in the ghetto need. Bishop eventually went crazy with power and killed his best friend, and injured another before falling to his death at the end of the film. Tupac fit this role eerily well. His persona made the character so believable that Tupac's image was now marked for life; people begin to believe that Tupac was that crazy, cold hearted and manipulative person that "Bishop" was. This could not have been further from the truth. But, as Appendices K illustrates with Tupac's involvement with the criminal justice system, if one was to follow simply the "facts" and the "stats" then they could only assume that "if the shoe fits…" Moreover, the fact that Tupac was Black only added to this.

---

[27] Also during this era there were several other major events that helped shape this era: 1) Tupac's run in with the Hughes Brothers in early 1994 in which Tupac was to spend 15 days in jail; he had admitted to the assault charges, 2) Late 1995 and early 1996 Tupac begins the feud between Bad Boy Record Company and Death Row Records; some suggest that this was an East vs. West Coast issue, but in an interview, Tupac said it was more a "beef" between artists and not the different Coast's, 3) In 1996, at the Soul Train Music Awards, Death Row and Bad Boy face off and cause civil disorder, 4), in the Summer of 1996 Tupac releases the song "Hit Em Up" that brutally attacks Biggie Smalls, Mobb Deep, and Nas. These were all considered in the ethnolifehistory of Tupac.

The media did not have any less pity on Tupac's image. They merely reinforced the stereotype that Tupac was a street hoodlum and "thug." Still, Hollywood was a perfect fit for Tupac, and it was during this era that Tupac's silver screen performances began to grow. The years spent at The Baltimore School for Performing Arts were paying off—even though Tupac never graduated. Tupac states about Bishop's character:

> Bishop is a psychopath, but, more true to his character, Bishop is a lonely, misguided young kid. His heroes are James Cagney and Scarface, those kinds of guys. Shoot'-em-up, go-out-in-a-blaze type of gangsters. I don't think acting is as technical as they try to make it. They try and make it technical so everybody isn't an actor. All you really have to do is feel for your character and relate to your character. Because when you act you satisfy inside of yourself. The character is me, I'm Bishop. Everybody got a little Bishop in them (Shakur 2003: 85).

Tupac wanted to give the public a glimpse into the harsh realities of ghetto life for young Black males. He wanted to let others know of the hardships, and Hollywood was just another open outlet for that expression. The early 1990's were filled with revolt, anger, political upheaval, and a nation that had to deal with the harsh realties of racism and a growing anger from the 'hood[28] These forces, coupled with The United States refusal to acknowledge a ghetto problem, helped to shape part of Tupac's worldview during this era of his life.

Tupac took another sharp turn in characters in the film *Poetic Justice* (1993) that put him opposite of Janet Jackson. The character, Lucky, took a direct opposite turn from Bishop. Lucky was responsible, talented, caring, and goal oriented. Tupac states:

> If Bishop was a reflection of young Black male today, I wouldn't be honest if I didn't show another reflection. All of our young Black males are not violent, they're all not taking the law into their own hands. Lucky is doing it the opposite way that Bishop did. He's working, he's very responsible. He's very deliberate about the things he's doing. He's taking care of his daughter. He's a respectful person, you know what I'm saying?

---

[28] It was during this time that the Los Angeles Riots occurred (April 29, 1992) and the O.J. Simpson murder trial (1994) that further divided a nation.

> He lives at home with his mother, he's not sweating it, that's where he wants to be. He wants to work (Shakur 2003: 86).

Hollywood gave Tupac more creative freedom. It also made him a stronger pop culture figure. Many young Whites were seeing Tupac on the silver screen for the first time and they loved him. During this era, there was also a shift in American pop culture from what was considered "White" to Black popular culture (Kitwana 2005). Tupac entered the homes of many young White Gen X'ers. This not only increased his record sales, but also gave him a voice from a different audience that was not primarily Black or Latino. White youth were seeing different sides of Tupac.

Tupac embodied the rebel, idealist, socialist, and social activist that so many White Gen X youth were craving. More importantly, White Gen X youth could relate to some of his pain in the sense that they too had been rejected, broken, and discarded by society. Poor White youth could especially relate to Tupac because they faced some of the same economic depravities that Blacks and Latinos face. Tupac was a hero for them as well. Hollywood gave Tupac an opportunity to express his voice and message to White Gen X youth.

Tupac completed work on six films: *Juice (1992), Poetic Justice (1993), Above The Rim (1994), Bullet (1996), Gridlock'd (1997),* and *Gang Related (1997).* All these films helped Tupac connect with a larger audience in America. These films are still classics for many urban audiences, not because of the excellent screen plays or directing—while some of the films were good in that area—but because Tupac was in the film. He brought realism to the cinema that was unrivaled. Tupac had dreams to write several different screen plays and was in the process of putting together several films that he was going to direct when his sudden death came in 1996. Tupac talks about his fame:

> Being famous and having money gave me confidence. The screams of the crowd gave me confidence. Before that I was a shell of a man. Now I believe that I'm my own man. I put it down, I put it down. If it's about rap music, if its about acting whatever—I want to get into the head set, I gotta be involved, I gotta excel at it (Shakur 2003: 101).

## THUG LIFE and Hollywood

Thug life only propelled itself while Tupac was doing film and gaining notoriety. Thug life[29] was at its height. The reasoning for this was that Hip Hop culture was in a Gangsta Rap genre.[30] America was coming to grips with how to deal with the image of the young Black male that said, "I don't give a fuck!" Hollywood, during this period, was releasing numerous gangsta films. Films such as *Boyz In The Hood (1991)*, *Menace II Society (1993)*, *and Belly (1994)* were just a few of the ones that made headlines. These hard core snapshots of first hand ghetto horror, gave Tupac and his thug life code a platform on which to speak. 1992-1994 was a tumultuous time for American culture; these years were filled with political stands from the inner city community and from activist voices such as Ice Cube and KRS-One.

Thug life had a home. And Hollywood, White Gen X youth, and Rap music fueled the flames. Still, this did not come without criticism. Tupac faced many critics that claimed he was only inciting hoodlum behavior. Even Civil Rights leaders such as Jesse Jackson criticized Tupac for the power and use of his lyrics in such songs as "Fuck the World" and "Outlaw." Delores Tucker publicly advocated that Tupac should be banned and that it was a disgrace when he won an NAACP image award. Regardless, through all of this, Tupac persisted.[31]

For Tupac, thug life was more than just an "era" or movement. For him, and the millions that loved him for it, it was a way of life. In a moving statement, Tupac says this about thug life and his image:

---

[29] See Appendix B for Thug Life Code.

[30] See Figure 9 to see the other sub-genres of Hip Hop culture and rap music.

[31] During this life event in Tupac's life, East Coast rappers such as Biggie, Nas, and Sean Puffy Combs were also considered "enemies" by Tupac. At one point, Tupac even mentions that he is at war with many.

I don't rap about sitting up eating shrimp and shit. I rap about fighting back. I make it uncomfortable by putting details to it. It might not have been politically correct but I've reached somebody; they relating to me. They relate to the brutal honesty in the rap. And why shouldn't they be angry? And why shouldn't my raps that I'm rappin' to my community be filled with rage? They should be filled with the same atrocities that they gave me. You have to be logical. If I know that in this hotel room, they have food everyday and I'm knockin' on the door everyday to eat and they open the door and let me see the party—see like them throwin' salami all over, just like throwin' food around—then they're tellin' me there's no food in there, you know what I'm sayin'? Everyday. I'm standing outside trying to sing my way in. 'We are hungry please let us in, we are hungry, please let us in.' After about a week that song is going to change to 'We hungry, we need some food.' After two, three weeks it's like 'Give me some food, we're bangin' on the door.' After a year its like, 'I'm pickin the lock, comin through the door blastin;,' you know what I'm sayin'? It's like you hungry you've reached your level. You don't want anymore. We asked ten years ago. We was askin' with the Panthers. We was askin' them with the Civil Rights Movement. We was askin', you know? Now those people who was askin' are all dead or in jail. Now what do you think we're going to do? Ask?...I have not brought violence to you or thug life to America. Why am I being persecuted (Shakur 2003:130-132)?

Tupac had decided long ago to fight his war using the weapons of media. He saw the power to reach the masses behind the camera and on the microphone. He understood the power of mass media, and used it to its full potential.

### Prison and Me Against the World

For Tupac, being in prison was a life changing event. His music, life, poetry, and countenance are adversely affected as a result of this. It is during this era and event that Tupac takes the popular stance that most who have not studied him know: namely "Fuck the world." In late 1994, Tupac released his album "Me Against The World." Tupac's life was changing and these life trials were taking a toll on him. People like Bob Dole, the C. Delores Tucker, and Dan Quayle were beginning to wear on Tupac. He states, "They don't even know what they talkin'. They just talking. They could be talking about Bob Marley for all they care…I know somebody geesed them up to attack Tupac, and now what it does is, they attacked a few famous rappers and now they themselves are famous" (Shakur 2003: 130).

Prison took its toll on Tupac. For those around him, they admit it was a turning point in his life. He was sent to prison in 1994 to serve a jail term for "forcibly touching the buttocks." During this time Tupac once again began to see the world differently. He felt as though he did not have friends anymore. He states,

> I don't have any friends anymore. I'm surrounded, but I don't have any friends. I have homies, associates. What relationship could I possibly have? Now I'm petrified; I can't mess with women. Now, I'm vulnerable cuz they all like, 'Ah ha! You're in trouble.' So I just decided to withdraw myself (Shakur 2003: 142).

Tupac's life was severely affected by prison and his life was changed. There were rumors that he was raped in prison. Rumors that he denies, but nonetheless exist; these hurt Tupac deeply. He further states:

> Prison kills your sprit, there is no creativity…I see a lot of it in other prisoners…but as for me, I am not there. I am reflecting back on life, prison doesn't inspire creativity.
> Do not come to jail, this is not the spot, I am surrounded with dudes that made a mistake when they were young and now in here for life. Do whatever you have to do to stay the hell out of here. I am a messenger, you know, if I go to a club I tell you the club is poppin' or the club is sorry…this ain't the spot, its like you an animal, no man don't wanna be here or a woman (Peters 2001).

For Tupac, this was a time to reflect on his life. He engrossed himself in reading and listening to music. Upon his release, he dropped the album "Me Against The World" and songs like "Me Against The World" made headlines. Tupac wrote only one song while in prison, he said that he could not write at the time. However, within a matter of two weeks after his release, he had written twenty-four songs. Below is the first lyric from "Me Against The World":

> Can you picture my prophecy?
> Stress in the city, the cops is hot for me

> The projects is full of bullets, the bodies is droppin
> There ain't no stoppin me
> Constantly movin while makin millions
> Witnessin killings, leavin dead bodies in abandoned buildings
> Carries to children cause they're illin
> Addicted to killin and the appeal from the cap peelin [32]

This album provided a release for Tupac. It was a release of his raw emotions that had been kept inside while in prison. This album was a way for his artistic side to come out and to exonerate his character. Tupac did not want to die before people knew that he did not commit the crimes that he had been sent to prison for. Tupac always maintained his innocence throughout all of this.

Tupac was bailed out of prison by Suge Knight, the president of Death Row Records.[33] It was late 1995, that Tupac entered into his final life era, ghetto saint. As Tupac drew closer to his death, his studio hours increased and between his release from prison and the time of his death on September 13, 1996, he recorded over 120 songs. His sainthood was forming and he entered into the final era of his life.

### *Ghetto Saint (1996-Present)*

Much of Tupac's work has been published and released posthumous. However, he wrote and produced that work during this era. This era finds Tupac's legendary status taking shape. This era deals with how Tupac's ghetto saint status took shape.

### All Eyez on Him

I am using the term saint as I defined it in Chapter 2, as a contextual saint that helped push his listeners closer to God in order to begin the evangelistic process. Tupac's ghetto saint status began to form in the last year of his life; 1996. Tupac's decision to sign

---

[32] Taken from http://www.ohhla.com/anonymous/2_pac/matworld/theworld.2pc.txt last accessed September 15, 2005.

[33] The amount paid was around $100,000.

with Death Row Records, after his release from prison, brought with it many problems and difficulties. During the beginning of this era, Tupac faced many moral and ethical decisions. Yet, because his face was in the public eye, more people got to know and love him because of his struggles. Tupac makes a poignant statement regarding his lifestyle during this era:

> I mean to me, I know what good morals are. It would seem you're supposed to disregard good morals when you're living in a crazy bad world. If you're living cursed, how can you live like an angel? If you're in hell, how can you live like an angel? You're surrounded by devils and you're supposed to live like an angel. That's like suicide, you know what I'm sayin' (Shakur 2003)?

Tupac's life was filled with turmoil at the beginning of this era. He wanted to do what was right, but he was also surrounded by with many "devils" which made it difficult for him to make the right decision. Tupac felt the weight of the world on him and his music reflected that burden too.

During this era we begin to see how Tupac's life was to be remembered after he was gone: as a martyr and saint. Tupac's martyrdom began the day he went to prison. For many, it was then that he was seen as someone who was being persecuted while remaining innocent. This was still overshadowed by his "outlaw" era, and his message of peace and unity was hidden under headlines such as "rapist," "cop killer," "sexist," and even "molester." [34]

Still, through all this, we begin to see Tupac's ability to survive and tenacious attitude to persevere through different life trials, even though Tupac's image was being tarnished and he was a public spectacle. Tupac managed to release another multi-

---

[34] It is important to note here that Tupac began to better develop his thug life message. He made distinctions about who was who and how things were to be handled. Tupac's message of thug life was for the downtrodden, the marginalized, the street solider, the pregnant teen mom, and the pimp. This was his message of hope to the ghetto community his message that would help unite the Black and ghetto communities as one. Moreover, thug life helped the new generation of young people that would have to grow up in conditions worse than Tupac's. This was unacceptable for Tupac. However, all this was overshadowed by his negative images in the media. The same "weapon" he used in his arsenal, was the same weapon that was used against him as well.

platinum album "All Eyez on Me." This album depicted his struggles that existed within Tupac. Tupac made it clear that only God would judge him:

> Perhaps I was blind to the facts, stabbed in the back
> I couldn't trust my own homies just a bunch a dirty rats
> Will I, succeed, paranoid from the weed
>
> Oh my Lord, tell me what I'm livin for
> Everybody's droppin got me knockin on heaven's door
> And all my memories, of seein brothers bleed
> And everybody grieves, but still nobody sees
> Recollect your thoughts don't get caught up in the mix
> Cause the media is full of dirty tricks
> Only God can judge me[35]

In Figure 15, we can simplistically see how Tupac's thug life code broke down. His message was two fold—both for the ghetto and for Black males. The idea to help Black males dated all the way back to 1991 on his "Strickly 4 My N.I.G.G.A.Z." album. In an interview with Davey D, Tupac states—regarding that album, that his vision for the meaning of the tracks on the album was to encourage the young Black male. Tupac felt as though the young Black male did not receive enough positive attention, so he was going to give them that positive attention that he himself did not receive.

Figure 15 also depicts Tupac's goals for thug life. The goals were rooted in the "Military Mind" era. And social concern was Tupac's top priority. Tupac knew the only way to make a difference was to sink his soul into this cause, and that is what he did.

Tupac used his fame and fortune to help many. Frank Alexander, Tupac's favorite body guard and now urban youth worker, recounts the many times that Tupac made time for the children of the ghetto (2000). Alexander also remembers the time Tupac took time to spend with his paraplegic niece; that was a time when he was real busy and under a lot of pressure, but Tupac did it anyway; his thug life code stretched far beyond the stereotypical image of "thugs."

---

[35] Taken from http://www.ohhla.com/anonymous/2_pac/eyezonme/godjudge.2pc.txt last accessed September 15, 2005.

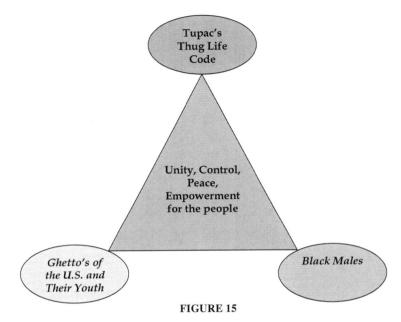

**FIGURE 15**

**TUPAC'S THUG LIFE CODE'S MESSAGE**

### Deathrow Records

There have been many accounts as to whether the move to Deathrow Records was a wise move for Tupac. But, at the time, he really did not have a choice. Suge Knight, Deathrow's president at the time, offered to pay his million dollar bail in exchange for his signing on the label. Tupac had recently started his own label, and was hoping to move into politics as well.[36] Nevertheless, despite the criticism, Tupac signed and went to Deathrow Records. Tupac states:

---

[36] It was Tupac's vision that by the year 2000, there would have been a third political party formed from Hip Hop culture. There has been no one to date to carry the torch for that vision.

Death Row is a successful record company. It runs efficiently. Everything they've released has sold in excess of four million copies. I'm saying, why not be there? I really like everybody on the record company. I like Suge. That's my homie. I like Snoop, Dre, and Nate, and all them. I hang out with them anyway, so now it's just official. Suge ain't no gangster, man. He's chillin. Me comin' to Death Row, one of the main reasons besides Suge was Snoop. The man's got so much style. I felt like since me and Snoop's music was often coupled together when we were being criticized and when we were being praised, we getting, you know, sales and all that. So I said it would be a wise decision to team up with them and make this allegiance that much stronger, and the vibe coming out the West Coast scene that much more heavier. I'm a super power. Death Row is a super power. Let's combine super powers and ally, and really hit ' em. And that's one of the biggest combinations you can get (Shakur 2003: 217).

This was a shaping moment for Tupac. Deathrow had the finances and the market to sell a lot of records. Moreover, Death Row was the king of West Coast Rap production. The sound of Hip Hop during this era came from The West Coast.[37] Tupac was Deathrow's crown jewel, and the fans were taking it all in. It was during this time that Tupac developed his theology for the ghetto. Songs such as "No More Pain," "Hail Mary," and "Black Jesus" were just some of the tracks that made many young ghetto youth feel that maybe Tupac was their own "Black Jesus." Deathrow's financing and marketing, helped foster and promote this image to ghettos everywhere.

Further, while there have been several independent investigations into the murder of Tupac, there have been no substantial leads in his murder. Some suggest that Suge had a part in the murder since Tupac was actually considering leaving Death Row and the fact that Suge was sitting less than a foot from Tupac when he was shot and did not endure any gunshot wounds. Tupac's death still remains a mystery.

---

[37] Currently, the sound for Hip Hop comes from what is termed "Tha Dirty South."

## I Wonder if Heaven Got A Ghetto

In the song "I Wonder if Heaven Got A Ghetto," Tupac makes it clear that things are hard, and that even he struggles with hope and a vision for a better tomorrow. Tupac, and several of his homies, rap on the track about a Heaven that can handle them. For Tupac, and many other young urbanites, the image of Jesus and of Heaven has not been one that could actually handle their sin. Most of the imagery that they receive about Heaven is one that can only handle the proper, secure, honest, pure, and righteous person. But Tupac challenged this view to say every one has in fact sinned, so how could Heaven only be for the "holy" and "righteous" person?

> Here on Earth, tell me what's a black life worth
> A bottle of juice is no excuse, the truth hurts
> And even when you take the shit
> Move counties get a lawyer you can shake the shit
> Ask Rodney, LaTasha, and many more
> It's been goin on for years, there's plenty more
> When they ask me, when will the violence cease?
> When your troops stop shootin niggaz down in the street[38]

In this verse, Tupac explains some of the issues that urbanites have to dwell in. He entreats that no one judges him when he "loots." He "loots" because he has to; much like the people in New Orleans had to after no help came for over a week. "Word to God" is a rap liturgical point that says God is the "man" and that God deserves all respect. Tupac is the messenger and participant (see Table 5) in this particular track and gives the listener first hand information about what is happening, while encouraging the people to hold on, much like Jesus did in John 15:18-27, to a brighter tomorrow rooted in Heaven.[39]

---

[38] "I Wonder if Heaven Got A Ghetto?" Album: <u>R U Still Down</u> (1997).

[39] I will go further with this issue in Part 4.

## Hold on Be Strong

In this song, Tupac reinforces his thug life message, and gives the listener hope for a brand new day. Tupac does not hold back, however, he uses the imagery of death and pain to get his point and message across. He made Heaven and Jesus out to be tangible for young people in the hood. And, Tupac made Jesus out to be someone who actually might care. This inspired hope in many, and a hope in Tupac as their mediator.

In this song, Tupac puts the listener right where he is: in the middle of the action. Tupac later discusses how God does not like ugly, and that he will catch up to all the "homies" in another life, that he was in "traffic." Tupac prophesied of his own death continually. Particularly in this era of his life. It was almost as if he knew his time was running out, and that death was around the corner.

## September 13, 1996

On the night of September 7, 1996, while driving with Suge Knight en route to Club 666, Tupac was shot four times in the chest by an assailant in a white Cadillac. Tupac was rushed to University Medical Hospital and underwent surgery, including the removal of his right lung. After six days in critical condition, Tupac was pronounced dead at 4:03 p.m. He was only twenty five years old.

This was the day the world stopped for many. Hip Hop artist after Hip Hop artist discusses the deep pain and mourning they went through the days following Tupac's death. In fact, the entire six days that Tupac was in the hospital, legions of fans waited outside to gather any passing news regarding Tupac.

Tupac's fans were devastated with the news of his death. Further, not just "ghetto" and "Hip Hoppers" mourned Tupac's passing. People like Tony Danza, Madonna, Jasmine Guy, Jada Pinkett-Smith, and James Belushi were among some of the many celebrities that loved Tupac.

Tupac had etched his mark in American pop culture. But, more importantly, he had carved his mark in the cultural continuum of Hip Hop culture. His death only raised his spiritual, thug, immortal, and Christ-like image even higher. Today, there are scores of fans who still believe he is alive. There are still several theories as to how he might be alive on some remote island.

Tupac symbolized a generation's anger, hope, love, hate, despair, and marginality. When Tupac died, it meant that they too could die. This explains why there are still so many people who hold on to the fact that he is alive; they do not want him to die because that would mean they too, are vulnerable to death.

*Summary*

This chapter has focused on the ethnolifehistory of Tupac. In it there have been five major eras that arose in Tupac's life. All of these eras are significant in the formation of Tupac's theology and musical message.

In the next chapter, I will focus on Tupac's musical message. I will elaborate on the major themes that arose from his music that were a reflection of all the cultural contexts he was a part of (Hip Hop, the 'hood, and BPC). This chapter will then set up part four which will focus on the conclusions and results of this study. Part four will provide Tupac's theological message and what his Gospel message was about.

# CHAPTER 9

# TUPAC'S MUSICAL MESSAGE

Tupac superseded the gangsta-rap label he was given. He was more complex than just one dimension. Tupac's songs contain many messages that include, but are certainly not limited to death, love, hate, anger, social politics, societal issues within the urban community, religion, spirituality, sexuality, women, encouragement, and even practical suggestions for everyday life.

There were four major themes that arose from Tupac's music. These themes were:

- Social and Political
- Spiritual
- Class
- Communal and Familial

Within these major categories, there are also sub-themes such as The Black male, Christological issues, and hermeneutics. These sub-themes helped to shape the overall theological and spiritual message of Tupac which will be discussed in section four. I use the term theological message as Tupac's own interpretation of the scriptures, Jesus, salvation, and Heaven using his own contextual hermeneutic. In contrast, Tupac's spiritual message is centered more on a both an idealistic and realistic message for living that is a part of this theological message, but not directly connected to any theological matters. A lot of Tupac's spirituality was shaped over his entire life, his theological understanding came during his Military Mind and The Ghetto is Destiny eras.

## *Tha Social and Political Message*

The social aspect of Tupac's music is extremely important. Tupac gave you his life and soul in every song. For the church to truly comprehend the affect and influence of Tupac's music, it must realize that Tupac was greater than just a simple "pop-star." His music fulfilled a large social hole that the church cannot seem to fill. Further, Tupac was able to help people see some hope through his social and political message by the mere fact that he was talking about difficult issues. This added to his ghetto sainthood.

### The Social Message within 2Pacalypse Now

2Pacalypse Now was Tupac's first album and was recorded during Tupac's The Ghetto Is Destiny era. This album dealt with many different social and political aspects of the 'hood. This album mainly focused on the Black male and how he lived. The introductory song "Young Black Male," states:

> Young black male
> I try to effect by kicking the facts
> and stacking much mail
> I'm packing a gat cuz guys wanna jack
> and fuck goin to jail
> Cuz I ain't equipped to stop how I look
> I don't sell ya-yo
> They teachin a brother like I was in books
> Follow me into a flow
> I'm sure you know, which way to go
> I'm hittin em out of the dopes
> So slip on the slope, let's skip on the flow
> I'm fuckin the sluts and hoes
> The bigger the butts the tighter the clothes
> The gimminy jimminy grows
> Then whaddya know, it's off with some clothes
> Rowd when the crowd says hoe[1]

---

[1] "Young Black Male," 2Pacalypse Now, (1992).

Within the song, Tupac alludes to the fact that life is "messed-up." Within the structure of the lyrics, there is a strong language connection to the culture in which it was inspired and formed. For example, in verse one, the word "gat" is a reference to a gun, "jack" simply refers to someone robbing you and beating you up. Moreover, the song is reflective of the cultural context; the song was recorded in 1991, most young urbanites do not still use the word "gat."

Inside this opening song, Tupac uses lyrical samples from other rap artists to make his point. "Hard like an erection...Young black male!" are both samples to illustrate Tupac's point that the Black male is still strong and vibrant. Tupac continues to insist that real "niggaz" cause fear and worry within many other people, especially Whites.

> I hate it when real nigga bust
> They hate when I cuss, they threaten to bust
> I had enough of the fuss[2]

The song following the opening track is about feeling "trapped" and marginalized. Tupac focuses on the social structure of the Black male and urban youth.

> You know they got me trapped in this prison of seclusion
> Happiness, living on tha streets is a delusion
> Even a smooth criminal one day must get caught
> Shot up or shot down with tha bullet that he bought
> Nine millimeter kickin' thinking about what tha streets do to me
> Cause they never talk peace in tha black community
> All we know is violence do tha job in silence
> Walk tha city streets like a rat pack of tyrants
> Too many brothers daily heading for tha big penn
> Niggas commin' out worse off than when they went in
> Over tha years I done a lot of growin' up
> Getten drunk thrown' up
> Cuffed up[3]

---

[2] "Young Black Male," 2Pacalypse Now, (1992).

Here, Tupac discusses the ails and struggles of growing up as a Black male. He calls out the higher powers that exist in society and asks the question, "Why?" Tupac's worldview—at this point during his Ghetto is Destiny era—was violent, so he began to pose the question that if one lives in a violent environment, will they then be a product of that violence?

Within the last verse, Tupac begins to allude to the fact that as a result of all this marginalization, deep hurts, and violence, he himself might just strike back at the system that created him.[4] Violence was a way of life for Tupac and the first five songs of the album are a reflection of that reality. This was part of the inspiration that Tupac has for this album.

Tupac wanted to give the general public a dose of reality about what was happening in the streets. Tupac was not about the violent product that he was living in, quite the contrast, he wanted to illicit change. He felt that through his music he was able to get that change in the urban community. Therefore, he decided to tell the most ruthless stories he could find about the inner city.

Tupac felt that the government did not really care about the inner city. Tupac calls out the political structures that are supposed to be helping out the "people."[5] Tupac, in this song titled "I Don't Give A Fuck," argues that there are many complex problems within the inner city and that they are not being alleviated by anyone, in fact they are getting

---

[3] "Trapped," 2Pacalypse Now, (1992).

[4] For Tupac, this was a constant theme. He would constantly ask why people were judging him as a thug when the biggest thug was the U.S. government. For Tupac, the "role models" around him (the social systems and networks at large) were corrupt, so what stopped him from doing the same just to survive? This is a significant question that is not simply answered particularly when we have a government that would seemingly appear to be no better than a common street gang.

[5] Also, keep in mind that this was all during the Reagan and Bush eras of politics. Many within the inner city feel that during this time, the inner city—especially Blacks—suffered the worst because of this regime.

even more horrific. In the last lyric this idea is reflected when he says, "Mama told me there'd be days like this, but I'm pissed cause it stays like this..."

## 'Hood Matters

Tupac's life was about a revolution. That revolution involved a revolt against the status quo, religious authorities that followed the status-quo, governmental agencies that ignored their people, poverty, and even pain. Tupac reflected this back to us in songs like "Panther Power," "Words of Wisdom," "Under Pressure," and "Lord Knows" to name a few.

Tupac wanted change in the urban community. He infused this message of change into every song. Tupac wanted the 'hood to matter to America. In the song "Lord Knows"—off the "Me Against The World" album—Tupac brings the listener face to face with the social conditions of the hood:

> I smoke a blunt to take the pain out
> And if I wasn't high, I'd probably try to blow my brains out
> I'm hopeless, they shoulda killed me as a baby
> And now they got me trapped in the storm, I'm goin crazy
> Forgive me; they wanna see me in my casket
> and if I don't blast I'll be the victim of them bastards
> I'm loosin hope, they got me stressin, can the Lord forgive me
> Got the spirit of a thug in me
> Another sip of that drink, this Hennesey got me queasy[6]

In this song, we are able to see that Tupac is giving the story from both an allegorical and first person point of view. This tells the listener that Tupac both understands the practical facets of 'hood living and the theoretical aspects of that same lifestyle. Later in the same song, Tupac gives you a gut check when he discusses the

---

[6] "Lord Knows," Me Against The World (1995).

realness of death in the 'hood. For him, he had seen too many friends die and no one really take notice, other than those around the immediate situation.

For Tupac, the 'hood was the source of music. Tupac questioned the social systems that were supposed to be helping but in reality were oppressing and subverting the 'hood even further.[7]

> Ain't nothing but another calculated scheme
> To get us locked up shot up back in chains
> To deny us of the future rob our names
> Kept my history of mystery but now I see
> The American Dream wasn't meant for me
> Cause lady liberty is a hypocrite she lied to me[8]

In this early track, entitled "Panther Power," Tupac wonders why the "American Dream" has not been passed on to Black people and urban youth all over. Tupac typically infused a story into his lyrics, making the listener both think and feel some kind of motivation to do something.

In the song, "Outlaw" Tupac infuses the harsh realties of outlaw living with the question, "Dear God, I wonder can you save me?" This was a fundamental issue for Tupac and for many urbanites in general: Will God "save" me even though I have had to do things that are not considered "right" in order to survive?

> Cause all I see is, murder murder, my mind state
> Preoccupied with homicide, tryin to survive through this crime rate
> Dead bodies at block parties, those unlucky bastards
> Gunfire now they require may be closed casket
> Who can you blame? It's insane what we dare do
> Witness an evil that these men do, bitches in, too
> In fact they be the reasons niggaz get to bleedin

---

[7] It is interesting to note that Tupac constantly stated that he owed everything to the 'hood and that the 'hood was his home.

[8] "Panther Power," The Lost Tapes (1989).

* Chorus *
Outlaw, Outlaw, Outlaw (They came in to sin)
Outlaw, Outlaw, Outlaw (Dear God, I wonder could you save me?)[9]

This question (do real niggaz go to Heaven?) was one that came up a lot in his music. On the streets, there is one overarching known theme: survival. Tupac even said, "I can't tell anyone how to live. Especially if I'm not even helping him or paying for nothin…"[10]

## Tupac's Politics

In the 'hood, there is a code of life and a code regarding how to live that life (c.f. Anderson 1999). Tupac understood this and wanted a little more order—being that no one else really cared about the situations within the 'hood. Tupac developed the T.H.U.G. L.I.F.E. code[11] that gave meaning and order to the 'hood and gang lifestyle.

This was an unprecedented move by Tupac. Until this point, not many people had attempted to deal with this matter head on. Most wanted to do away with gangs and get rid of gang violence without ever dealing with the individual. Tupac dedicated an entire album to it, "Thug Life: Volume 1."

In this album Tupac began to, once again, lay out the realities of 'hood life. However, his lyrics took on a morbid feel. Death was around every corner; in fact, death was the ultimate rest and something to actually look forward to.

In the song "How Long Will They Mourn Me?" Tupac challenges the optimistic and individualistic United States view that states "everyone can make it if they work hard enough:"
All my homies drinkin liquor, tears in everybody's eyes
Niggaz cried, to mourn a homie's homicide
But I can't cry, instead I'm just a shoulder

---

[9] "Outlaw," Me Against The World (1995).

[10] Tupac Shakur in *Tupac Vs*. Spirer (2001)

[11] See Appendix D for the complete code.

> Damn, why they take another soldier?
> I load my clip before my eyes blurry, don't worry
> I'll get them suckers back before your buried (shit)
> Retaliate and pull a one-eight-seven
> Do real niggaz get to go to heaven?
> How long will they mourn me? Bury me a motherfuckin G
> Bitch don't wanna die; then, don't fuck with me
> It's kinda hard to be optimistic
> When your homie's lyin dead on the pavement twisted
> Y'all don't hear me doe, I'm tryin hard to make amends
> But I'm losin all my motherfuckin friends.. damn!
> They should've shot me when I was born
> Now I'm trapped in the motherfuckin storm
> How long will they mourn me?

Tupac was letting each listener know that life in the 'hood was more complex than the "American dream." There were many different layers of social ills that held back young people, particularly Black males. Therefore, that "dream" took on different aspects within the 'hood. For Tupac, the reality and ending result of that dream was death itself.

Death, to the average person, is something that is feared, avoided at all costs, and will hopefully happen when the person is older. But, for the urbanite, it is something that is an everyday reality. Tupac made this apparent. Tupac also suggested that the government might not actually care about the situation in the 'hood:

> Killing us one by one
> In one way or another
> America will find a way to eliminate the problem
> One by one
> The problem is
> the troubles in the black youth of the ghettos
> And one by one
> we are being wiped off the face of this earth
> At an extremely alarming rate
> And even more alarming is the fact
> that we are not fighting back
> Brothers, sistas, niggas
> When I say niggas it is not the nigga we are grown to fear
> It is not the nigga we say as if it has no meaning
> But to me
> It means Never Ignorant Getting Goals Accomplishs, nigga

> Niggas what are we going to do
> Walk blind into a line or fight
> Fight and die if we must like niggas
>
> This is for the masses the lower classes
> The ones you left out, jobs were givin', better livin'
> But we were kept out
> Made to feel inferior, but we're the superior
> Break the chains in our brains that made us fear yah
> Pledge a allegiance to a flag that neglects us
> Honor a man who refuses to respect us
> Emancipation, proclamation, Please!
> Nigga just said that to save the nation
> These are lies that we all accepted[12]

Death is never an easy topic to discuss. But, for many urban youth, they have already planned ahead, bought their own casket, written out their eulogy, and paid for the minister in the wake of their death. Tupac knew this and it provoked his sprit; this provocation was seen in the song "If I Die 2Nite:"

> Pussy and paper is poetry power and pistols
> Plottin on murderin motherfuckers 'fore they get you
> Pray to the heavens three-fifty-sevens to the sky
> And I hope I'm forgiven for Thug Livin when I die
> I wonder if heaven got a ghetto for Thug niggaz
> A stress free life and a spot for drug dealers
> Pissin while practicin how to pimp and be a playa
> Overdose of a dick, while drinkin liquor when I lay her
> Pistol whippin these simps, for bein petrified and lame
> Disrespectin the game, prayin for punishment and pain
> Goin insane, never die, live eternal, who shall I fear?
> Don't shed a tear for me nigga I ain't happy here
> I hope they bury me and send me to my rest
> Headlines readin MURDERED TO DEATH, my last breath
> Take a look picture a crook on his last stand
> Motherfuckers don't understand, if I die tonight

The resounding statement in this lyric is the last line. Who really understands without judging and wanting to completely change the individual? Tupac knew this, and argued

---

[12] "Words of Wisdom" 2Pacalypse Now (1992).

for a new understanding and new social and political structure what would have an urban agenda. Tupac's wish was for a new political party that would represent the 'hood and give voice to the reality that young people were dying too young.

### *Tha Familial and Communal Message*

Tupac was deeply connected to his family, a value that was embedded in him during his Military Mind era. For him, that was the last line of defense. This was one of the reasons he was so hurt and depressed after his arrest and imprisonment in 1995; he felt as though his urban and Black family had abandoned him. He also felt as though good friend—Biggie, Puffy, even Dr. Dre, had abandoned him in his moments of need. Many thought Tupac was paranoid, but in an interview in 1995 he revealed his hurt and disappointment in his extended family. His songs post 1995 were a reflection of that as well.

### The Women of the Family

Tupac connected many different songs to the family. One of those connections was women. For the outsider looking in, it would appear that Tupac did not have a real concern for women with his flagrant use of the word "bitch." Yet, Tupac was raised by women, loved women, dated women, and loved the most important woman in his life, his mother Afeni Shakur.

Unlike other rap artists, Tupac distinguished between a bitch, a hoe, and a woman (see Table 6). For him, there was a great disparity between the three, while all three were necessary for 'hood life to continue—it was part of the culture, as Tupac would say.

Women, the ultimate female, were people that Tupac wanted to spend the rest of his life with. The other two—hoe and bitch—were someone that Tupac used for his own sexual pleasure. [13]

In the song "Wonda Why They Call U Bitch," Tupac wrote the song with his sister in mind. Why? You may ask. Because his sister, at the time, was addicted to crack and was prostituting herself. The song itself was a call for her to wake up:

> Look here Miss Thang
> hate to salt your game
> but yous a money hungry woman
> and you need to change.
>
> In tha locker room
> all the homies do is laugh.
> High five's cuz anotha nigga
> played your ass.[14]

Tupac wanted to call out his sister and encourage her to change the way she was living. While Tupac had his issues with women—sexually speaking—he did have a heart and a passion to see women empowered and for them to gain a better footing in society—even more after having witnessed his mom be discriminated against in the Black Panthers.

---

[13] Now, this is a harsh reality, but a fact of the inner city for many men. Sexuality in the 'hood is a subject that deserves further research.

[14] "Wonda Why They Call U Bitch," All Eyez on Me (Disc 2; 1996).

## TABLE 6

## TUPAC'S DISTINCTIONS OF THE FEMALE GENDER

| | |
|---|---|
| **Bitch**[15] | A woman that was out for money and would stab anyone in the back to get it, i.e. a "gold digger." A woman that lied to get her way and manipulated others to get her way. A woman that did not value herself highly and allowed others to use her. |
| **Hoe** | Someone who was extremely sexually active and did not care very much who they had sex with, i.e. a "hood-rat." |
| **Woman** | The highest of all females. The woman who knew herself, was outspoken, knew what she wanted and got it without using "shady" tactics, an educated woman—not necessarily from a traditional college or school, but someone who knew "what wuz up." A woman that could hang with real niggaz. Tupac's mom is an example of a woman. |

### Community

Tupac was never happier than when he was with his niggaz (or his family), as he would put it. Tupac made many references to his real friends and homies that made him feel connected and grounded. Tupac was a huge proponent of "clicks" or units of people that helped each other when there was trouble in the lives of other members.

Tupac would give you the shirt off his back, as many around him would regale (Hodge 2005). In the song, "If My Homie Calls" Tupac makes that apparent in the first verse:

---

[15] Tupac did agree that there were male bitches too and that they too fir into this category. In the Better Dayz album track 3, Tupac asserts that he would no longer call women bitches.

> Ever since you was a pee-wee, down by my knee with a wee-wee
> We been coochie-coo all through school, you and me G
> Back in the days we played practical jokes on
> everybody smoked with they locs and the yolks on
> All through high school, girls by the dozens
> Sayin we cousins, knowin that we wasn't
> But like the old saying goes
> Time goes on, and everybody grows
> Grew apart, had to part, went our own ways
> You chose the dope game, my microphone pays
> In many ways we were paid in the old days
> So far away from the crazies with AK's
> And though I been around clowning with the Underground
> I'm still down with my homies from the hometown
> And if you need, need anything at all
> I drop it all for y'all, if my homies call

Tupac was a man of his word and would give all he had for his family and homies. For him, the real niggaz were the ones that could hang with him through the good, the bad, and the ugly. Someone who was just around during the good times was not worthy of his time or energy.

In another song, "I Ain't Mad At Cha" written during the latter part of the Outlaw era, Tupac wrestles with the fact that things have changed between he and his childhood friend. This was a reality for Tupac and it did affect him. Moreover, this is an aspect of life we all have to face. Tupac, however, dealt with it through song and connected this to a story, which in turn made the listener connect to the overall message of the song.

> Now we was once two niggaz of the same kind
> Quick to holla at a hoochie with the same line
> You was just a little smaller but you still roller
> Got stretched to Y.A. and hit the hood swoll
> Member when you had a jheri curl didn't quite learn
> On the block, witcha glock, trippin off sherm
> Collect calls to the till, sayin how ya changed
> Oh you a Muslim now, no more dope game
> Heard you might be comin home, just got bail
> Wanna go to the Mosque, don't wanna chase tail

> It seems I lost my little homie he's a changed man
> Hit the pen and now no sinnin is the game plan
> When I talk about money all you see is the struggle[16]

Here we see the importance of friendship and family. In the 'hood, there is no stronger bond—outside of the mother-child bond—for the urbanite. For Black males, this is a strong connection to the heart of life in the 'hood. Tupac knew and understood this, and therefore made it a theme in his music.

Community, along with family, was a predominant concept that Tupac had within all of his music. The overarching community that Tupac discussed was the urban community. However, he did distinguish between different sub-cultures within the urban community.

In the song, "Something to Die 4" Tupac encourages the Black community to take a stand and stand up for the right. He calls for what Spike Lee would say, a "wake-up-call!"

> You know what my momma used to tell me
> If ya can't find something to live for..
> .. then you BEST, find something ta die for
>
> (Richard Pryor: "If there's hell below, we're all gonna go!")
>     (*repeat the above throughout*)
>
> Deep deep
>
> La'tasha Hardings, remember that name...
> Cause a bottle of juice... ain't something to die for
>
> Young Quaid, remember that name...
> Cause all you motherfuckers
> That go to your grave with that name on your brain
> Cause jealousy and recklessness is NOT, something to die for
>
> All you niggas out there (*echoed laughter*)
> Got a crack that crumbles

---

[16] "I Ain't Mad At Cha," All Eyez on Me (Disc 1 1996).

>When I say all you niggas (all you niggas)
>Unite
>One nigga, teach two niggas
>Four niggas teach more niggas
>All the poor niggas
>The pen niggas
>The rich niggas
>The strong niggas
>UNITE

Tupac connects the social and political to the community and brings out current events to spark a movement that will ignite a change in the community that he loves: the 'hood.[17]

Another aspect of this community for Tupac was that he allowed for many young artists to appear on his albums. The Outlawz, Big Syke, Snoop Dogg (At the time), and Tretch were just some of the artists that Tupac would collaborate with and keep within his own personal community. Each of Tupac's albums had numerous artists on them and Tupac allowed others to take the first verse of the song—an unprecedented move on an album that has the artist on the title.

Within the Hip Hop community, there is an overall strong element to "represent" and "shout-out" to those who have helped you. Tupac knew this, understood this, and was an extreme supporter of this ideology. In his song, "Representin 93" he made that clear:

>Peace to Redman, Tretch, Vin Rock, K-G the great one
>Mary J. Blige, Pete Rock and sure you're late son.
>Heavy D, CL Smooth, and Queen Latifah.
>Too Short, Tony Toni Tone,
>And the Special motha fucka, Ed Lover, the Tribe, A Tribe Called Quest,

---

[17] One of the urges that Tupac, as well as Ice Cube, would call for was that niggas need to start "locking" up. In other words, the 'hood community needs to take their education and role in society more serious and take action.

## Tha Class Message

Class and social position is a familiar topic for Tupac. From his Criminal Grind era, Tupac began to realize that poverty, class, and social injustices were a reality for Blacks, Latinos, and urban individuals in general (Hodge 2005). Tupac's music took on this ideology and worldview—that the world, particularly the U.S. was not equal and fair for people of color. It truly hit home for Tupac when he and his family moved to Baltimore Maryland:

> And we moved to Baltimore which was total ignorance town to me. It gets me upset to talk about it...Baltimore has the highest rate of teen pregnancy, the highest rate of AIDS within the Black community, the highest rate of teens killing teens, the highest rate of teen suicide, and the highest rate of Blacks killing Blacks. In Baltimore, Maryland. And this is where we chose to live (Shakur 2003: 34).

Tupac was not convinced that we were all living the "American Dream." He saw first hand how money can make or break a family in the 'hood. Tupac hated poverty, and hated the fact that there were castes in society. Tupac once said that if there were no money and if everything depended on morals and standards, most people would be millionaires and wealthy (Shakur 2004). But, as Tupac states, it is not this way, and we (Blacks, Latinos, and poor Whites) are "Stone broke" (Shakur 2004). Tupac was clear about class and the different castes of society, especially how those castes relate to the 'hood's socioeconomics.

### 'Hood Poverty

One clear issue that Tupac knew and comprehended was 'hood poverty. This kind of poverty is right next to third world in other countries. Tupac was clear about the harsh realities of growing up poor. In the song "Cradle to The Grave", Tupac and the Outlawz paint a dim picture of inner city life:

[Chorus]
From the cradle to the grave
Life ain't never been easy, livin in the ghetto
From the cradle to the grave
Life ain't never been easy..

[2Pac]
June 16th, 1971
Mama gave birth to a hell-raisin heavenly son

In this compilation, Tupac and the Outlawz laid out several key issues of growin up in the 'hood. For Tupac, as with others, there were several different echelons of poverty and how one might fit in; chiefly if you were young. In Table 7, we see the different areas a person could possess living within 'hood poverty.

For Tupac, these seven areas were the prevailing classes within the 'hood. Poverty is a reality and pushes people to do things that they would not normally do. In the song, "Ballad of a Dead Soulja" the realities of people living within a poverty-stricken area and the different things they have to do in order to survive are discussed. In this particular verse, we see Tupac discussing the difficulty of a hustler, gang member, and baller:

## TABLE 7

## TUPAC'S CLASS ORDER IN THE 'HOOD

| Class Position | Ensuing Class Results |
|---|---|
| Baller | Make money and survive; money is often gained in an illegal manner, but you will live and eat; the risk is great, but starvation is even greater; money is big, depending on what you sell and what your product is. |
| Hustler | You make money off other people's ignorance; most of the time the money earned is illegal; money can come in great amounts if you can "hustle" others well. |
| Gang member | The gang takes care of you; community above the individual; collectivist society; money is rationed out by your gang leaders; protection is high, but so are death and incarceration; making money this way is typically illegal, but you will eat and possibly be able to help your family. |
| Dope dealer | Quick and easy money; high rate of incarceration; very competitive; utilizes the principles of capitalism; money can be big, if you make it high up in the ranks. |
| Rapper | Good way out of your class position and making money; you have to be good; extremely competitive; can be a lucrative way to make money if you can market yourself well. |
| Athlete | Another good way out the 'hood; don't get hurt; competitive; can be a way to make good money and support your family if you can make it to the pros. |
| Good Student | A sensible way out; you will be picked on or "punked" by most other people; money is not guaranteed, nor is a job; the longest way to get money and get paid to help your family and survive; if you can make it and make it well, you may be able to create a nice future for you, but not the norm. |

[2Pac]
The plan, to take command of the whole family
Though underhanded, to be the man it was planned
All my road dawgs, official mob figures love to act up
The first to bomb we rob niggaz
I can be, lost in my own mind
To be the boss only thought's grip on chrome nines
Niggaz get tossed up, war scars, battlefield memories
Swore I saw the devil in my empty glass of Hennesey
Talkin to a nigga on a tight leash
Screamin "Fuck the police," as I ride through the night streets
Lil' child runnin wild, toward his danger
What's the cause don't be alarmed death to all strangers
Maybe I'm a madman
A pistol grabbin nigga unleash the Sandman
Promisin merciless retaliation, nothin is colder
Close your eyes, hear the ballad of a dead soldier

Once again, Tupac presents the listener with the realties of the harmful effects of 'hood poverty. Notice the connection to survival and what street life is about for these people. The use of explicit language, gives the listener a dose of 'hood life.

'Hood poverty is a poverty that few ever see, much less understand. Most would argue, "How could this be? This is the United States?" But, Tupac made it a reality that there were people that lived in the U.S. that had two pennies short of nothing. Tupac described this in great detail in different stories and fables within his music. What was interesting, though, even if the song itself was fictional about an event in the 'hood, it was still relatable because someone had experienced something similar. Tupac knew this, and this is another reason why his music was so popular with so many people. It was relatable; Tupac knew he had the underdogs on his side (Shakur 2003).[18]

---

[18] A strong motivation in creating the T.H.U.G. L.I.F.E code (see Appendix B) was poverty and the organization of that poverty. The code was set up for the hustlers, gang members, and balers. The code was set up for the marginalized in society. Thug Life—the ideology and doctrine of Tupac's Outlaw life era— was about the marginalized and the lower classes. For Tupac, Thug Life was about helping those lower classes and helping those in society that were not looked upon as ideal members of that society; i.e. pimps, gang members, hustlers, prostitutes, and thieves—a Gospel message for those people. Thug Life was a means to make these people legit, Thug Life was not the traditional definition of a thug, and it was

## Niggaz

Nowhere else did Tupac use the word nigga as he did in his music. Tupac connected the lower class, blue collar, and working class individual to the word nigga (c.f. Kelley 1996:209-214; 1997: 15-42; Neal 2002: 23-56). For Tupac the word nigga was not the conventional definition of the word to mean a derogatory racist statement toward Blacks. For Tupac, it was class status and a class identifier. This was a way for Tupac to label the classes within the 'hood and society in general. Arthur Spears states, "Likewise, the use of nigga in an utterance does not necessarily mean that it is racist or reflective of self-hate. Terms such as these are used sometimes simply to refer to individuals without any evaluative implications" (1998: 227).

Tupac knew the negative connotations the word itself carries, this was one of the reasons he changed the last letter of the word from an S to a Z. The Z gave it a class meaning rather than a cultural or ethnic meaning (See Table 8).

For many older folks, characteristically from the Civil Rights Generation,[19] it is difficult to get past the fact the root of the word niggaz is nigger itself. For them, that is an entirely different meaning and connotation. During their generation, there was no nigga or niggaz; everyone was a nigger if they were Black. Therefore, Tupac was greatly misunderstood and mistaken by the Civil Rights Generation. The mere utterance of the word, made them feel as though Tupac did not have concern for their struggles to rid the word all together. Once again, the power of the word: Nommo (Smitherman 1998: 203-212).

---

the opposite. Tupac knew better. Tupac wanted to give a voice, face, and power to those who had been forgotten in the 'hood.

[19] The parallel of this generation is the Boomer Generation (Born between 1943-1969) which reflects a White, middle class type of person.

## TABLE 8

## TUPAC'S DEFINITIONS FOR THE WORD NIGGA

| Term | Meaning |
| --- | --- |
| Nigga | A Black person meaning, but not limited to, a friend, a true friend, a person who is acting up, the "crew" in which you are a part of; typically associated with cultural and ethnic backgrounds, i.e. Blacks or young Blacks. |
| Nigger | The derogatory racist term used to describe Black people in a negative and unconstructive way; typically used by Whites towards Blacks. |
| Niggaz | Your class status; typically a blue collar, working, lower class individual who is marginalized and has very little to look forward to; the reject of society; could be someone who is White, Latino, Asian, or Black; is limited to a class position rather than an ethnic identifier; for Tupac, this was where a majority of his help and attention was given in his music. |

Still, this was not a deterrent for Tupac. He insisted that there were different meanings for the word, and that over time, the word changes. And what was once used for evil, was now used for good.

Tupac even titled his second album with the word, "Strictly for my N.I.G.G.A.Z." This album dealt with personal issues that urban youth dealt with on a daily basis. This album was aimed toward the lower class and niggaz of society. This was a first for any artist at the time. For many rap artists, the word niggas simply meant the literal definition of the word (See Table 8). But, Tupac took things a step further and made it known that niggaz were more than an ethnic group and more of a class status and position. Tupac's main message was for them.

Tupac utilized the power of words once again, to carve new ground and new definitions of old terms and conditions. In other words, Tupac created a new language for the marginalized, broke down, and disenfranchised. Tupac's use of the word niggaz took on new levels of identification for the marginalized and helped bring much needed cultural identification for a group of peoples that are rapidly growing into urban youth culture.[20]

## The Marginalized

Here I contend that Tupac once again, is strengthening his ghetto saint status with his message to the marginalized. Much of his "marginalized" message comes during both his The Ghetto is Destiny and Ghetto Saint eras.

Within many of Tupac's songs, there was a message for the marginalized: keep ya head up and there is a better way. The album "Thug Life: Volume 1" laid that message out.

Within that album, Tupac created doctrine for the thug and the person who does not have much in life. Tupac's lyrical message stretched beyond the song. One of the "shout-outs" that rappers give is on the album cover and within the album sleeves. Tupac made this album a creed and message for his own doctrine Thug Life. Within the album sleeve, Tupac thanks all the thugs and gives them their "props" or better put, respect.

This was important because it sent a strong message to those who felt as though they did not have a voice in society. This message was not limited to just Black youth

---

[20] While this term can be ambiguous, what I contend here is that the growing population of urban youth is diverse both ethnically and culturally; creating a new generation of Hip Hoppers that can still identify with Tupac's struggles and message within his music. This culture is also connected to Black popular culture.

either. Latinos, Asians, Whites, Pacific Islanders were all included and Tupac's message of hope.

The opening song, "Bury me A G" sets the tone and gives the basis of Tupac's philosophy. One may even think about it as Tupac setting up his methods and literature sections of a thesis. Below is a sample of the first lyric and chorus:

\* Walker sings and harmonizes over the Chorus

[2Pac]
Bury me a G.. Thug Life, feel me

Thinkin back, reminiscing on my teens
A young G, gettin paid off a dope fiends
Fuckin off cash that I made
Nigga what's the sense of workin hard if you never get to play?
I'm hustlin, stayin out 'til it's dawn
And comin home, at 6 o'clock in the mornin
Hands on my glock, eyes on the prize
Finger on the trigger when a nigga ride
Shootin craps, bustin niggaz out the do'
Pick my money off the flo', God bless the tre-fo'
Stuck on full, drunk again
Sippin on gin with a couple of friends (ha ha)
Say them Thug Life niggaz be like major pimps
Stickin to the rules wasn't made for sin (beotch!)
And if I die, let it be
But when they come for me, bury me a G

[Chorus 2X: 2Pac]
I ain't got time for bitches
Gotta keep my mind on my motherfuckin riches
Even when I die, they won't worry me
Mama don't cry, bury me a G

[Mopreme]
More trouble than the average
Just made 25 and I'm livin like a savage
Bein a G it ain't no easy thing
Cause you could fuck around get crossed and get stuck in the game
And for the rest of your life you will sit, and reminisce
Wonder why it had to end like this

> And to the G's you can feel my pain
> until the motherfucker gets born again

Tupac ends the first lyric with a mandate to be "born again." This touch's on the Thug Life spirituality that replaces traditional and conventional Christian religion and gives spiritual connectivity to the marginalized and left behind.[21] Nevertheless, Tupac allows the listener to know two things: the reality of the violence in the streets, and the resulting consequences of that violence.

For the marginalized, this provided hope. For someone looking in from the outside—an etic perspective—might look upon this hope as dark and "gloomy." But, when you have nothing else to hope for and no other dreams, Tupac's message was a godsend.

For example, in the song "Stay True" on the same album, Tupac lays out the basic creed for living the "Thug Life." This is a common practice of rappers to connect with their audience with some type of precept that most everyone is aware of. For example, a rapper might talk about drinking liquor every time there is a party or death, the audience then recognizes that as a common practice and event; therefore making the cultural identification even deeper with the song. Tupac understood this, and within this song, he takes that connection and identification even deeper, giving a louder voice for the marginalized:

> Big Stretch represent the real nigga
> flex, Live squad and this mutha fucker catch wreck
>
> (Stretch)
> Thug Life
> sharp as a roughneck
> Shakin' the dice, we roll long, ain't nothin' nice
> so the vice wanna follow us around (raize up)
> Got 'em runnin' as we clown thru the town (blaze up)
> Another one, had to throw another gun

---

[21] More on this subject in Chapters 10 and 11.

> Don't need another case
> you can see it on my face son
> But I ain't fallin' yet
> And I gotta give a shout to where my ball is at

In the song "War Stories," Tupac takes this identification with the marginalized a step further. Here he and other rap artists utilize the power of the compilation – the art of putting many artists on one song to bring out multiple perspectives—to actually bring the message of stories from the perspective of those that lived and still live the life. Tupac ends the song with a benediction of sorts:

> [2Pac talking]
> War stories nigga; hahaha, what players do
> Thug Life, Outlaw Immortalz
> Motherfuckin Tupac a.k.a. Machiavelli
> Can you feel me? Just so you know, it's on Death Row
> My niggaz love that shit
> Dramacydal in this motherfucker, heheheh
> Yea nigga! Shout out to my niggaz Fatal and Felony
> C-Bo, the bald head nut, what?
> You know what time it is

In this track, Tupac uses his inspiration and composition to create a physical and emotional response within the listener. This song illustrates the message to the marginalized and gives voice to the overall struggle they have to face in the form of stories.

Within the song, "Lord Knows" written during his Outlaw era, Tupac begins to ask the deep theological question, "What is sin?" What constitutes sin and transgression of the law? Tupac began to make that connection to what almost every urban youth faces: is there a Heaven for me if I have done "wrong" things? This was a powerful message and line of questioning that would eventually lift Tupac to saint status in the 'hood. This song makes the results of the violent life a reality:

> I wonder if the Lord will forgive me or bury me a G
> I couldn't let my adversaries worry me

>and every single day it's a test, wear a bulletproof vest
>and still a nigga stressin over death
>If I could choose when a nigga die, figure I'd
>take a puff on the blunt, and let my trigga fly
>When everyday it's another death, with every breath,
>it's a constant threat, so watch yo' step!
>You could be next if you want to, who do you run to?
>Murderin niggaz, look what it's come to
>My memories bring me misery, and life is hard
>in the ghetto, it's insanity, I can't breath
>Got me thinkin, what do Hell got?
>Cause I done suffered so much, I'm feelin shell-shocked
>And drivebys an everyday thang
>I done lost too many homies to this motherfuckin game
>and Lord knows...
>
>(Lord knows, Lord knows, Lord knows!)
>Lord knows[22]

Tupac discusses the death of a friend from a drive by—an image and event that I can personally connect to myself. I watched as one of my good friends was shot and killed right in front of me. When I listened to this song, I felt the same way. He asked me if things were going to be alright, and I too, lied. He died as we held him there on that street corner. Moreover, the alcohol, at the time, was the only pain reliever. This song hits home.

For many living in the inner city, this is a haunting reality and Tupac brings it out into the open. Once in the light, those things not talked about, gave voice to the experiences and events of the marginalized. He made it "cool" to be a nigga and to be marginalized—if one can ever be "cool" being that. In other words, Tupac brought the reality of the marginalized to the homes of millions in suburban America.

---

[22] "Lord Knows," Me Against The World (1995).

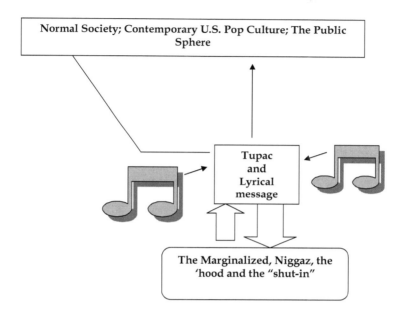

**FIGURE 16**

**CULTURAL IDENTIFICATION PROCESS THROUGH TUPAC**

In a simplistic way, Figure 16 displays how Tupac connected the 'hood to the rest of the world, and how the world was connected to the 'hood through his lyrical message. Now this is not to say that Tupac was the sole connecter, but he was a major piece in the rise of Black popular culture. Moreover, his lyrical message permeated from his music and lyrics, which preceded his reputation. Many different types of cultures and people within urban communities were able to identify with the thug and marginalized because of the lyrical content.

### *Tha Spiritual Message*

Tupac pioneered the dialogue about theological matters in the 'hood and Hip Hop culture. Tupac became a lighting rod for those theological matters, both positive and negative. Once again, Tupac connected the profane to the sacred. Moreover, Tupac made religion, God, church, and community attainable for comprehension and understanding by the masses.[23] Once again, I use the term theological message as Tupac's own interpretation of the scriptures, Jesus, salvation, and Heaven using his own contextual hermeneutic. Here, Tupac's spiritual message is centered more on both an idealistic and realistic message for living that is a part of this theological message, but not directly connected to any theological matters. A lot of Tupac's spirituality was shaped over his entire life, his theological understanding came during his Military Mind and The Ghetto is Destiny eras.

Additionally, James Cone describes a blurring of the sacred and profane with the musical genre of the blues (1991: 97-113). Cone states, "The blues depict the 'secular' dimension of black experience. They are the 'worldly' songs which tell us about love and sex, and about that other 'mule kickin in my stall'" (1992: 68). Further, he states, "The power of song in the struggle for black survival—that is what the spirituals and blues are all about" (1991: 1). While I would agree that the blues do depict much of the struggles and life of the Black experience, Tupac's music was not completely "secular" (i.e. devoid

---

[23] This was no different from what music did for slaves during the time of slavery. The music was a way to help slaves escape, connect, and hope in a savior that was not seen, but had been through what they had been through; Tupac comes from this line of historical music (Southern 1983; c.f. Hustad 1981; Burnim 2006). DuBois was himself fascinated with the tension in the spirituals between hope and despair and sorrow and joy; Tupac's music was very similar (1961: 182-189)

of God). Tupac's music presented a myriad of deeper theological understandings that could and did bring people closer to God. This "blurring" of lines, however, was certain and the debate whether Tupac was just a "popular" rap artist or an actual saint will continue to be debated.

This section strengthens my argument that Tupac was a ghetto saint. Here I will illustrate Tupac's own understanding of Jesus, suffering, hope, and vision.

### The Suffering Jesuz

Tupac insisted that people not reduce their hopes, dreams, and vision to the level of the event. For someone living in the inner city, this meant the vile living conditions you were in at the time. For others, that event might be poverty or a "broken home." Whatever the event, Tupac insisted that people keep their heads up. Hopelessness occurs when one cannot imagine a different future. Tupac encouraged his audience to keep believing for a better day, and that Heaven itself might have a "ghetto." Simply put, there is a place that will accept "us" as we are.

Tupac represented two sides of the coin. On one side, you have extraordinary hopefulness with songs like "Keep Ya Head Up," "Dear Mama," and "Black Jesuz." We have a representation of a Black Jesus that looks like we look, eats like we eat, smokes and drinks like we do, and is now on our level; a saint in the ghetto to whom we can pray. On the other side, you have the deep pain and suffering that he himself endured during much of his childhood. This is reflected in many of his songs. Tupac was searching for a pure theology. Tupac was also searching for a Jesus that could deal with his type of pain and suffering, this is seen in the song "Searching for Black Jesuz":

> [2Pac]
> Searching for Black Jesus
> Oh yeah, sportin jewels and shit, yaknahmean?

> (Black Jesus; you can be Christian
> Baptist, Jehovah Witness)
> Straight tatted up, no doubt, no doubt
> (Islamic, won't matter to me
> I'm a thug; thugs, we praise Black Jesus, all day)[24]

From this particular verse, one thinks immediately to that passage in Hebrews,[25] that tells us we have a savior and deity that can identify with us and has been through what we have been through. Tupac, made that same correlation:

> Searchin for Black Jesus
> It's hard, it's hard
> We need help out here
> So we searchins for Black Jesus
> It's like a Saint, that we pray to in the ghetto, to get us through
> Somebody that understand our pain
> You know maybe not too perfect, you know
> Somebody that hurt like we hurt
> Somebody that smoke like we smoke
> Drink like we drink
> That understand where we coming from
> That's who we pray to
> We need help y'all[26]

Tupac gave the listener the suffering Christ. For Tupac, Hebrews 4:14-16 demonstrated to him that Jesus knew of the suffering of the 'hood, cared for the individuals there, and was able to identify with the person going through that trial.

Suffering is nothing new within Black music and the 'hood community. However, when songs do not fall within the norms, values, and morality of the "church" advocated by church tradition, there becomes a problem (Pinn 1995: 118-119). Tupac came under

---

[24] "Black Jesuz" from the album 2Pac +Outlawz: Still I rise (1999); lyrics written during his Outlaw era.

[25] Hebrews 4:14-16 (ESV) Since then we have a great high priest who has passed through the heavens, Jesus, the Son of God, let us hold fast our confession. [15] For we do not have a high priest who is unable to sympathize with our weaknesses, but one who in every respect has been tempted as we are, yet without sin. [16] Let us then with confidence draw near to the throne of grace that we may receive mercy and find grace to help in time of need.

[26] "Black Jesuz" from the album 2Pac +Outlawz: Still I rise (1999).

criticism because of his "seductive" and "profane" lyrics, yet Tupac continued to commit to the rap about the unpolished expression and lifestyle of both Black and 'hood life which made segments of not only the United States uncomfortable, but also many Blacks (c.f. 1995: 118).

Tupac is a "non-standard"[27] representation of a much bigger religious debate of a God who became who we are; the Black Jesus that could identify and connect with the marginalized and the suffering (c.f. Cone 1997 a; 1997 b). Not the blue eyed blonde haired embedment of White pious perfection, but a Jesus that understood the issues and accepted those with these issues. That Black Jesus for Tupac meant a Jesus that relates to the downtrodden and the poor. This figure is a new figure, both literally and figuratively in theological literary responses to suffering both black and white (Cone 1997a).

For Tupac's issues, however, we have an irreverent Jesus that most people who identify with Jesus cannot understand. The black Jesus is NOT the Jesus of history…it is the Jesus that has never been talked about. We do not want a perfect God, we do not want a too neat God, we do want a God that smokes marijuana, drinks like we drink; a God that smokes a blunt, a blunt smoking Jesus? That is not the catechism of the irreverent that is pure blasphemy![28] We sees some of that blasphemy in the song "Black Jesuz" with Tupac and the Outlawz:

> I do my shootin's on a knob, prayin to God for my squad
> Stuck in a nightmare, hopin he might care
> Though times is hard, up against all odds, I play my cards
> like I'm jailin, shots hittin up my spot like midnight rains hailin
> Got me bailin to stacks more green; God ain't tryin to be trapped
> on no block slangin no rocks like bean pies
> Brainstorm on the beginnin

---

[27] By this use of the word I mean that Tupac was not a traditional "Christian" or formally trained theologian, he was a non-standard representation of Jesus.

[28] Michael Dyson in *Tupac Vs.* (Peters 2001).

> Wonder how shit like the Qu'ran and the Bible was written
> What is religion?
> Gods words all cursed like crack
> Shai-tan's way of gettin us back
> Or just another one of my Black Jesus traps

Here Tupac and the Outlawz question what kind of God it is we all really serve. Whether most would admit it or not, this is a fundamental theological question about the identity of God.

Still, within that blasphemy there is something larger at work: a fundamental attempt to make God more accessible to humankind especially in the 'hood.

> Bow down, pray to God hoping that he's listenin
> Seein niggaz comin for me, to my diamonds, when they glistenin
> Now pay attention, rest in peace father
> I'm a ghost in these killin fields[29]

In the verse above from, "Hail Mary," Tupac wonders if God will forgive him for all of his sins. Using the traditional framework of sin and salvation, which is the standard dogma for many Christians and churches, the answer is no. For Tupac, that was not good. Tupac then asked, "If what 'you' say I have to do to be saved is true, then I am in hell already and we're lost. But what if there is another way and Jesus really did die so that everyone could be saved?" This was one of the fundamental and foundational elements of Tupac's spiritual message within his lyrics and music: a new ideology for salvation and a new definition for sin.

> [Makaveli]
> Makaveli in this... Killuminati, all through your body
> The blow's like a twelve gauge shotty
> Uhh, feel me!
> And God said he should send his one begotten son
> to lead the wild into the ways of the man
> Follow me; eat my flesh, flesh and my flesh[30]

---

[29] "Black Jesuz" from the album 2Pac +Outlawz: Still I rise (1999).

[30] "Hail Marry," Makaveli - The Don Killuminati: The 7 Day Theory (1996).

Tupac would have his listeners connect to Jesus through different stories and allegories. [31]These stories and allegories became theological reference points to people who otherwise never set foot in a church. Moreover, Tupac presented his audience with a Jesus that could relate to their needs and hurts. In fact, the simple changing of the letter "S" to "Z" at the end of "Jesus'" name meant that this was the suffering and downtrodden Jesus that could identify with those who were the same.[32]

Figure 17 illustrates a way of seeing how Tupac took old values and gave them new meaning for a new way of understanding Jesus and His purpose on this earth. Tupac contextualized the Gospel message[33] and made it "digestible" for those who were otherwise shunned by the church (the pimps, prostitutes, gang members, street thugs).

### The Profane

Tupac's connection to the profane was inevitable. He was faced with both the ideal life of "living right" and being a perfect "role model," while on the other hand having the reality of street life in which the code of the street says if your too "right" and "nice" you will be taken advantage of. Tupac once raised the question: how could he live like an angel when he was amongst devils.

---

[31] Tupac's ultimate criticism was not of Jesus, but of the organized church. None of his lyrics ever blasphemed the name of Jesus. However, Tupac did have sharp criticisms about the organized church, a parallel with Jesus' life.

[32] This was a common practice throughout history. In slavery days, many slaves could not relate to Paul and his letters in the New Testament because of his perceived stance on pro-slavery. Instead, the Gospels were used to describe a Jesus that loves all and cared for them. This made it easier for slaves to identify with Jesus; especially through song (Burnim 2006; Reed 2003; Southern 1983).

[33] Figure 19 illustrates the process in which Tupac made Jesus more accessible for his audience through song.

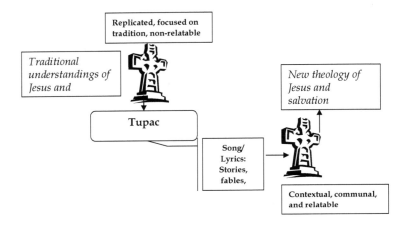

**FIGURE 17**

**NEW THEOLOGICAL FOUNDATIONS THROUGH TUPAC'S LYRICS**

In the song, "Blasphemy" Tupac questions the societal foundation in the 'hood called the "church." The "church" was a community beacon and an inspiration for many—within the Civil Rights and Boomer Generations. Tupac questioned this "church" and drew much negative attention and controversy in the song "Blasphemy":

> [Tupac]
> We probably in Hell already, our dumb asses not knowin
> Everybody kissin ass to go to heaven ain't goin
> Put my soul on it, I'm fightin devil niggaz daily
> Plus the media be crucifying brothers severly
> Tell me I ain't God's son, nigga mom a virgin
> We got addicted had to leave the burbs, back in the ghetto
> doin wild shit, lookin at the sun don't pay

Criminal mind all the time, wait for Judgment Day
They say Moses split the Red Sea
I split the blunt and rolled the fat one, I'm deadly -- Babylon beware
Comin from the Pharaoh's kids, retaliation
Makin legends off the shit we did, still bullshittin
Niggaz in Jerusalem, waitin for signs
God promised, she's just takin her time, haha
Living by the Nile while the water flows
I'm contemplating plots wondering which door to go
Brothas getting shot, comin back resurrected
It's just that raw shit, nigga check it (that raw shit)

And I remember what my papa told me
Remember what my papa told me, blasphemy

Chorus

[Tupac]
The preacher want me buried why? Cause I know he a liar
Have you ever seen a crackhead, that's eternal fire
Why you got these kids minds, thinkin that they evil
while the preacher bein richer you say honor God's people
Should we cry, when the Pope die, my request
We should cry if they cried when we buried Malcolm X
Mama tell me am I wrong, is God just another cop
waitin to beat my ass if I don't go pop?

As the lyrics roll out of Tupac's mouth, he shakes every foundational being from within traditional Christian foundations. Just the mere fact that he addresses God, as a "She" would raise eyebrows. Tupac even wonders if God is just another figment of our imaginations. Moreover, he calls out the theology of the very pastor that is supposed to be helping the people they are working with when he asks why the preacher is warring against their own youth.

This all falls into the category of the profane. Most Christians (especially those converted within two years) have little to do with "unsaved" people and the profane areas of life. But Tupac did not overlook these "gray" areas of society—he himself realizes that he is a part of that "gray."

232

Tupac deconsecrates the sacred[34] world and gives it back to the marginalized and downtrodden. That is a sin worthy of a beating from the Spanish Inquisition. Moreover, Tupac brings out the dirty laundry of not only the Black community, but of the Black church. He even begins to have more popularity than the "pastor" or "reverend" of that church; not because he is more holy or without sin, but because of the very fact that he is not perfect. Tupac was simply transparent and open about his profanity. So much so, that it offended many around him and made him the scapegoat for many people's own unresolved sins. Tupac replaced the traditional way of coming to Christ and salvation, with the Thug Life and a type of thug theology of sorts (c.f. Dyson 2001). For Tupac, this needed to be a part of his "new church" because it was a part of the community that he and so many others were a part of.

In the song "I Wonder if Heaven got a Ghetto," Tupac challenges the typical way to salvation. Upon first hearing this song, and without the proper context for it, one may see it as a syncretistic approach to the Gospels. However, with a second and possible third and fourth look, we are able to see that this is not the case at all in the song "I Wonder if Heaven got a Ghetto":

>  Here on Earth, tell me what's a blick life worth
>  A bottle of juice is no excuse, the truth hurts
>  And even when you take the shit
>  Move counties get a lawyer you can shake the shit
>  Ask Rodney, LaTasha, and many more
>  It's been goin on for years, there's plenty more
>  When they ask me, when will the violence cease?
>  When your troops stop shootin niggaz down in the street
>  Niggaz had enough time to make a difference
>  Bear witness, own our own business
>  Word to God cause it's hard tryin to make ends meet
>  First we couldn't afford shit now everything's free

---

[34] About the time of Bach and also during the middle Ages, there was no distinction between the sacred and the secular in terms of music. Music was just music; many hymns that we sing today were derived from "bar-songs" (Grout and Palisca 2001: 31-65; 465-500).

> so we loot, please don't shoot when you see
> I'm takin from the, cause for years they would take it from me
> Now the tables have turned around
> You didn't listen, until the niggaz burned it down
> And now Bush can't stop the hit
> Predicted the shit, in 2Pacalypse
> And for once I was down with niggaz, felt good
> in the hood bein around the niggaz, yeah
> And for the first time everybody let go
> And the streets is death row, I wonder if heaven got a ghetto

Tupac makes reference to current events and issues that make the song relevant. He also uses his lyrics to illustrate that his first album predicted, or better, prophesized, the "mess" that the 'hood was currently in. To escape all the pain, Tupac proposes a Heaven that accepts him and others that look and act like him.

### Sinner's Prayer

One of the better theological songs that Tupac ever did was "So Many Tears."[35] This song was a theological masterpiece. Laced with a sinner's prayer underneath the vocal track, Tupac takes the urbanite on a ghetto version of the Lord's Prayer.

The opening lyrics to the song itself have Tupac asking God for forgiveness and mercy while he lives this daily life of sin. Here Tupac reveals his deepest self and gives his audience something more to connect with:

> I shall not fear no man but God
> Though I walk through the valley of death
> I shed so many tears (if I should die before I wake)
> Please God walk with me (grab a nigga and take me to Heaven)

This particular verse is derived from Psalm 23 and for one of the first times you have a "secular" artist discussing spiritual matters within a rap song. This was unprecedented

---

[35] See Appendix H for the complete song.

and made Tupac's audience love him even more. [36] Much of Tupac's deepest sorrow came from his Ghetto is Destiny era when he saw first hand the hardships of both his mother's life and the broken lives around him.

The opening verse lays out the harsh realties of the street while contending those realties with the actuality that there is a need for Jesus amidst the pain and hurt:

> Back in elementary, I thrived on misery
> Left me alone I grew up amongst a dyin breed
> Inside my mind couldn't find a place to rest
> until I got that Thug Life tatted on my chest
> Tell me can you feel me? I'm not livin in the past, you wanna last
> Be tha first to blast, remember Kato
> No longer with us he's deceased
> Call on the sirens, seen him murdered in the streets
> Now rest in peace
> Is there heaven for a G? Remember me
> So many homies in the cemetery shed so many tears

Here you can see that Tupac is not really sure of what to make of all this. Tears fill his eyes with the thought of another life lost.

Tupac, is an irreverent, yet natural, theologian,[37] connecting a Black and urban quest for meaning in the midst of suffering. The song "So Many Tears" parallels much of the Lord's Prayer as seen in Table 9. While Tupac does not directly address each verse, the song deals with parallel themes within the Lord's Prayer that help the young struggling urbanite, make sense of their world. More importantly, it provides a contextualized message for them.[38]

---

[36] Some would argue that this was a marketing ploy to get money and sell albums. While I do not disagree with the fact that Tupac was a businessman and did sell records for profit, this was not the case for this song. This was Tupac's attempt to make Christ more accessible for not only him, but for his listeners.

[37] I use this term to refer to Tupac as an unrefined, organic, grassroots, pre-evangelistic type of 'hood preacher that can begin conversations about God with hard core Hip Hoppers in which most traditional pastors cannot.

[38] This is extremely controversial. Even what I am doing here could be considered heretical because it does not follow standard exegetical methods, and parallels Jesus' words with words considered

## TABLE 9

## LYRICAL CONNECTION TO THE LORD'S PRAYER

| Verse | Connection to The Lord's Prayer<br>Luke 11:2-4<br>Matthew 6:9-13 (NLT) |
|---|---|
| I shall not fear no man but God<br>Though I walk through the valley of death<br>I shed so many tears (if I should die before I wake)<br>Please God walk with me (grab a nigga and take me to Heaven)<br><br>And fuck the world cause I'm cursed, I'm havin visions of leavin here in a hearse, God can you feel me? | "Father, may your name be honored, may your kingdom come soon" |
| Take me away from all the pressure, and all the pain<br>Show me some happiness again, I'm goin blind<br>I spend my time in this cell, ain't livin well<br>I know my destiny is Hell, where did I fail?<br>My life is in denial, and when I die, baptized in eternal fire I'll shed so many tears<br><br>Lord, I suffered through the years, and shed so many tears..<br>Lord, I lost so many peers, and shed so many tears<br><br>Now I'm lost and I'm weary, so many tears<br>I'm suicidal, so don't stand near me<br>My every move is a calculated step, to bring me closer | "Give us our food day by day." |

---

to be profane. Still, I argue, we must deal with the issue head on if we are to be relevant and missional in this 21st century.

| Verse | Connection to The Lord's Prayer<br>Luke 11:2-4<br>Matthew 6:9-13 (NLT) |
|---|---|
| They planted seeds and they hatched, sparkin the flame<br>inside my brain like a match, such a dirty game<br>No memories, just a misery<br>Paintin a picture of my enemies killin me, in my sleep<br>Will I survive til the mo'nin, to see the sun<br>Please Lord forgive me for my sins, cause here I come...39<br><br>Lord, I suffered through the years (God) and shed so many tears..<br>God, I lost so many peers, and shed so many tears | "And forgive us our sins just as we forgive those who have sinned against us." |

Further, in the song "Blasphemy," Tupac leads the listener on a basic plan of salvation:

> God has a plan -- and the Bible unfolds that wonderful plan
> through the message of prophecy
> God sent Jesus into this world to be our savior
> And that Christ is returning, someday soon
> to unfold the wonderful plan of eternity, for my life and your life
> As long as we're cooperating with God
> by accepting Jesus Christ as our personal Lord and savior
> And as the Lord does return in the coming seven days
> We'll see you next time here on This Week in Bible Prophecy

Tupac lets you know from the beginning of the song, that this is serious business, and that the 'hood needs salvation too. As the song is set up, you are left wonder if Tupac is really serious about this. Moreover, one wonders if this is a ploy to sell more records? However, lest we forget, Tupac was raised in the Black church. Tupac was raised to believe in Jesus The Christ; that being coupled with being raised as a revolutionary. Therefore, Tupac knew and understood the basic principles to salvation. Here, he merely allows the listener

---

39 One of the things that Tupac does, though not often, is to forgive his transgressors.

to make a decision; Tupac never once claimed that he had all the answers. If Tupac was anything, he was a beacon of light and hope. He was not, as I argue, a direct scholar or theologian; moreover, I do not believe he was the reincarnate of Jesus as some believe. He was merely a connecter and interpreter and acted much as a pastor would over their congregation that would incarnate the Gospel message (Kraft 1991).

### Hope and Vision: Gospel

Overall, Tupac wanted to inspire people to live differently. Through all the gloom, anger, frustration, pain, and hate Tupac still flourished; his "rose" grew from the concrete of pain. That rose represented hope and vision for a brighter tomorrow. Tupac knew this and wanted others to experience the same.[40]

In the song, "Letter to my Unborn Child" Tupac gives life lessons to his younger child—which was in fact never born because Tupac never had children. In this song, Tupac gives life instructions and lessons to instruct and encourage a younger generation—it was as if he knew he would not be around to see them:

> Seems so complicated to escape fate
> And you can never understand 'til we trade places
> Tell the world I feel guilty to bein anxious
> Ain't no way in hell, that I could ever be rapist
> It's hard to face this, cold world on a good day
> When will they let the little kids in the hood play?
> I got shot five times but I'm still breathin
> Livin proof there's a God if you need a reason

In this particular verse, Tupac is giving out quick one-liners to a new generation of youth that will have to face even stronger battles on the 'hood front.

---

[40] Many times, the media portrayed Tupac as a thug that had no concern for normal life and decency of life. This was simply not true. It was, in fact, quite the opposite.

In the song, "Ghetto Gospel" Tupac encourages the people in the 'hood to remain strong through all the hurt and pain, and that there is a brighter day coming. He extends the Gospel message of Jesus and contextualizes it for a contemporary audience:

> [Verse Two]
> Tell me do you see that old lady, ain't it sad
> Livin out of bags, plus is glad for the little things she, has
> And over there there's a lady, crack got her crazy
> Guess who's givin birth to a baby?
> I don't trip and let it fade me
> From out of the fryin pan, we jump into another form of slavery
> Even now I get discouraged
> Wonder if they take it all back, will I still keep the - courage?
> I refuse to be a role model
> I set goals, take control, drink out my own bottles
> I make mistakes, but learn from every one
> And when it's said and done, I bet this brother be a better one

Tupac even lets his audience know that he himself gets weary and worried at times, but that in the end, there is hope. There is a connection here to Matthew 11:27-30 where Jesus encourages his followers to take their problems and pains to Him, and that He will carry them for you.[41] Much of Christian music connects the audience with that higher level of hope and vision. Many of the songs just use different words, but the principals remain basically the same (Hustad 1981: 62-78). Tupac, once again, extends Jesus' Gospel to an unreached people that most churches cannot do with a Hip Hop culture. Later in the song, Tupac asks God if He hears him speaking. Does God even care?

> [2Pac]
> Lord can you hear me speak? ..
> The pain and strife of bein hellbound

---

[41] Matthew 11:27-30 (ESV) All things have been handed over to me by my Father, and no one knows the Son except the Father, and no one knows the Father except the Son and anyone to whom the Son chooses to reveal him. [28] Come to me, all who labor and are heavy laden, and I will give you rest. [29] Take my yoke upon you, and learn from me, for I am gentle and lowly in heart, and you will find rest for your souls. [30] For my yoke is easy, and my burden is light."

Tupac raises an elemental theological question as old as Job. Job himself argued with God for over fifteen chapters until God finally interrupted him. Tupac is asking the same thing about life and salvation. Tupac's spirituality then becomes blurred with his theological hermeneutic and the two seem intertwined. Yet, Tupac himself did not come to any solid conclusions regarding salvation and Heaven. Tupac both extends the Gospel message of Jesus by giving hard core Hip Hoppers a message of good news, and begins a pre-evangelistic discussion with Hip Hoppers. The next step is up to us to help move that person forward, more on this in chapter thirteen.

There is yet another message of hope from Tupac. In the song "Hold on be Strong" Tupac directly tells his audience that they need to hold on and find their trust in God. This connects with yet another scriptural verse found in Philippians 4:12-14.[42]

>Hold on, be strong, hold on
>Be strong, hold on
>When it's on it's on
>
>There's, never a good day, cause in my hood they
>let they AK's pump strays where the kids play
>And every Halloween, check out the murder scene
>Can't help but duplicate the violence seen on the screen
>My homies dyin 'fore they get to see they birthdays
>These is the worst days, sometimes it hurts to pray
>And even God turned his back on the ghetto youth
>I know that ain't the truth, sometimes I look for proof
>I wonder if heaven got a ghetto, and if it does
>Does it matter if you blood or you cuz
>Remember how it was, the picnics and the parties in the projects
>Small time drinkin gettin high with them armies
>Just another knucklehead kid from the gutter
>I'm dealin with the madness, raised by a single mother
>I'm tryin to tell you when it's on
>You gotta keep your head to the sky and be strong, most of all hold on

---

[42] Philippians 4:12-14 (ESV) I know how to be brought low, and I know how to abound. In any and every circumstance, I have learned the secret of facing plenty and hunger, abundance and need. [13] I can do all things through him who strengthens me. [14] Yet it was kind of you to share my trouble.

Tupac, connecting to the pain and misery of 'hood life and just life in general, still brings it full circle at the end of the verse and tells the listener to keep their focus on the "sky" or, as it can be interpreted, God.

Allan Merriam states, "Song texts can be used as a means of action directed toward the solution of problems which plague a community" (1964: 201). Tupac did just that, his song texts gave light to the many problems in the 'hood, yet pointed the listener to find solutions to these problems. Tupac did not simply want to leave his audience with just problems, there needed to be solutions, and for him, those solutions were primarily found in God, which equaled hope for tomorrow.

### *Summary*

In this chapter I have analyzed Tupac's musical message. Four major themes arose in his music that speaks to people: the social and political message, the familial and communal message, the class message, and the spiritual message. All four of these areas combine to form Tupac's lyrical message that spoke of the 'hood's issues, problems, spirituality and theology.

This chapter is a solid reflection of the major messages within Tupac's lyrics. His lyrical message, from both his poems and music, is a reflection of the context in which Tupac grew up. Moreover, Tupac, being a product of Hip Hop culture, the 'hood, and BPC gave you his version of what he saw happening in those three areas. This chapter summarizes those.

Tupac took things out of the profane world and made them sacred; deconsecrating what was once a sacred world. People would hang Tupac, metaphorically speaking, for his engagement with issues that could be construed as profane. But, for Tupac this was necessary in order to reach a new generation. Tupac even developed a way for those listening to his music to accept Jesus as their savior and find hope in Him. Tupac was still considered a profane person. He was the irreverent theologian.

Lastly, Tupac inspired others with his message of hope and vision for a brighter future. Tupac wanted people to believe that there was hope and that hope came in Jesus, if you could be open to that.

All of these major themes can now be synthesized to form Tupac's theological message, which can be seen in Table 10.

## TABLE 10

### TAXONOMIES OF TUPAC'S MUSICAL MESSAGE

| Social and Political | Familial and Communal | Class | Spiritual |
|---|---|---|---|
| Within the 'hood there exists another track of living that does not get spoken of very often. Tupac gave you that message continually while presenting a musical score that made you bob your head. | Tupac was deeply connected to his family both extended and nuclear. Nowhere else would he let you know how he cared for them than in his music Further, Tupac was extremely giving and help his family and community both financially and emotionally. | Tupac was aware of class in the United States. Tupac was not ashamed to call out the powers and give voice to the great class divide that exists in our country today. | Tupac, while providing a great rhythm, would infuse deep theological messages with street knowledge and street sense, which lifts up the name of the Lord, while connecting people to Him. |

In Part 4, I will present Tupac's theological message. In other words, I will present his Gospel message. I will also present an evangelistic tool for reaching Hip Hop youth.

# PART IV

## HERMENEUTICAL SHIZNIT:
## TUPAC'S GOSPEL

Based on the findings, I am able to make recommendations pertaining to better understating Tupac from both a missiological and theological point of view, and provide tools for Hip Hop youth evangelism as seen through the eyes of Tupac. Furthermore, these recommendations have broader missiological significance in that they enable me to contribute to the missiological objectives for the manifold ministry of Christ and His Church in an urban context.

In this section, we will be moving into both the biblical and church context as seen in Figure 18. This is the last part of this book, and reflects the conclusions and recommendations from the findings on Tupac as it relates to evangelism and missions to Hip Hop youth. It also extracts the theological themes that arise in his music.

The first chapter discusses Tupac's theological framework and how it is broken down. This chapter sets the stage to discuss Tupac's Gospel message for both the church and Hip Hop youth, and to provide crucial recommendations for the urban church. The chapter will offer up new theory for reaching a Hip Hop generation in the 21$^{st}$ century.

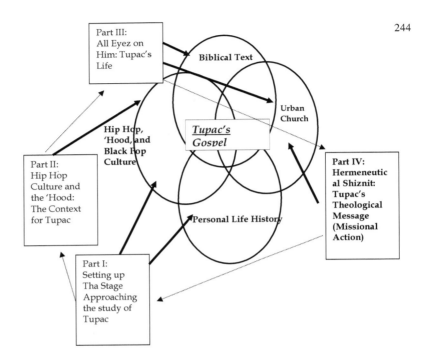

**FIGURE 18**

**FLOW OF BOOK PART FOUR**

# CHAPTER 10

# INTERPRETING TUPAC'S THEOLOGICAL MESSAGE

Tupac presented a conundrum of sorts. On one hand, he represents the hope, vigor, and excitement of a generation. Yet, on the other, he represents the despair, depression, and marginalization of several generations all gathered into one person. Tupac presented both sides. His half brother asserts that he represented both the good and evil in people (Peters 2001).

Tupac spoke of the harsh realities of the street, and connected those realities to larger societal issues. If you were to sum up Tupac's major "fault" it was that he "kept it real." Tupac spoke about things as they were, and did not hold back. In the song "Blasphemy" he calls out the pastor, the church, and urban Christians as he pushes for a new understanding of Jesus.

### *Theological Frameworks*

To begin, we must first delve into the theological mainframe which will guide our discussion. This will "set the stage" and give a foundation in which I will base my conclusions on Tupac.

### Reversing the Hermeneutical Flow

First, beginning with Larry Krietzer's concept of reversing the hermeneutical flow, we see how Tupac and his musical message can interpret the Bible and Jesus. Krietzer (2002) uses film to analyze and study scripture. Krietzer uses film, in essence, to interpret the Bible as opposed to using the Bible to interpret culture—hence, reversing the hermeneutical flow. In this work, he views several films to interpret different biblical messages from the Old Testament to the New Testament. Krietzer (1993, 1994, and 2002) argues that when we hold the Canon of God in comparison with pop culture, we can—at first glance—not find any "Christological message" within the "mess." However, if we were to hold that the meaning of a text is not some invisible substance inserted in it as the moment of its origin (rather like the immortal soul that mysteriously appears in a human fetus), but rather that the meaning of the text must be negotiated and continually re-negotiated between that text and its reader, then Tupac's crucifixion and image of Black Jesuz becomes a more interesting theme in order to study. And the hermeneutics could therefore be reversed (Krietzer 2002) using Tupac to study the Bible.[1] The meaning, therefore, lies between the texts, within culture, and not 'in' the text at all. This, Krietzer would argue, is reversing the hermeneutical flow. We can apply not only the stories of Christ to interpret Tupac, but we can shift and use Tupac's stories to interpret Jesus.[2]

Songs such as:
- Young Black Male
- Brendas Got A Baby
- How Long will They Mourn Me?
- Cradle to the Grave
- I Ain't Mad at Ya
- Hail Mary
- Black Jesuz

---

[1] This is not to say that orthodox theology is bad or wrong, merely a new way to interpret Jesus.

[2] While this could be interpreted as "heretical" and blasphemous, I, along with Krietzer, would contend that we continue to use the Bible as a reference point in order to maintain a Christ like feel.

The songs listed here reflect Krietzer's framework. These particular songs deal with issues such as death, social justice, poverty, life after death, and the connection between man and God—in other words: a Christ figure for the Ghetto. These songs also deal with the fact that things in the ghetto are "different" and cannot be looked at with the same lens that someone could look at regular issues in mainstream America. Tupac uses scripture and his theological understanding to bring illumination to a Christ that has been muddied and marred by a "White" theology and a theology that states you have to be "perfect" in order to enter Heaven. Therefore, Tupac asks the question, "Does Heaven got a Ghetto, and if so, can I come, because it sucks down here?" These songs can be used to better understand the Bible, salvation, Jesus' deity, and Heaven; reversing the hermeneutics using Tupac.

This type of framework connects with Shaw and Van Engen's "hermeneutical spiral" concept (2003: 80-82). In this concept they assert, "The spiraling process of missiological hermeneutics begins with missional intention" (2003: 80). In this framework, both the divine and human level at some point meet through a spiraling process over time which includes new missiological perspectives, a new view of the Gospel in the midst of a missional church, and a knowing of God in a new context. This ultimately ends with a converging praxis between the divine and human level (2003: 80-81). Shaw and Van Engen further state, "The purpose is Gospel proclamation through crossing barriers" (2003: 80). Krietzer's position is similar in that he suggests that we find God in contextual ways that bring us closer to Him using culture—in this case Tupac (1993:11).

248

Krietzer's view of "reversing the hermeneutical flow" is exactly what Tupac's message is about. Using everyday life to interpret what God is trying to tell us. This will lay the basic groundwork for understanding Tupac's theological message.[3]

## Nitty Gritty Hermeneutics

Second, we have Anthony Pinn's nitty-gritty hermeneutics (1995). In this, Pinn uses hermeneutics as a model for understanding culture and theology. He states, "hermeneutics denotes interpretation of the meaning submerged in events, texts, etc. That is, words and texts contain valuable information that must be recognized and processed within one's system of values and concerns, hermeneutics makes this possible" (1995:115). Here Pinn argues that there are greater issues at work in society, especially when it comes to Black culture. Pinn states, "Only the broadened frame of reference will allow for a full explanation of all vital materials relevant to the problem of evil" (1995:114). In other words, the nitty-gritty allows the person to state that there are forces larger than the simplistic answers given to us by many pastors that "God just allows evil and evil has to exist." God is in the details. For Tupac, yes, that is true; however, Tupac uses his own nitty-gritty interpretation from life that tells him that things in life are not as simple and easy to explain away. Although Pinn's framework of the nitty-gritty was developed independently, it does bear some resemblance to Henry Mitchell's use of nitty-gritty as descriptive of the Black preacher's exposition of the Gospel. In other words, Mitchell was describing how the Gospel for Blacks was a "tell-it-like-it-is" style Gospel

---

[3] While some would argue that this is a blasphemous way to interpret who Jesus is, and, the majority of Krietzer's work deals with a White upper middle class perspective, I would argue that the basic tenets of his conceptual framework are exactly what Tupac was and still is doing with theology. All of Tupac's songs are connected to a greater story in some shape or sort. None of his music was ever done haphazardly or by coincidence. Many rappers today cannot say the same thing. In order to gain a basic understanding of Tupac's theological message, we are impressed to reverse the flow of hermeneutics and peer closely and deeper into that theological meaning from the "outside" in.

and the nitty-gritty was the details of it all. For more, see Henry H. Mitchell (1979: 23-31).

For Tupac, the nitty-gritty helps explain the entire *context* behind each event and why Brenda had the baby in a restroom, and was left out in the cold—from the song *Brenda Got A Baby*. For Pinn, the Blues and Rap music begin to explain away this detail and context behind the issues are areas of life. Therefore, there is a higher meaning to why evil exists and how it comes about in the hearts of men. For Pinn, the Blues and Rap being to put "feet" and details onto the meaning of life.

Tupac was no different. Tupac, as a ghetto saint, wanted people in the world to be aware of what was happening in the hood. He decided at a young age that his music would show the more graphic details and images to evoke change.[4] Tupac's music was not simply interpreted either. There were "nitty-gritty" details to many of his songs. Songs such as:

- The Hearts of Men
- Skandalouz
- All Eyes on Me
- Trapped

These particular songs are examples of songs that delved deeper into matters that could not be easily explained nor easily dealt with. These are examples of Tupac's nitty-gritty hermeneutic. While Pinn himself has a humanist viewpoint on theological matters, he still covers the areas that I feel are important to Tupac's theological message. Tupac, himself, was part humanist and saw himself as a community servant. Therefore, Pinn's view on the nitty-gritty serve for another solid theological framework to interpret Tupac's theological message through his music.

---

[4] Unfortunately it did not work the way Tupac had planned.

This particular conceptual framework is also closely related to Kraft's "Dynamics of Revelation" (1979: 239-253). Here Kraft contends that through different life events, beginning with an unacceptable starting point in life (love for another God, idolatry), through different situations and life events that point to God, one ultimately comes to a point where they see God in a different way, all the while using those past life events and situations to build on their new found place in life (Kraft 1979: 243-245). Through different specific events, that are sometimes unexplained and mundane, God is seen much clearer and the person is able to grow closer to Him. The nitty-gritty of life is used to draw closer to God. This will further be discussed in chapter twelve.

## Jesus and Hip Hop

Third, I use James Cones' framework in his classical book, *The Spirituals and the Blues*, for a broader understanding of using the "secular" to interpret the sacred. James Cone, a noted scholar and expert in the areas of Black theology, states: "Theologically, there is more to be said about the music of black people than what was revealed in the black spirituals. To be sure, a significant number of black people were confident that the God of Israel was involved in black history, liberating them from slavery and oppression. But not all blacks could accept the divine promises of the Bible as a satisfactory answer to the contradictions of black existence...The blues depict the 'secular' dimension of black experience. They are 'worldly' songs which tell us about love and sex and about that 'mule kickin in my stall...the blues are about black life and the sheer earth and gut capacity to survive in an extreme situation of oppression" (1991:97).

In this framework, Cone argues that the blues are used to greater explain the larger and more complex issues that arise within Black culture and life. Cone argues here that the blues express a certain Black outlook and perspective on life, culture, society, economy, sex, and even theology and attempt to make meaning in a situation fraught with contradictions (Cone 1991:102-110).

Tupac's musical message was no different. The only thing I would add is that the term "secular" needs to be redefined. I contend that Tupac's musical message is, in fact, a spiritual and theological message infused in samples, deep baselines, and a West Coast sounding rhythm that infringes into the deep social and psyche of human-kind and forces them to see life differently and broadly as a result of the message that Tupac gives.

### *Black Jesuz*

> Searchin for Black Jesus
> It's hard, it's hard
> We need help out here
> So we searchins for Black Jesus
> It's like a Saint, that we pray to in the ghetto, to get us through
> Somebody that understand our pain
> You know maybe not too perfect, you know
> Somebody that hurt like we hurt
> Somebody that smoke like we smoke
> Drink like we drink
> That understand where we coming from
> That's who we pray to
> We need help y'all

In the opening lyric to the song "Black Jesuz" above, we are able to see a theology of liberation for ghetto peoples (e.g. Cone 1991, 1997a, 1997 b; Early 1997; Edwards 1975; Floyd 1995; Blackwell 1999). This was connected with Tupac's thug life message as well. In the documentary film on Tupac, *Tupac Vs* (Peters 2001), Dyson states:

> Pac is deconsecrating the sacred world....that is a blasphemy that would get you killed.
> Don't reduce your hope, dreams, and experiences, to the level of the event. (Talking about slavery). But one must foster, encourage, the future vision that allows one to escape the disparity. Hopelessness occurs when one can't imagine a different future. Pac represented 2 sides of the

> coin. On one side of the coin you have a spiritualness and hope in songs like "keep your head up", and others...we have a representation of a Black Jesus that looks like we look, eats like we eat, smokes and drinks like we do; and is now on our level. But a saint in the ghetto to whom we can pray. Tupac is representation of a secular figure to a much bigger religious debate of a God who became who we are. We are searching for Black Jesus. That Black Jesus for Pac meant, a Jesus that relates to the downtrodden and the poor. That figure is a new figure. Both in the literature and in literal responses to suffering both black and white...we have an irreverent Jesus that most people who identify with Jesus cannot understand...the black Jesus is NOT the Jesus of history...it is the Jesus that has never been talked about.

For Tupac, the image of the Black Jesus was one that could connect with the downtrodden, the sick, the hungry, the hurt, the marginalized, and the despairing. Tupac imagined a Heaven with a ghetto—the figurative and metaphorical image of a Heaven that was made for "real" people. Tupac believed that there had to be a better place than this.

For many years, Blacks and urbanites in general, have had to deal with the image of a White, blonde, blue-eyed Jesus that was shaped in an image that was foreign to them. Cone (1997 a and 1997 b) argued that there needed to be an image of a Black Jesus: one that Blacks in America could relate to, one that was socially aware of the struggle that Blacks had to go through, and one that would have compassion on them because of their hardships (Cone 1997 b: 99-105).[5]

Tupac took the ideology of the Black Jesus a step further and talked about a Christ figure for the ghetto. A Christ that smoked weed, drank liquor, kicked it, and had compassion for the 'hood; a human link to deity, which referred back to the literal image of The Christ—God incarnate. This is a difficult image of Jesus. This is not the traditional form of Jesus, both literarily and figuratively. For many traditional Blacks—including many other evangelical Christians—Tupac was simply too irreverent and sacrilegious. Once again, Tupac was deconsecrating the sacred world; this was an act

---

[5] C.f. Reed (2003).

worthy of death in the Spanish Inquisition. People would hang Tupac for what he was saying—and they did, metaphorically and lyrically.

The image of the Black Jesus was one that could connect with the downtrodden. This image was connected back to his thug life message and carried a messianic message of hope, vision, blessings, and cares for the downtrodden and hurt that dwell in the inner cities of The United States. Tupac was the irreverent natural theologian that gave voice to a suffering community (Dyson 2001).

It was during this era that Tupac began to write songs that had a messianic message rooted in Christianity. Tupac fashioned himself off of the great scripture in Hebrews 4:14-16:

> 14 That is why we have a great High Priest who has gone to heaven, Jesus the Son of God. Let us cling to him and never stop trusting him. 15 This High Priest of ours understands our weaknesses, for he faced all of the same temptations we do, yet he did not sin. 16 So let us come boldly to the throne of our gracious God. There we will receive his mercy, and we will find grace to help us when we need it.

In this passage, we can begin to see where Tupac was heading. Jesus was a connection to a greater hope that lay in Heaven. The ultimate peace and rest was with God. Tupac knew he had to pass this message on to the streets of America, especially the young people. This became part of Tupac's mission in the latter part of his life.

### *The Image of Black Jesuz*

Tupac's life resembled the image of the Black Jesus (Dyson 2001; Reed 2003; Ramsey 2004). A Jesus figure that is not merely the skin color or that way in which Jesus speaks and acts, but a figure that goes beyond the blue eyed, blonde haired image of a White deity that had been presented to so many ghetto neighborhoods for decades. This image of the Black Jesus was one that Tupac embraced and also emulated throughout his music and poems. This image is rooted in Black theology, one that James Cone states as objective and socially aware (1997 a: 15-20). Cone further states about this phenomenon:

> We cannot afford to do theology unrelated to human existence. Our theology must emerge consciously from an investigation of the socioreligious experience of black people, as that experience is reflected in black stories of God's dealings with black people in the struggle for freedom (1997 a: 15).

This is what Tupac was aiming for in a street, pimp, hustler, thug, irreverent and Black Panther sort of way. James Cone argues that there is no truth for, and about, Black people that does not emerge and root itself out of the context of their experience. Tupac was no different. He lived and breathed his music that was socially, politically, and religiously aware of the situation many Blacks were in and are still in. Tupac's message was one of hope, salvation, healing, and freedom. This is a central issue in Black theology—how much longer must we live in this hell?

One of Tupac's tattoos was Exodus 18:11 which was symbolically tattooed on his back. It reads, "I know now that the LORD is greater than all other gods, because his people have escaped from the proud and cruel Egyptians" (NLT). James Cone argues that the Black experience is a source for Black Theology (1997 b: 16-28). This was Tupac's thought as well.

For many Blacks, however, theology comes from a White perspective; a perspective that is not contextualized for the Black experience. This perspective also argues for a "peaceful" and "safe" theology; one that is void of political and social upheaval. This is one of the reasons why White Christians today, have a better time identifying with Martin Luther King rather than Malcolm X. While Dr. King protested and marched, he advocated non-violence and was a self-proclaimed Christian, while Malcolm X advocated justice by any means necessary, including violence at some points. Moreover, Malcolm X was not a Christian and spoke openly about the White image of

Jesus. While Malcolm X did believe and follow in God's word (later in life), he vigorously opposed White theology and advocated for a more contextualized theology for the Black and urban communities. This is where Tupac rooted his theological foundations: a theology contextualized for Blacks and urban people.

### *Sorrow, Misery and God for Tupac*

Sorrow, misery, and hope all go together in Black music (c.f. Cone 1997a, 1997 b, 1991; Floyd 1995; Spencer 1990; Southern 1993) Tupac's music was no different. His lyrics were infused with a distinct and acute awareness of pain, suffering and misery that was derived from his childhood and existed well into his adult hood. Each of these songs demonstrates some type of pain and hurt in Tupac's life:

- So Many Tears
- I Wonder if Heaven Got A Ghetto
- Trading War Stories
- Ballad of A Dead Soulja
- Teardrops and Closed Caskets

Many could connect with this pain and misery. Moreover, Tupac questioned the formal institutions that were supposed to care for him. Churches, the government, and social institutions were all establishments that Tupac challenged to help him and the ghetto.

For Tupac love was a fragile thing. A heart can be broken by a woman the same way it can be broken by difficult situations. Tupac was also able to attest to the hard realties of the dating world. Listening, one can then correspond to that lament and either attest to it or consol with the pain themselves having been through it. Tupac is a masterful craftsman when it comes to placing lyrics and musical scores that match those lyrics. Few artists are this way.

For many rap artists, they hear a rhythm or musical score and match the words to that rhythm and/or musical score. This is not to say that this process is wrong, however, to perform that process within Hip Hop culture the opposite way is the mark of a true rap artist.[6] Tupac was this way. He would write, and then choose the musical score that best matched his lyrics. If the rhythm was not a match for the words, then the song would not be good. Stevie Wonder, Quincy Jones, Marvin Gaye, and Ray Charles were the same as well; producing some of the best songs that ever came out of Black popular culture; songs that not only Blacks could listen and relate to, but also Whites.

Tupac's music connects with many slave narratives and spirituals.[7] All of these songs connect to the pain and misery that many feel within the 'hood. This same pain and misery is dealt with in many ways, but one of the most popular ways to deal with it, is through music. Ray Charles, and artists like him knew this. Women, drugs, sex, money, work, and social misfortunes were all themes that arose from Charles' music. Charles, suffering himself from many years of drug abuse and his struggle with women, knew first hand of the pain one feels being a Black man. Many could relate, making Charles a musical giant, much like Tupac.[8,9]

---

[6] Composers typically attempt to wed words and text with the rhythm and melody in ways that fit well. Further, cultures will vary in their approach to composition styles. Some, most commonly among White musical cultures, begin with melody while others, specifically Black musical cultures, begin with the text and allow the melody to arise out of the words. Musically speaking, either method of bringing the words and music together are viewed as valid. However, within Hip Hop culture, the mark of a true M.C. is that they begin with the text and then find a matching rhythm that fits the text.

[7] See Appendix E for a brief view of Tupac's connection to slave music.

[8] Several other themes arise in the music of BPC and Tupac that, for project length reasons, I am not able to illustrate more in depth here. For example, the issue of death, fornication, adultery, sexuality, and male female relationships are all areas that BPC deals with on a daily basis. These themes are seen clearly within all of the music I researched. Terms like baby, bitch, ho, slut, chicken head, baby-mama's, and freak are just some of the terms used to name women. For men, there are much fewer. This posed a double standard that is another subject, not covered in the scope of this study; still, Black popular culture is not without its issues and problems.

[9] Great resources for connecting slave narrative to contemporary Black popular culture and Tupac is (Floyd 1995, Odum and Johnson 1968; Fisher 1969; and Cone 1991).

Out of suffering and sorrow in the ghetto, Tupac felt the freedom to question God. Through his music he asks if God was just another cop waiting to give him a beating.[10] Tupac continually asked God the life long human question "Why?" Tupac wanted to know why there was so much hate, brokenness, murder, death, misery, pain, suffering, and despair in the ghetto and in the world, much like Cone (1997 b) discusses how we as Christians have a deity figure that Himself was broken, hated, spat on, and murdered and who Himself asked if the brutality of the cross could be passed onto someone else. Tupac was able to identify with Jesus in His suffering, pain, and sorrow. Tupac continued to ask the questions, to gain a deeper understanding of who God really was, and what His purpose was for Tupac's life. This was seen through his music and poetry.

### *Summary*

In this chapter, I have discussed the various areas of theology for Tupac. This chapter focused on gaining an understanding into why Tupac could have asked the question: Is there a Heaven for a G? Tupac's discussion of the Black Jesus was a Jesus that could identify and connect with a downtrodden society.

More importantly, the Black Jesus is a Jesus that is new, both literally and figuratively. The Black Jesus, for Tupac, could connect with the pain, sorrow, and misery of thugs, the poor, the 'hood, the marginalized, and the person who has lost all hope.

Tupac wanted to connect with these people and bring them hope. In the next chapter, I will focus on Tupac's theological and missiological message and how we can learn from it and thereby develop new evangelistic structures to reach the Hip Hop

---

[10] "Blasphemy" in *Makaveli - The Don Killuminati: The 7 Day Theory (1997).*

generation. The next chapters will give both insight and depth to Tupac's missiological and theological message.

## CHAPTER 11

## THE GOSPEL OF CHRIST ACCORDING TO TUPAC:
## REVERSING THE HERMENEUTIC WITH TUPAC

As we enter the 21$^{st}$ century, there are many hopes and desires that this century will bring about a new and better society. For Christians, those hopes are often that the United States will return back to the "good ol' days" and that our moral state will return—whatever that means. Still, there has been a lot of good forward progress within the last thirty years in America in terms of society and religion. Blacks are considered "human" and can be "saved" as Christians in God's kingdom. Women are allowed to vote. Blacks can vote. We have terror alerts to make us aware of the threat on our country and make us feel "safe."

Still, with all of these magnificent advances, there remain many deficits in our society today, particularly in the 'hood. The 'hood still has not received the aide and help it truly deserves and needs. Moreover, the urban church has not made many significant advances in the realm of "missions" toward Hip Hop youth and their culture. Many of those churches remain vastly ignorant of the issues, concerns, beliefs, and values of Hip Hop youth and their culture. What compounds this even further is the problem of tradition which runs so deep it paralyzes many into not being able to see anything other than what has "always been done."

However, what I see as the most significant issue as we look towards evangelism toward Hip Hop youth is the generational divide that exists between the Hip Hop generation and the Civil Rights Generation. This divide causes many conflicts, communication problems, misunderstandings, and theological variances. The outcome is a generation of young people that not only distrust the church, but despise the older generation; this feeling is reflected back to the younger generation from the older, and the Hip Hop generation is blamed for many of society's ailments. This cycle, manifests itself in the church as well.

That being said, Tupac had a Gospel message of sorts for his fans, community, and society. Tupac embodied both the sacred and the profane of this world. This world is just that; both sacred and profane. In fact, we ourselves embody much of the sacred and profane—much to our disapproval. In Romans 3:23, we are told that all are sinners and have trespassed on God's law. Tupac owned up to this. He was open about it. I would argue that one of the reasons why people have so much trouble with him is the fact that those people are more like Tupac than they would like to admit.

With that in mind, we begin with Tupac's "good-news" about life, the 'hood, and for people. Tupac is an indirect missiologist.[1] Jamal Joseph (2006) notes that Tupac had a huge heart for people to understand a better way of living, know positive role models, and to be critical thinkers (60-61).

What follows here is a reversal of the hermeneutic using Tupac to interpret the Bible and the message of Christ's Gospel as seen through the eyes of Tupac. This, I argue, is imperative for the church to begin missions to Hip Hop youth.

### *Hold On: Matthew 11:27-30*

If there was ever a message that was needed in the 'hood, it is the message to hold on. Far too many times I have seen young people, particularly Black males, loose their grip on hope and dreams and turn to pessimism, despair, cynicism, and doubt of the

---

[1] While Tupac was not a trained "Missiologist" in the orthodox sense, Tupac's heart was to reach out to those who society has given up on. Tupac was also concerned with educating people in the ways of Jesus which connected him to The Great Commission in Matthew 28:16-20.

future (Iverem 1997). The Gospel of Matthew[2] recounts Jesus telling His disciples and the crowds, to come unto Him when they were broken, poor spirited, dismayed, and marginalized.

The "hold on" message from Tupac was to encourage those who have given up or were about to give up. Within this message, Tupac encourages his listeners to see that there is hope for a brighter tomorrow:

> God
> When I was alone, and had nothing
> I asked for a friend to help me bear the pain
> No one came, except God
> When I needed a breath to rise, from my sleep
> No one could help me... except God
> When all I saw was sadness, and I needed answers
> No one heard me, except God
> So when I'm asked...who I give my unconditional love to?
> I look for no other name, except God (Shakur 1999)

Here in the poem, entitled "God," Tupac lets the reader know that God does help, care, and love His people. Tupac tells you that God comes when we call on Him and comes when no one else is there.

For Tupac, there is a sense of optimism in the midst of extreme pain, hurt, despair, and violence. Still, Tupac continually calls the person to a higher plain; as Jesus would also do. It is in this higher level of understanding God that we will find a deeper connection to God and His plan for our lives.

This "hold-on" message, however, was contrasted with the constant reality that the streets and 'hood context were present. For Tupac, there was the everlasting knowledge that this earth was not the final resting place, and that things were, as he put it,

---

[2] Matthew 11:27-30: 27 All things have been handed over to me by my Father, and no one knows the Son except the Father, and no one knows the Father except the Son and anyone to whom the Son chooses to reveal him. 28 Come to me, all who labor and are heavy laden, and I will give you rest. 29 Take my yoke upon you, and learn from me, for I am gentle and lowly in heart, and you will find rest for your souls. 30 For my yoke is easy, and my burden is light."

fucked up! Still within all of the despair, Tupac encouraged you to look for deeper signs of God and peace here on earth. For Tupac, there were too many signs of God in the world not to hold on for something deeper. Signs such as a mother's love for her children, the miracle of birth, a sunset, natural beauty in clouds, and the simple fact that Tupac knew he was put here on this earth to do something more than just take up space.

This ideology connected with a concept that Rudolf Otto calls "The Mysterium Tremendum" (1925: 12-24). For Otto, this meant the mysteriousness of what God did in spite of an appalling situation. For Otto, this meant that, "A God comprehended is no God" (1925: 25). In other words, holding on, does not always mean it will make sense or will even "feel right." This was an area for Tupac that helped him deal with the bigger picture of sin and the brokenness of humankind.

Holding on, for Tupac, meant that he could live with a little ambiguity and that God would come, even if it meant He would come when Tupac was dead. This was a hard concept to comprehend, but, holding on and taking our "burdens" to a figure we have never physically felt or seen could also be construed as incomprehensible.

### *Keep Ya Head Up: Matthew 28:20*

Tupac wanted his fans to know that the ideology of "keeping ya head up" was not done in vain. In the face of extreme opposition and hurt, there was still a way to move forward, even when things seemed as though they could not get any better, Tupac would tell his fans that there was a better way. And life did not end on the experience of the event; in other words, one's errors and successes were not necessarily their defining moment (c.f. Cone 1997 b; Kain and Abel 1996).

Keeping your head up was to encourage the masses to know that God still cares. Further it is a message that God is still with you, even when you do not feel Him with you. This connects to the latter part of Matthew 28:20, "And be sure of this: I am with you always, even to the end of the age" (New Living Translation). Tupac let you know that, even though you might be being beat down, God was still there for you. Moreover, there was a bigger plan at work.

This was one of the reasons why Tupac was so calm, almost at peace, with the knowledge of his imminent death (Joseph 2006). Tupac was fully aware that life did not end here. Even though he did not have it easy here and his situation was nefarious, there was a better place in Heaven set for him.

What the urban church must realize is that there are, more important issues than saggin pants, thongs, spaghetti straps, and "foul" language. You see, these are merely symptoms of a larger problem that exist in the inner city. Tupac constantly tried to tell you about that "problem." Keeping your head up during this process of educating the rest of the masses was merely encouragement as the "fight" does get hard.

Moreover, Tupac attempted to bring a pragmatic type of hope for the 'hood. Instead of the traditional hymns that are out of date and irrelevant for this culture, Tupac replaced them with the Thug Life mantra and his message of encouragement in hard times.

For some in the urban church, like T.D. Jakes, they feel as though someone like a Tupac gets mistaken for a messiah in a generation that had lost their way and desperately needs "direction" beyond lyrics that excite them. This is the typical viewpoint of those from the Civil Rights generation. On the extreme side of that view point you have people who would actually say that if the word "Jesus" is not in the song, lyric, or prayer it is not from God. But who determines what *is* from God and what is not from God?

Regarding the authority of what is from God and what is not, Dyson (2001) writes:

> Yet countless sacred narratives are hardly distinguishable from contemporary rap by this standard. The prophet Jeremiah belched despair from the belly of his relentless pessimism. And the Psalms are full of

> midnight and bad cheer. This is not to argue that the contrasting moral frameworks of rap and religion do not color our interpretation of their often-opposing creeds. But we must not forget that unpopular and unacceptable views are sometimes later regarded as prophetic. It is a central moral contention of Christianity that God may be disguised in the clothing—and maybe even the rap—of society's most despised members (208-209).

For Tupac, keeping your head up, while as "great" and "uplifting" as it may sound, did not resonate well with traditional Christians. However, resounded greatly with the Hip Hop generation and continues to touch people today.

The church must begin to look outside of its confined view of what a Christian looks like. Lest we forget, Jesus Himself was considered a heretic, a blasphemer, and a profane individual for his views on spiritual matters (e.g. Miles 2001). Jack Miles (2001) gives an excellent treaty of Jesus as a blasphemer in his context and time period. Miles argues that Jesus flagrantly violates the Sabbath (145-147), he refuses to condemn an adulteress (152-159), and gives new commandments such as kindness to strangers (178-184). Miles argues that, in the context, Jesus was a problem and a theological paradox; something to consider as we look at emerging prophets, like Tupac, today.

Nevertheless, Tupac sounds out, that in times of trouble, God is with you, so keep your head up. Even the words in that phrase, "head up" is meant to persuade one to look unto the Heavens in which our help comes from.

### *Heaven's Got a Ghetto: John 3:16-17*

John 3:16-17 is a paradoxical passage in the Bible. It is paradoxical because it presents a God that actually wants everyone in Heaven and not just those types of people that look, act, smell, and talk good. This goes against some theological views that contend only a certain type of person can enter in God's Kingdom and that everyone has to be a Christian in order to be "saved." This passage presents a hope that God cares and wants to save all. For Christians and other religious traditions, there is a hard time believing that God actually came and died for a person like Hitler to be saved. Further, in a post 9/11 world, do we really believe, here in the United States, that a person like Osama Bin Laden can be saved if he were to accept Christ? Do we even want him in the same "heaven" with us?

These are spiritual conundrums that echo vagueness and ambiguity of who God is. For Tupac, he could no longer sit by and accept a traditional view of Jesus nor Christianity. Tupac needed a stronger theology than that. Further, he needed a Christ who could accept the thug and the marginalized person. This was the outcry in songs like "I Wonder if Heaven Got A Ghetto?" and "Black Jesuz." These were expressions of a deeper search for God and spirituality. These were also fundamental questions of who God really is; questions that many of us ask ourselves are we really "saved?"

Tupac's answer to his own question, "Does Heaven got a ghetto?" is yes! But, not in the literal sense Tupac never said that there is poverty, crime, gentrification, and homelessness in God's Kingdom. The term is used figuratively as if to ask, in a different manner, "Is the Gospel big enough to fit everyone who wants to fit in, and can God handle me if He really created me?" Tupac resoundingly said yes.

He encouraged his audience, as a pastor would their flock, to see that there was a different image of Heaven and that there was room for those "other" types of people. Those "others" for Tupac consisted of: The Lost, The Marginalized, The Thug and The Nigga.

The Lost: Those who have been searching for meaning, identity, and community but have found it elsewhere (i.e. gangs, prostituting, pimping). Snoop Dogg once said, "Tupac attracted the lost souls and the lost to him. It was as if he were a magnet for the lost" (Lazin 2003). Tupac wanted these types of people to find community and to be fulfilled through Christ. This was one of the reasons that his home was like a refuge for these types of people.

The Marginalized: This is the type of person that has been set aside by society. The homeless person, the displaced family, the wounded soul, and the single parent are all types of people that society in general has decided to just "throw away" (Kirkland et al. 2004). Tupac wanted these types of people to know that someone had not put them aside, and that someone who had money and fame, cared.

The Thug: The straight up street hustler, pimp, gang member, 'hood person. This person is just trying to survive and has embraced a sort of ruthless capitalistic approach to that survival. This person is feared by many, and in many churches, the only response they have is to completely change this person and not allow any remnant, good or bad, to remain from their former life. Tupac, while not advocating violence and crime, simply said, "I can't tell no one how to live if I ain't feedin em. I mean, I think gangs can be positive, if they are just organized" (Peters 2001). For Tupac, this was the type of person that needed the most help because society and the church combined could not comprehend the complexity of this lifestyle. In Tupac's opinion, Jesus had a large place for this type of person.

The Nigga: The person who is a blue-collar, simple minded, hard working individual who does not take any bullshit from anyone. Tupac was raised in this type of environment. This is one of the reasons his work ethic was so high. Tupac was about the working class. He knew that much of his base was from the working class—racial identities aside. In other words, Blacks, Whites, Latinos, Asians, and Africans could all be classified under this term. Tupac let them know that there was a safe spot for them in Heaven.

Heaven has a place for all of these types of individuals who live in the 'hood. Tupac was like a theological "middle man" of sorts. He relayed what he interpreted as the Gospel, and in turn gave it back to the people for them to better understand. To look at it another way was to call Tupac, what Dyson calls, a "Natural Theologian."[3] The street theologian is someone that sees God, life, society, religion, the church, and the Gospel from a street perspective. This person, like Tupac, is able to relate to people in an untraditional unorthodox way. These methods could be construed as blasphemous and heretical, but, one person's blasphemer is another person's saint (Dyson 2001:210-215). In other words, it is incarnating the Gospel—Jesus modeled this and Tupac pointed people of the 'hood to see Jesus as the Christ (Kraft 1992; Shaw and Van Engen 2003).

Tupac's "natural" theology can be seen in Figure 19. In Figure 19 Tupac represents the center cross. With his interpretation in the word of God, he is able to connect larger, broader, more difficult theological concerns to the different types of people in the 'hood. Within all of this, there is sin, and the swaggering lines represent the fact that we, as fallen humans, do not always get "it" right. God, using anything[4] He can to reach us, used Tupac to help the lost, the thug, the marginalized, and the nigga to see God better and ultimately, be saved in His kingdom. Kraft asserts, "Effective communicators learn to fit code to message in such a way that they guide receptors to interpret the main message plus the paramessages to square with their intent" (1991: 113). Tupac, as an effective communicator, learned to theologically code the word of God, so that others were able to interpret that message, thereby allowing them to grow in Christ.

---

[3] Michael Eric Dyson referred to Tupac as a natural theologian in the DVD *Tupac Vs.* (Peters 2001).

[4] To better understand this concept of a God that transforms culture, we must first believe that God loves and cares for everything He created. God uses everyday people and everyday items to catch our attention. Richard Niebuhr (1951) argues that in order for us to truly experience God, we must begin to loosen our constraints on a God that is totally against culture and a God that has nothing to do with culture and society (190-196). This is my understanding of God and how He used Tupac to spread his word, even with all of Tupac's faults, sins, and shortcomings.

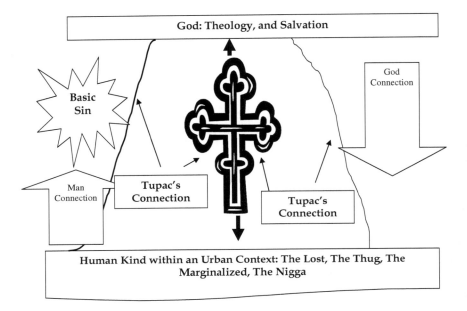

**FIGURE 19**

**TUPAC'S GREATER CONNECTION IN THEOLOGY**

### *The Paradox of the Sacred in the Profane*

Tupac was not perfect. He was not Jesus incarnate either. Nor was he the "perfect" role model for everyone. Tupac's life was altered between his outlaw era and ghetto saint era. Before he left for prison, he told Jada Pinkett Smith that he wanted to quit thuggin and give up on the rap thing and solely do acting (Dyson 2001: 215-216).

However, Tupac ended up embodying the same Black male image he had fought against for so long: the cyclical prison inmate. Tupac struggled in his time at Death Row Records. He was conflicted with past demons and a lifestyle that he himself knew would catch up with him.

It is within that conflict that this paradox between the sacred and the profane arises. Tupac embodied both sin and deity in him. If we truly believe that we are all shaped and formed in sin, that all have sinned and fallen short of the Glory of God, and that we are born again through Jesus the Christ, then we ourselves are living this paradox as well.

When the good and the bad collide in a super nova of ideologies, worldviews, and pedagogies, we have the paradox of the sacred within the profane. Tupac embodied this. One of the questions I get asked most often when speaking is, "How can you study someone like a Tupac and find anything good in him?" Now, part of this is just ignorance by the person asking. The other part of this is the struggle represented in each of us in relation to the Gospel of Christ. And that struggle is how we contend with sin and our own holiness in an everyday world.

Tupac shot straight with you and told you where he was coming from. Another one of Tupac's big "sins" was that he was transparent and open about his own "mess." This bothers a lot of people. Especially those who live a facade and try to fake a lifestyle they think people want to see. For example, before it made the news, Tupac was challenging Jessie Jackson on his extramarital affairs (Shakur 2003). Tupac gave you all of his "crap" and asked that you deal with it. People who like living the fake life despised that quality about him.

Within this paradox, there is both good and evil, sin and salvation, dirt and cleanliness. This is the human struggle. Jesus knew this, God knew this, and so did the writers of our Canon. We all struggle with the human nature to sin and do what is wrong.

Tupac, in this sense, was no different than Paul. What Tupac knew to do right, he did not do because the flesh was weak (Romans 7:7-24). Still, within that weakness, Christ is made strong and His love and grace for us is shown through our own faults. In other words, when we "mess up," it is by Jesus' grace alone that we are not smitten down and burned to a crisp.

Once again, Tupac gave you this and let people know that he was not the way, he was only pointing the way to the one most high: Jesus.[5] Tupac's account of Christ's Gospel is to say that:

- God desires a relationship with all types of people in the 'hood.
- The message of hope and salvation that people traditionally receive is not a "one size fits all," there are many different areas to that and God is open to different paths that leads to Him.
- To grow means to fail, and to fail means to grow. That in mind, we all embody both a sinful and a holy side (i.e. the paradox of the sacred in the profane)

### *Summary*

In this chapter I have covered Tupac's Gospel message for the 'hood. I have demonstrated how that message has played out for the people that loved Tupac. Tupac had a message to hold on that connected to Matthew 11:27-30. This passage tells us that we should bring our problems and burdens to Christ. Tupac encouraged his people to do just that.

The message to keep your head up in times of darkness and despair connects us with one of the last things that Jesus said to His disciples when leaving this earth in

---

[5] This connects back to John in his Gospel account in 1:19-32, where he denies that he is the One and that the one who comes after him is Jesus who gives life eternally.

Matthew 28:20. Jesus said, He is always with us. Tupac pointed people towards that, and made them aware of a greater power in Jesus when things are bad.

Tupac also let people know that there was a Heaven for people from the 'hood. The lost, the marginalized, the thug, and the nigga all had a place in God's Kingdom and could sit at the right hand of God. Tupac worked as a mediator who always pointed people to Christ, for God, to bring a Gospel message to people in order that they might see God in a different light.

Lastly, the paradox of the sacred in the profane exists in all of us and Tupac let us know that. We are all shaped in sin yet are saved by the Blood of Christ. Still, life occurs and we all need help from Jesus in order to continually see His redeeming power.

The next chapter provides insight in using Tupac as an evangelistic tool in reaching Hip Hop youth. I will be discussing new theoretical constructs for reaching Hip Hop youth in a postmodern pedagogy. Further, the next chapter will deal with Tupac's own evangelistic methods as well. This will set up the ending chapter which will focus on recommendations for the urban church for to reaching this new generation.

## CHAPTER 12

## BLASPHEMY:

## TUPAC AS A PRE-EVANGELIST

Tupac was not a trained theologian, pastor, or evangelist. However, having a formal degree and training never qualified anyone from doing "God's work." Still, Tupac never really came to any solid conclusions about a theology of the 'hood. He began the discussion, but because of his early death, never finished the mantra of a ghetto Gospel. What follows here is a conversation about using Tupac as a pre-evangelist to begin the conversation about who Jesus is to an individual's life. Tupac did that for many, but he was not the "finish" line for people's walk with Jesus; he was the concrete foundation of the step that begins the journey with Christ.

Within a postmodern culture emerges a new kind of prophet— a prophet that is able to engage culture, deal with conflict, create connective narrative, generate community, dispel the traditional powers, and call people to a higher level. Tupac fulfills that prophetic role.[1] He provides a new theological mainframe that follows Herbert Edwards (1975)[2] tenants of establishing a new theological foundation.[3]

---

[1] Even though no young people were interviewed for this project, all 25 of the youth that I interviewed for my M.A. research told me that Tupac was their "pastor" and connection to theology. They told me that Tupac was a prophet because of the way he could interpret theological matters and make it "clear" for them (Hodge 2003).

[2] Edwards (1975), while discussing Black Theology, argues that in order for theologies to have a concrete basis they must, 1) prove the inadequacy of the last, 2) establish and prove its own adequacy for the present, and 3) must establish continuity with the primordial, normative expressions of the faith (46-47).

Tupac's message and theology proves the inadequacy of the previous and existing theologies for the present Crisis. Tupac never once questioned, called out, blasphemed, or cursed the name of the Lord. Not once did he refer to Jesus in a negative or blasphemous way. However, Tupac did call out the church, traditional forms of religion, irrelevant orthodox methods, and current methods of evangelism. Tupac challenges youth workers, pastors, and church officials in their morals, ethics, values, and theological understanding. Moreover, Tupac argued that the current Christian theological mantra was not working and needed major changes in order to reach a new generation—and this was over a decade ago, imagine what he would say now!

Tupac's message and theology establishes and proves its adequacy for the present crisis: Tupac set up the mantra of Thug Life, this mantra was not about robbing, violence, or street life, but more about connection to the people who the church has deemed "sinners." Tupac called out the old theologies of the modern[4] church, and replaced the former with the Thug Life, Black Jesuz, and his own Gospel message. Tupac critically challenged the traditional fibers of theology while giving solid solutions for 'hood matters. Tupac also raised such questions as:[5]

- Why is the pastor the only one who can know and talk to God?
- Where is the older generation when we need their help?
- Why does the pastor have to preach these heaven and hell sermons to scare young people into following God?
- Where is He or She at when we need a Jesuz we can pray to,?

---

[3] The best theology is done in community; Tupac did have a small community that surrounded him who encouraged him. This crowd included Jada Pinkett-Smith and his mother, Afeni.

[4] By this term I mean the literal definition of the modern in a postmodern modern sense. The period that occupied the years between 1700 and 1960 (Lash 1990).

[5] These questions are derived from Tupac's inner struggle when he personally raised these theological questions at different points in his life.

Tupac's theological view establishes its continuity with normative expressions of faith. Tupac was not preaching a "new God" or saying that Jesus was not the Christ. In fact, quite the opposite was happening with Tupac's theological view. Tupac was merely establishing a new theology for the 'hood, Hip Hop youth, and for those people that are considered to be marginal and "outside" the church's view of salvation. Tupac wanted these types of people to have salvation too. But, the traditional means of obtaining that "salvation" were blocked by Christians who could not see a different way to the Cross—this continues today. Tupac, if he had lived, wanted to establish not only a Hip Hop political party, but a "church" community for the 'hood; a church that was contextualized for the inner city and with leaders who came from the community, but more importantly, also understood that the "old-way" was not working and that there needed to be a change.

With this framework, we now enter the discussion of using Tupac as an evangelist and an urban prophet for reaching Hip Hop youth and urban youth as well. These next sub sections deal with what that might look like while using Tupac as an evangelist in an urban Hip Hop setting.

### *Tupac Explaining Culture*

Tupac had a vast understanding of culture in general, especially regarding the inner city. No doubt he was an authority on this culture because of his upbringing. Further, Tupac could see and interpret things using a different lens than other people. Tupac saw life in a different way, and in each era of his life there were different interpretations of life.

Tupac had a passion for life in general. For example, he loved being out with people and engaging with them on their level. One of the many reasons that Tupac was so famous was the mere fact that he "hung-out" with normal people without all the cameras and security guards. Friends recount him going to clubs and just walking in to "kick-it" without the entire glamour and "Hollywood" image surrounding him. To put it another way, he was transparent and open with the people around him.

Tupac made it a point to help people feel at ease when near him,[6] to feel connected to him and to the context in general, and to see the potential within their own life. Should the church not also do the same? Should the church not be a beacon of light helping to explain culture? Should the church community not be transparent with each other and be open with the people they serve?

What happens far too often is that the church community gets "caught-up" with rules, by-laws, tradition, and the acute fear that somehow culture will over take Christ, and we must be wary of it. In order to properly engage with culture, using Tupac as a model, we must begin to look at three major areas of engaging culture.[7]

First, we must begin with a *dialogue* of culture that engrosses all of culture, not just the nice and neat areas. In dialogue we are able to learn more about each other and ask the hard questions of each other. In dialogue we are able to move beyond the basics and into the deep levels of culture where we find that not all that we think is "bad" and "evil" is really neither bad nor evil.

In fact, there are many aspects of culture that help explain Christ (Detweiler and Taylor 2003; Krietzer 1994). This is where we reverse the hermeneutical flow and use culture to interpret the Bible. In his music and poetry, Tupac gives us a new understanding of culture and how to engage it on a spiritual level. Tupac guides his listeners on a new understanding of the sinners and Lords prayer in the song *So Many Tears* (See Appendix H for the entire song). From this song we are able to better

---

[6] While Tupac was not connected to a single Christian faith community, he was a part of a spiritual network that encouraged him and kept him sane during times of trouble. This network included his mother Afeni, Dr. Mutulu Shakur, Snoop Dogg, and Jada Pinkett Smith.

[7] These concepts are derived from Richard Niebuhr's (1951) five views of Christ and culture: 1) Christ against culture, 2) the Christ of culture, 3) Christ above culture, 4) Christ and culture in paradox, and 5) Christ the transformer of culture.

understand God on an entirely different level; at a level that a conventional church cannot begin to understand simply because most, who view theology simplistically, will have a difficult time engaging culture (Niebuhr 1951).

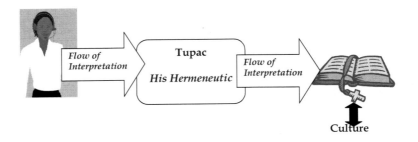

**FIGURE 20**

**REVERSING THE HERMENEUTIC USING TUPAC**

In Figure 20 the illustration uses Tupac to interpret scripture and thereby interprets culture. Tupac, at a basic evangelistic level, can provide basic interpretations of who God is and how God can redeem life. Moreover, with his appeal and transparency, Tupac is able to connect with a new generation that would otherwise not be interested in the Bible or in critically looking at culture from a theological standpoint. Figure 20 illustrates how Tupac can help to interpret culture and its surrounding context for Hip Hop youth

It is within this reversal that a deeper dialogue is formed with God, human kind, our fellow peers, culture, creation, and newcomers to the faith.

Second, if we are able to make it, we move into *appropriation*, or better put, a worldview of Christ above and within culture; Christ as the transformer of culture. Here, in appropriation, we can use Tupac as a model demonstrating how Jesus can transform a person's life.

No one is really saying that Tupac was perfect or without fault. In fact, quite the contrary. All of his family, close friends and most fans would admit that Tupac had some serious issues that he was dealing with since childhood. I would agree and add that Tupac was a kind-hearted person who really did not want to be caught up in the fame and popularity he had. In spite of his shortcomings, Jesus can use someone as broken as Tupac to proclaim His message and thereby expand His kingdom. That gives hope for someone on the street.

Appropriation moves beyond the "talk" of it all into the "real deal," in which people are transformed. Let us "keep it real." The only "Christ" that new believers see is the "Christ" they see in us at first. When people are coming to know Jesus, their main reference point is the person walking with them. Tupac is that example.

Now, one may add that he was killed and that there was not really any physical example of Jesus redeeming Tupac. However, who are we to really judge the situation in those last moments of Tupac's life? Moreover, Tupac's music has been used for good and many more have come closer to God as a result of both his life and his music.

In this area of appropriation, we are able to see a Jesus figure that deals with the profane and the sacred, the good and the evil of culture, and transform it all for His good. After all, do not all things work together for the good of the Kingdom?[8]

Third, is the area of *divine encounter*. In this area Jesus comes into culture and not only transforms it, but also breathes new life into it. Tupac dreamed of a time like this. For Tupac, his divine encounter came when he was making music, dialoging with God, and realizing that He was doing the same with him (Kraft 1979: 345-353).

---

[8] Romans 11:35-36

To be even clearer, divine encounter means that something within culture causes you to have a deep revelation of who Jesus is. That encounter can come in many different forms. For Tupac, music was the means. But how great would it be if we could encourage Hip Hop youth to discover God in the arts, rap music, films, and even the "bad" things in life. Divine encounter is the highest level you can experience. In divine encounter you are able to see God and His divine love, mercy, judgment, and salvation in a totally different light. It is within this area that we begin to see that there are deeper questions to life, therefore even more complex answers or lack of answers.

### *Nit Grit 'Hood Theology*

This is my rendition of Anthony Pinn's "Nitty Gritty Hermeneutics" (1995: 113-138). What differs is a more intense focus on the 'hood and Hip Hop youth.

Tupac raises deep questions about life, death, sin, and grace. What Tupac does not do, is give many simplistic answers to complex situations. Tupac is not trying to tell his audience that life is easy and that all we have to do is go to church. For Tupac, there is something much deeper and more complex to life. This is where nit Grit 'hood theology enters.

Answers are not the single most important issue within nit grit 'hood theology and neither are simplistic explanations. Simplistic answers like, "God wanted it this way," are not tolerated nor should they be. Nit grit 'hood theology gets at the real issues that no one really wants to discuss. For example, the issue of gay marriages is an open topic. Healthy explorations of scriptures are examined during this dialogue. Nit grit gets at the details of what is going on. Nit grit does not stand for the traditional answers that say the devil is behind every bush so you had better beware.

Nit grit 'hood theology encourages personal responsibility, because sometimes the devil is not to blame, and really *we* are the true culprit. Tupac would challenge pastors and theologians to think deeper about issues such as poverty, social justice, and suffering. In three DVD interviews,[9] Tupac is seen challenging the older generation to act as opposed to just "preach" and talk more at young people. Tupac is seen asking for deep help from institutions like churches. Moreover, Tupac does not always accept that the simple answer is the only answer.[10]

If God really knows all our needs, why are we still asking Him to "bless" us with a new home, car, boat, cat, or dog when we know that there is someone who has none of that? More importantly, if we are using the model of prayer laid out for us in the Gospels, where do we find that individualism is more holy? Tupac posed this question and was shunned as a heretic and blasphemer. Most Christians are not ready to face the fact that God cannot be explained in three sessions. In addition, many Christian churches are not ready to deal with complex issues that require more attention than just traditional "prayer" such as racism? Yet, Tupac went there.

If we are going to evangelize in the 21$^{st}$ century, then we must be ready to deal with a postmodern, Bling-Bling, I-Pod generation that will not take "let's just pray about it" for a final answer; we may be able to begin there, but we sure as hell cannot end there![11]

Nit grit 'hood theology engages this generation and pushes for deeper answers and solutions to complex issues. Nit grit 'hood theology is able to deal with ambiguity

---

[9] *Tupac Vs* (2001), *Thug Angel* (2002), *Tupac Resurrection* (2003).

[10] This raises the issue of prayer. Does prayer really work? Or, to put it another way, are we spiritually lazy sometimes and just say, "Oh, I'll just pray about that," rather than truly acting on an issue such as poverty. While there are countless examples of God answering prayer in and out of the Bible, I would argue that the model of prayer we have today is nothing like the biblical model of prayer. Many of the prayers uttered today are more a reflection of individualistic appeals to God that have nothing to do with reaching out into the community, social injustice, and evil social systems.

[11] This connects with Shaw and Van Engen's assertion that, "Presenters of the Gospel who effectively communicate God's Word in today's world…are involved in the flowing development of truth through time and space" (2003: 196). To effectively communicate the Gospel message, we must, as young people state, "Go there!"

and the unknown because it knows that God is still in control. Nit grit 'hood theology engages in tough dialogues and is ready to deal with the issues head on. The simple "sinners prayer" is out because after that is over, while I may be "saved" and feeling tingly inside, if I live in the 'hood, the reality is that I still need to eat, sleep, love, and live in a place where I can grow in Christ. Most evangelistic programs are over once a person stands up and confesses Christ as their savior.

Nit grit 'hood theology says, we are with you for life; through the good, the relapses, the failures, the successes, the backsliding, and the getting back up. This evangelism is designed for a lifetime and not just a program. Tupac believed in, and he lived it out daily.

Table eleven lists out the key tenets of nit grit 'hood theology. Keep in mind that evangelism is a key component in this framework. The "Mission of God" or, "Missio Dei" is being carried out within Hip Hop culture. Here, I argue that nit grit 'hood theology is central to a new generation of evangelism within and to Hip Hop youth.

Table 11 explores some of the basics of this new way of evangelizing Hip Hop youth. Hip Hop youth are not concerned so much with "the right answer" as much as they are concerned with community and shared life experiences. Tupac was an example of that. Even though he himself struggled with God's ways at times, had issues with sexuality, and "sinned" abundantly, Tupac knew God still cared for him and welcomed him back in His Kingdom at the end of the day, just as the Father did with his prodigal son.

## TABLE 11

## NIT GRIT 'HOOD THEOLOGY KEY PRECEPTS

| **Nit Grit 'Hood Theology** |
|---|
| • Engages in a deeper conversation about God. This conversation is not merely discussion on the personhood of God, but an active conversation about how to actually help people in their need so that they can live life better than their current situation.<br><br>• Is concerned with the person's post salvation experience. In other words, the real excitement comes in the daily life of that person not merely "living" for God, but simply "living." Basic life needs are taken care of and the community of God is helping to provide that.<br><br>• Simple answers are not tolerated. Life is complex and therefore many solutions are therein complex as well. The nit grit gets down into the details of events and searches out the truth and evidence to explain issues and events. Nit grit is concerned with helping get at complex issues such as divorce, sex, gay marriage, immigration, and drug abuse—to name a few.<br><br>• Ambiguity is a constant reality. In the search to find answers, a person will inevitably (at times) come up without answers. Moreover, God works in ambiguity and at odd times. When dealing with people, this needs to be emphasized—that at times, things cannot be explained, they just are.<br><br>• Community is a must. Whether it is online or in person, this style of evangelism needs to be performed in community and with others around. This is what the body of Christ is about. |

## Thug Life Theos

Where Tupac left off was fully developing the mantra of Thug Life. It is not clear whether or not Tupac would have completed a full theological scale of sorts with this mantra if he had lived. What is clear, though, is that in order for the 'hood and hard core Hip Hop youth to be reached, the church as a whole must be able to identify with and accept the "shitty" aspect of life that exists in the 'hood and ensuing "shitty" lifestyles of individuals that are engrossed in those living conditions.

Thug Life Theos discusses The Street is a Code of Life: This means that while we all may live by a set moral standard, there is an entirely different set of cultural rules that apply when living on the street. While I am not advocating violence, stealing, and/or immoral behavior, the 'hood evangelist must be ready to live in that element and present a Gospel of Christ, while resisting the urge to force people to change their lifestyle; the Holy Spirit will do that. The code of the street (Anderson 1999), will remain with individuals, moreover, there are certain street principles that can apply to "normal" life. Hustling, watching your back, standing your ground, dealing with O.G.'s, and pimping are all translatable skills that can be used when trying to compete for a job, scholarship, and even a position in the academic academy. The difference is, as opposed to hustling to "cheat" someone out of their money, the person would hustle to stay ahead and be assertive.

Thug Life Theos also argues that Christianity needs a Facelift: The standard Christian approach to salvation, evangelism, and the Bible are not valid approaches in the 'hood. As stated in the last bullet point, the rules are different. If Christianity is to be the religion that helps people see Jesus better, then salvation, Bible study, evangelism, and "coming to Christ" are going to need some changing. What I mean is that coming to church does not work with Hip Hop youth, the church must go to them, and therefore salvation may happen on a street corner with a bottle of Malt Liquor still in the hands of the individual. Bible study may take place in a strip club to further be a witness to the club itself. Evangelism might evoke the help of a Fiver Percenter or the Nation of Islam; controversial indeed!

Thug Life Theos also understands and sees Jesus as the foremost presentation of good news. Jesus is far too often overlooked, neutered, and dulled by many Christians. What happens in place of Jesus' divine authority & living relationship with us is that we create by-laws, rules, and imposed "moral behavior." Hard core Hip Hop youth need to know that Jesus stirred up a lot of shit in His day and took no shit from anyone. Hard core Hip Hoppers need to know that Jesus got angry and actually whipped people as they disgraced His Father's temple. Hard core Hip Hoppers also need to know that Jesus focused on twelve individuals; He himself did not overwork Himself. Making money, health and wealth Gospel messages, and the prosperity Gospel is not valid to Hip Hop youth; only pure Jesus is relevant.

Thug Life Theos understands that pain, love, sorrow, anger, and joy are entwined. Christianity tends to sell people this story that when you receive Christ every element of life will be solved, taken care of, and "great." What people soon come to realize is that life is not the simple and problems are complex and need complex resolutions. Many times people become frustrated and simply leave the faith. Hard core Hip Hop youth deserve the truth that living a life for Christ is not only difficult, it is impossible without solely relying on not just Jesus but community. Pain will come, and when it does, it is important to let the person know that it is normal and that as Tupac would encourage us to hold our heads up, so does Jesus.

Thug Life Theos wants A Return to Liturgy, Monasticism, and Corporate Prayer. This can be hard to believe from a culture that despises conformity and traditionalism. However, hard core Hip Hoppers attain these principles at Hip Hop concerts, why not bring that element into the 'hood with Jesus at the center. Hard core Hip Hoppers want this type of discipline, and I can personally testify that young Hip Hoppers enjoy "quiet times" and refection. It is a well needed break from the constant noise and movement in their world.

These are the main doctrines of Thug Life Theos. If the urban and multicultural church is to reach hard core Hip Hop youth, then I argue these are imperative in their missional advancements. What follows next is a connection to the narrative of Christ and its importance.

### *The Narrative of Christ*

One of the things that we must begin to understand is that this current generation wants narrative[12] and strives for different forms of narrative in films, music, and friends (Detweiler and Taylor 2003; Miyakawa 2003). This is one of the reasons people are so into narrative, mythic films; they connect with a larger story and bring you, the audience, into that story. Tupac knew this and did this well.

Tupac opened up stories from the Bible and put them into context. For example, Tupac lived out the tattoo scripture on his back (See Appendix D for a pictorial image of Tupac's tattoos), Exodus 18:11. Tupac was about helping free the mind, body, and spirit from oppression no matter what age, sex, or ethnicity you were. Tupac wanted people to know truth. Tupac did not say that he himself was the "savior" but at times did connect himself with biblical figures that struggled like he did in life, society, and theology. Figures such as Moses, Abraham, and David were just some of the Biblical characters that Tupac would connect himself to.

---

[12] The story of life that many postmoderns are in search for. This is why films such as *The Matrix, Harry Potter, and The Lord of the Rings* are so popular; they give people narrative and story. Moreover, they put people right into the story of the bitter struggle between good and evil. This generation seeks narrative and the Gospels are laced with plenty of it. It is our responsibility to help people find their story in Christ.

If we are to move forward in bringing the Gospel to Hip Hop youth, narrative is paramount and necessary for people to understand that there is a larger story that involves them and Jesus The Christ. Within the narrative, people are allowed to journey on the path with Jesus. People are allowed to experiment with different methods in understanding Him. People are also allowed to fail and get back up, as the Proverb tells us: "For a righteous man falls seven times, and rises again…"[13] This type of new path to Christ can be frightening and alarming to many who see Christ one dimensionally.

For many who see religion in terms of being black and white, then Jesus is also that: very clear and simple. This view says, there is definitely clear evil and clear righteousness that exists and the Bible is *our* only guide in life. The problems with a black and white view of life, is that most people live in the gray of life. In other words, evil, righteousness, love, anger, and hate all have blurry boundaries. Tupac's life was not perfect. In fact, his life was a walking contradiction if we are to examine it carefully. But, Jesus still cared for him and loved on him the same way He does with us when we sin.

The gray of life is where Tupac lived. The story of Jesus helped him through that gray. The fact that Jesus himself was a profane prophet in His time and context gave Tupac hope (Miles 2001). Tupac found comfort that Jesus Himself was crucified by his own people. Tupac was able to see how his own life fit into that crucifixion, narratively and metaphorically speaking, and was able to articulate the pain, hurt, and angst that he felt when his community "crucified" him.

God Himself gives us all the power to choose. He is not concerned with power nor control. If He were, then we would all be following Him to begin with, since He could force us to follow Him. Still, many churches have not been able to comprehend this simple concept and feel it is their duty to construct, control, and order how a person comes to Christ and lives the "saintly" life. Tupac destroyed all those parameters and

---

[13] Proverbs 24: 16 NASB.

Christ still used him for good—despite his profane attributes. Jesus Himself is concerned with our own personal ethnolifehistory. He wants to be involved with every major and minor era in our lives. This is the reason why our lives have a variety of seasons.

What we must begin to do is understand that people are people and that no one outside of Jesus is perfect. We never will be perfect until we are given a new body and life from God. Until that time, we are all shaped and formed in sin. And there is a story that Jesus wants to connect us to. What seems to bother most people about Tupac is the fact that they are more like him than they care to admit. To make this even clearer, there is a little Tupac in all of us whether we care to admit it or not. Most of us love, get angry, hurt, care, and have emotions that do not always *seem* "right." Tupac was not just a reflection of his generation, but also a symbolic figure for humankind in that he represented the constant struggle for the Holy in Christ yet still struggling with the profanity of everyday life. Although he did not always get it right, he kept trying.[14]

### *Summary*

In this chapter I have discussed how Tupac's different philosophies can be utilized to draw evangelistic lessons from him. This chapter focused on using Tupac's ideals as a tool for reaching Hip Hop youth and engaging them in their environment and in their context. Tupac presents a new theological understanding using Herbert Edwards' (1975) three components of new theological establishments.

In this Chapter I also discussed how Tupac was able to help interpret culture. Using Tupac, we are able to reverse the hermeneutical flow, and we are able to better interpret scripture and the Bible for use on the streets with Hip Hop youth.

---

[14] It is interested to note that the week prior to Tupac's death; he was witness rededicating his life to Christ at Faithful Central Church in Inglewood, California. It is also interesting to see that a week later he died. Some attribute this fact that God was preparing him and then releasing him from his earthy duty, thereby giving way to his ghetto saint status.

This leads to a nit grit 'hood theology which basically gets at the details of life and sees God in a grander scheme rather than a systemized God done in three classes. Nit grit 'hood theology is also a way of evangelizing Hip Hop youth and presents new tenets for doing just that.

Lastly, this Chapter focused on connecting people, particularly Hip Hop youth, to the story of Christ. Christ is concerned with the whole life and not just one era. Using Tupac as an example, we are able to see the ups and downs along with the failures and achievements.

In the final Chapter I will focus on some concluding remarks. I will also discuss the missiological significance of Tupac Shakur in order to better reach Hip Hop youth.

# CHAPTER 13

## CONCLUSION:

## FINAL THOUGHTS ON OUR GHETTO SAINT

This book has been concerned with one major theme: discovering the missiological significance of Tupac Amaru Shakur. Part one presented an overall view of the study on Tupac. Part two set up the context in which Tupac lived and operated. This gave me an appreciation for Tupac's ideology and helped me better understand his identity and purpose. Part three was concerned with Tupac's ethnolifehistory. From there we were able to grasp the five eras within his life. The findings within part three suggest that Tupac's life was complex, filled with hurt and confusion, hope, love and care, as well as theology. Part four focused on the hermeneutical aspects of Tupac's life. These theological frameworks were derived from the findings in part three and suggested that in order to truly engage Hip Hop youth, there must be fundamental changes in the church's approach to evangelism, theology, engaging culture, and understanding 'hood culture in general. On the basis of the findings from this research, I now recommend several significant missiological imperatives that may challenge the urban and multicultural church to move in the direction of missional engagement with Hip Hop youth.

This research project utilizes my understanding of Tupac's lyrical messages, as interpreted from the data, and now presents a basic evangelistic tenet for the urban and multicultural church as a whole to reach Hip Hop youth.

## *Missional Essentials*

I suggest six urgent missiological directions that the urban church needs to address if it is to evangelize Hip Hop youth, deal with the reality of the streets, and address the deep issues of the inner city (Thug Life Theos). These suggestions emerge from the significance and analysis of the data and will enable the church to be missional in the 'hood. These missiological directions are also connected to Tupac's overall missiological message from findings within the research.

## Preparing the Way

The first and fundamental missiological essential is that the urban church must *prepare the way*. David Bosch asserts that missions to the poor and the city were always looked at as missions to the "heathens" and the "evil" (1991: 290-291), and that cities were looked upon with "pity" and "shame.". He discusses how missions to the inner cities have been distorted by guilt, pity, and a sense of shame on the part of the group going there (Bosch 1991: 290). In my tenure as a minister in the inner city, I have seen this to be shockingly true. The role of the church needs to change and the outlook the church holds about culture, and people in general, needs to shift (Bosch 1991: 299).

The church must be the beacon of light that opens up the door initially and re-invites the people back in. For too long the church has been a symbol of distrust, corruption, lies, sexual misconduct, and misappropriating Christ. A solid missional church opens up doors, and helps the people they are working with; not decide for them or act in the place of God for their lives, but allow them to think for themselves.

Further, Wilbert Shenk (1999) states:

When the church lives in conscious response to the reign of God, its life is governed by only one criterion. Indeed, the power of the church's witness depends on the extent to which God's kingdom defines and shapes that witness. When the church attempts to make its ministry relevant by rendering 'respectable' service, it has adopted an alien criterion and it becomes merely mundane (16).

In this perspective, the church has become irrelevant and the message of God is "watered down" so much that the people do not have a clear perspective of God. Part of preparing the way means that we must keep God in the forefront of the message, while remaining contextual, but never sacrificing "program" for true relationships (Shenk 1999: 189).

For a church to open its doors and actually prepare the way, it must begin by engaging culture in all its profanity and sacredness. A church that prepares the way is a leader in innovation and is not conjoined to one idea. They are open to new ideas and new ways of thinking, while not loosing sight of biblical epistemology.

## Announcing Good News

The second missiological essential is *announce good news*. The good news of Jesus Christ: that He loves you no matter what and that He will forgive you is what people need to hear. Moreover, they need to see it more than they need to hear it. Announcing good news, within a postmodern context, is not so much about speaking, as much as it is about living a lifestyle that reflects the good news.

We live in a nation that knows about hell and the brimstone that awaits them; urban churches are great on making sermons that make you feel the very flames of hell. But people do not need to hear that. They need to know more about the loving grace of Jesus. Tupac connected with that grace and acceptance. What the concept of "hell" does is keep people in the pews, and not live out the good news of what Jesus commissioned us to do in Matthew 28 by making disciples. Within the 'hood many people are already living in hell. What they need to hear is that Jesus still cares for them.

## Identify With Sinners

The third missiological essential is being able to *identify with sinners*. The church is typically concerned with appearing good and often loses that connection with the reality that we are all still sinners in process. Everyone makes mistakes, other people need to know about those mistakes, and it needs to be transparent to the people in the community of the church.

Further, we as a Christian body must have friends outside the church family that are not believers. We grow when this happens and we are stretched in different areas when we have friends that do not always think and act the way we do. Jesus knew how to engage and identify with sinners. In John 4, Jesus is seen talking with a Samaritan woman, in the middle of the day, and to a woman known to have had many husbands; all cultural "no-no's" of His day. Still, Jesus engaged and identified with the woman while holding her accountable. In the end, she was used to save many in her village (4:39-42).

## Confronting Social Injustice

The fourth missiological essential is *confront social injustice*. For too long churches everywhere have ignored the problems of the inner city (e.g. Dyson 1996; Dyson 2001; Cox 1965). If we are going to move forward in a positive way, the church must be a leading authority in confronting social injustice within the 'hood. This confrontation should even come at the cost of loosing donors that do not agree with this policy. Jesus continually confronted the injustices of His day and made it a point to help individuals see their own justice issues. This is seen in his dealing with the rich young ruler.[1]

The church will be a place that can confront the problems in the context they are in. The church will be place that deals with problems both inside the church and outside,

---

[1] Mark 10: 17-26.

problems of social justice and social welfare, gender issues, economic matters, and engaging culture. Jesus knew how to do this and was not worried about saving face. John 6:66 record that many disciples that once followed Him left Him because what He had told them was too hard to hear. Jesus, in verse 67, did not miss a beat, turned to the twelve, and asked if they would leave Him too. If we are going to "go" into the city we must be ready for people to hate us, disagree with us, and quite possible try to kill us; but we must stand our ground and confront the opposition.

## Power of the Holy Spirit

The fifth missiological essential is *operate in the power of the Holy Spirit*. This is a simplistic sounding missiological essential, however, far too often churches move out in mission without ever truly listening to the voice of the Holy Spirit. Moreover, the church must be willing to hear that voice in unfamiliar voices—such as Tupac.

One of the most important aspects of living in the hood is knowing when to move on certain issues and when to wait. If we are to move forward in the urban church, then we must be lead by the Holy Sprit and not the "holy ego" we all have inside us. In other words, take a gut check and ask yourself why you are even there in the first place. There will be many temptations in the field and as we move forward, we must be led by the Holy Spirit as we confront those temptations.

## Accepting and Dealing with the Nature of the 'Hood

The sixth and final missiological essential is *adequately accept and deal with the true nature of the 'hood*. Elijah Anderson (1999) argues that the 'hood lives by a different set of rules, or "codes," than the rest of society. These codes are from and about the streets. They are a part of everyday life and they govern the daily life of many. These codes are present in every 'hood. If the church is to be a missionary figure, then understanding, accepting, and then dealing with that code is essential.

When many pastors looks at the city, the first reaction he or she gets is to "change" those "sinners." That has been the reaction of most churches and para-church organizations; barbarically, they enter into neighborhoods and mow down and destroy any cultural artifacts that may exist, because they are forms of the "old-life."

While part of that "old-life" may be true, the fact remains that we cannot control anyone other than ourselves (and even that can be hard). What the inner city church has attempted to do is to clone, and control the "saved" people in their congregation. There is a certain culture that comes with living in a city. We must let people express that culture and express their way of living without imposing our belief system. For example, if a young person is "saved" and still listens to Tupac, then let them. Ask them what the message is that they hear in that music. Probably the most important thing is to *ask* that person what it is they need and want.

There are many issues facing the city and one church cannot solve them all. There must be a networking within that neighborhood. It must be a true networking that does not involve jealousy over numbers that the other ministry or organization possesses. This network means working with organizations outside the Christian realm and not assuming that Christian organizations are the only ones *helping* young people.

Tupac strongly criticized the formal church and Christian that refused to change for a "new day." Tupac's criticism should not be taken lightly and should be heeded as we begin to move forward and reach out to hard core Hip Hop youth.

### *From Street Sainthood to Jesus*

Tupac's message can be taken as a pre-evangelistic conversation that begins on the street, and is then used to enter into a richer conversation that connects the person closer to Christ. Tupac presented many different messages that could be taken in many different ways. Sexuality, death, love, drugs, and life itself are all categories Tupac discussed in his music. However, to help the listener move from that pre-evangelistic conversation to one that is deeper in Christ will require a critical eye and mind.

To begin this process, the urban and multicultural church needs to approach this conversation by taking on what I suggest are four important principles. These principles are a beginning evangelistic tool for the urban and multicultural church:

Engage Culture: This is of paramount importance. If culture—particularly Hip Hop culture—is not understood, dealt with, connected with, and critically engaged then relationships with people are at jeopardy. One of the most essential skills that any Christian must learn is the skill of engaging culture. That means studying it and suspending judgment until the culture has been studied. There are many different elements of culture that are nefarious, ugly, and appalling. However, Jesus went where the people were and dealt with them on their level to bring salt and light to their lives. Zacchaeus was a despised and detested person, but Jesus called to him and broke bread with him because one, He understood the culture of the time in which breaking bread was important, and two He gained a deeper relationship with Zacchaeus by showing him that his sin was no different than everyone else's and that change was needed in his life.

Relationships over Programs: While I am not arguing that programs should be done away with, they are to be secondary and at times, third. In this postmodern world, community and personal touch is a high priority. One of the things that Tupac understood well was that relationships are sacred. Jesus knew this too. Jesus lived, breathed, ate, and worked with twelve individuals that did not really comprehend His message until He was gone; one of which betrayed Him. Still, Jesus "stuck it out" because He understood the power of relationships through rough times and even rougher times. Too many times when people do not live up to a certain mark, by-law, doctrine, or commandment, the church community would treat and view them as a failure, sinner, and heathen. Failure and disappointment is inevitable when dealing with people. But, when there is a true relationship, those let-downs and frustrations are able to be absorbed in the relationship and dealt with; no program can do that.

Get Passed Saggin' Pants and the F Word: Far too many times the "symptoms" of people get dealt with rather than the real problem. There are greater issues in the 'hood that need to be addressed than a young person's pants that are riding below their knees. I would pose the question, "Why are the pants that low?" Style and fashion only reflect the current context and time. Saggin' pants are a type of fashion and the individual wearing them typically has greater needs than someone constantly tell them to pick up their pants. The F word generates much discussion, however, I once again ask a question, "How is the word being used and why is it being used?" When the church can begin with a question rather than immediate judgment and sentencing, the real issue can then be revealed. The real issues lie deep within culture. Below the surface level reside matters in which so many churches get wedged.

Listen to the Story of People: This book project, beyond the formality, has ultimately been concerned with telling a story about a person's life. In order to move from street sainthood and closer to Jesus, the story of individuals in the 'hood are important. It is simple to merely view a person at the physical level and judge them. But, every human in this world was carried for nine months and birthed by a woman; a story comes with each person. While not all stories are neat and end well, Jesus has created each of us and has placed us here on this planet to fulfill His mission which is to, simplistically, call people to His Kingdom. Listening begins with us being able to truly accept and deal with the diverse stories of people.

These are suggestions that are a result of the findings from the data. These are the beginnings of an evangelistic tool for the urban and multicultural church. There is still research that is needed as the church begins to deal with the profane and the multifaceted elements of Hip Hop culture.

## *Concluding Remarks*

Tupac gave his heart in everything he did. Tupac spoke authentically from his heart, oftentimes getting himself into trouble. However, one of the most significant things that Tupac did was bring people together in a way that no church service could. I want to be a part of that. I want to understand that. In addition, more importantly I want the church to be about that. However, to create that, there must be a deeper engagement with culture. There must be a deeper engagement with Hip Hop if we are to really begin to see what it was that drew people towards Tupac.[2]

Tupac was a prophetic voice for many young people in the Black community, suburban community, Asian community, global community, and the 'hood. He not only spoke to Black kids, but he spoke truth to White and rural kids. His legacy of authenticity, a love for Christ, a passion for truth, and a tension between profanity and the sacred left many in awe of his raw talent. Tupac did not settle for anything other than authenticity and the truth. He questioned the very moral fibers of the church. Tupac[3] engaged with the secular in ways that eventuated his lyrics wherein he wrestled with the profanity of inner city living and the sacredness of Jesus and the cross. His death in 1996 made him into a martyr. Dyson writes:

> In Tupac's raps all parties to death, evil, and suffering get a hearing—and lashing—including the crack addict, the welfare mother, the hustler, the thug, the pimp, the playa, the bitch, the ho, the politician, the

---

[2] I personally have spoken with 10 young people between the ages of 16-19, who came to Christ as a result of listening to Tupac.

[3] Tupac's mantra: T.H.U.G. L.I.F.E= The Hate U Give Little-ones Fucks Everyone. N.I.G.G.A= Never Ignorant Getting Goals Accomplished.

rapper, the white supremacists, the innocent child, the defenseless female, the crooked cop, the black sellout. If his love for his people and his God were intertwined with the cruel and self-defeating impulses of the lost, one must remember Tupac's proclamation of 'Black Jesus': 'In times of war we need somebody raw, rally the troops like a Saint that we can trust.' At the end of the song, one of his comrades prays for a Black Jesus who is 'like a Saint that we pray to in the ghetto.' By both rejecting and embracing suffering, Tupac offers a complex prayer that does not merely glorify violence but interrogates its meanings and howls at the pain it wrecks (2001: 230).

Pac gave way to a new breed of Hip Hop artists.[4] Now, we have artists such as Common, The Roots, Mos Def, Eve, and Jill Scott who rap about Jesus walking with the hustler, the pimp, the drug addict, and many others that the urban church has deemed as "evil" and "demonized." These, and many other artists, come to the table and state at the introduction, "I'm not here to argue about his facial features, or to convert atheists into believers, I'm just trying to say the way school needs teachers and the way Kathy Lee needs Regis, y'all need Jesus!"[5] The urban church cannot ignore this outcry for a decentralization of Jesus, and a privatization of the cross, that is regulated only to certain groups of people that "act" the right way.

My vision is that the new church be a church that is open to change and open to new voices in obscure places. My vision is for a church that leads cultural reform and transforms culture so that Jesus is at the center and people are able to see Him. More importantly, those people are able to live by His commandments and connect to the larger story of Christ. I see a church that is connected to its community in a way that promotes strong and healthy relationships with the 'hood environment, and surrounding systems. A "pie in the sky?" I hope not. All I can do is keep my head up!

---

[4] See Appendix G, Figure 21 for Tupac's effect on the Hip Hop cultural continuum.

[5] Kanye West, *Jesus Walks*, High School Dropout: (2004).

# APPENDIX A

# PICTORIAL VIEW OF TUPAC

## APPENDIX B

## T.H.U.G. L.I.F.E. CODE

**"I didn't create T.H.U.G. L.I.F.E., I diagnosed it." – Tupac Shakur.**

In 1992 at the 'Truc Picnic' in Cali, Tupac was instrumental in getting rival members of the Crips and Bloods to sign the Code Of THUG LIFE.

He and Mutulu Shakur had helped write up the 'code', with help from other 'og's'.

The Code of THUG LIFE is listed here. It details do's and don'ts for being a righteous thug and banger.

**Code OF THUG LIFE:**

1. All new Jacks to the game must know: a) He's going to get rich. b) He's going to jail. c) He's going to die.

2. Crew Leaders: You are responsible for legal/financial payment commitments to crew members; your word must be your bond.

3. One crew's rat is every crew's rat. Rats are now like a disease; sooner or later we all get it; and they should too.

4. Crew leader and posse should select a diplomat, and should work ways to settle disputes. In unity, there is strength!

5. Car jacking in our Hood is against the Code.

6. Slinging to children is against the Code.

7. Having children slinging is against the Code.

8. No slinging in schools.

9. Since the rat Nicky Barnes opened his mouth; ratting has become accepted by some. We're not having it.

10. Snitches is outta here.

11. The Boys in Blue don't run nothing; we do. Control the Hood, and make it safe for squares.

12. No slinging to pregnant Sisters. That's baby killing; that's genocide!

13. Know your target, who's the real enemy.

14. Civilians are not a target and should be spared.

15. Harm to children will not be forgiven.

16. Attacking someone's home where their family is known to reside, must be altered or checked.

17. Senseless brutality and rape must stop.

18. Our old folks must not be abused.

19. Respect our Sisters. Respect our Brothers.

20. Sisters in the Life must be respected if they respect themselves.

21. Military disputes concerning business areas within the community must be handled professionally and not on the block.

22. No shooting at parties.

23. Concerts and parties are neutral territories; no shooting!

24. Know the Code; it's for everyone.

25. Be a real ruff neck. Be down with the code of the Thug Life.

26. Protect yourself at all times..

**Some other Interpretations**:

**Thug Life** means - The Hate U Gave Lil' Infants Fucks Everyone.

**NIGGA** means - Never Ignorant Getting Goals Accomplished.

**OUTLAW** stands for 'Operating Under Thug Laws As Warriors'

**MOB** stands for Member Of Bloods and /or Money Over Bitches

# APPENDIX C

# BLACK PANTHER 10 POINT PROGRAM AND PLATFORM

1. WE WANT freedom. We want power to determine the destiny of our Black Community.

WE BELIEVE that black people will not be free until we are able to determine our destiny.

2. WE WANT full employment for our people.

WE BELIEVE that the federal government is responsible and obligated to give every man employment or a guaranteed income. We believe that if the white American businessmen will not give full employment, then the means of production should be taken from the businessmen and placed in the community so that the people of the community can organize and employ all of its people and give a high standard of living.

3. WE WANT an end to the robbery by the CAPITALIST of our Black Community.

WE BELIEVE that this racist government has robbed us and now we are demanding the overdue debt of forty acres and two mules. Forty acres and two mules were promised 100 years ago as restitution for slave labor and mass murder of black people. We will accept the payment in currency, which will be distributed, to our many communities. The Germans are now aiding the Jews in Israel for the genocide of the Jewish people. The Germans murdered six million Jews. The American racist has taken part in the slaughter of over fifty million black people; therefore, we feel that this is a modest demand that we make.

4. WE WANT decent housing, fit for the shelter of human beings.

WE BELIEVE that if the white landlords will not give decent housing to our black community, then the housing and the land should be made into cooperatives so that our community, with government aid, can build and make decent housing for its people.

5. WE WANT education for our people that exposes the true nature of this decadent American society. We want education that teaches us our true history and our role in the present-day society.

WE BELIEVE in an educational system that will give to our people knowledge of self. If a man does not have knowledge of himself and his position in society and the world, then he has little chance to relate to anything else.

6. WE WANT all black men to be exempt from military service.

WE BELIEVE that Black people should not be forced to fight in the military service to defend a racist government that does not protect us. We will not fight and kill other people of color in the world who, like black people, are being victimized by the white racist government of America. We will protect ourselves from the force and violence of the racist police and the racist military, by whatever means necessary.

7. WE WANT an immediate end to POLICE BRUTALITY and MURDER of black people.

WE BELIEVE we can end police brutality in our black community by organizing black self-defense groups that are dedicated to defending our black community from racist police oppression and brutality. The Second Amendment to the Constitution of the United States gives a right to bear arms. We therefore believe that all black people should arm themselves for self- defense.

8. WE WANT freedom for all black men held in federal, state, county and city prisons and jails.

WE BELIEVE that all black people should be released from the many jails and prisons because they have not received a fair and impartial trial.

9. WE WANT all black people when brought to trial to be tried in court by a jury of their peer group or people from their black communities, as defined by the Constitution of the United States.

WE BELIEVE that the courts should follow the United States Constitution so that black people will receive fair trials. The 14th Amendment of the U.S. Constitution gives a man a right to be tried by his peer group. A peer is a person from a similar economic, social, religious, geographical, environmental, historical and racial background. To do this the court will be forced to select a jury from the black community from which the black defendant came. We have been, and are being tried by all-white juries that have no understanding of the "average reasoning man" of the black community.

10. WE WANT land, bread, housing, education, clothing, justice and peace. And as our major political objective, a United Nations supervised plebiscite to be held throughout the black colony in which only black colonial subjects will be allowed to participate, for the purpose of determining the will of black people as to their national destiny.

WHEN, in the course of human events, it becomes necessary for one people to dissolve the political bonds which have connected them with another, and to assume, among the powers of the earth, the separate and equal station to which the laws of nature and nature's God entitle them, a decent respect to the opinions of mankind requires that they should declare the causes which impel them to the separation.

WE HOLD these truths to be self-evident, that all men are created equal; that they are endowed by their Creator with certain inalienable rights; that among these are life, liberty, and the pursuit of happiness. **That, to secure these rights, governments are instituted among men, deriving their just powers from the consent of the governed; that, whenever any form of government becomes destructive of these ends, it is the right of the people to alter or abolish it, and to institute a new government, laying its foundation on such principles, and/organizing its powers in such form, as to them shall seem most likely to effect their safety and happiness. ** Prudence, indeed, will dictate that governments long established should not be changed for light and transient causes; and, accordingly, all experience hath shown, that mankind are more disposed to suffer, while evils are sufferable, than to right themselves by abolishing the forms to which they are accustomed. **But, when a long train of abuses and usurpations, pursuing invariably the same object, evinces a design to reduce them under absolute despotism, it is their right, it is their duty, to throw off such government, and to provide new guards for their future security. [1]

---

[1] Taken from http://www.itsabouttimebpp.com/home/bpp_program_platform.html last accessed Tuesday September 6, 2005.

# APPENDIX D

## TUPAC'S TATTOO'S

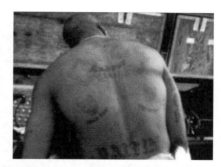

| | |
|---|---|
| **Tupac's Chest** | Top Left: 2pac<br>Top Right: Queen Neferetete (Egyptian Queen) with "2.DIE.4" below it.<br>Middle: A machine gun and tha words "50 Niggaz".<br>Stomach: The words "Thug Life", with a bullet as the "i". |
| **Tupac's Arms** | |

| | |
|---|---|
| | Left Shoulder: Panther head<br>Left Upper arm: Jesus' head on a burning cross. Off to the left of the Cross it says "Only God can judge me". On his left inner arm is written "Trust Nobody".<br>Left Forearm: The word "Outlaw", underneath which is another "Crown" that you can see in the movie "Gang Related".<br>Right Shoulder: The word "westside".<br>Right Upper arm: Skull and crossbones. Under the word "heartless". Under the skull and crossbones written in small print it says "My only fear of death is coming back reincarnated".<br>Right Forearm: Written in old English lettering, the word "Notorious".<br>Back Arm: On the back of the arm it says "MOB". |
| **Tupac's Neck** | Right Side: In the movie "Gang Related" and "Gridlocked" you will see the name "Machiavelli".<br>Back Side: There is a Crown and then under that is the word "Playaz". Under "Playaz" are the words "Fuck the World". |
| **Tupac's Back** | A BIG cross is on his back with the word "Exodus 18:11, meaning, "Now i know that the lord is greater than all gods: for in the things wherein they dealt proudly he was above them" in the middle of the cross. On each side of the cross is a clown mask. The mask on his right is crying and under it, it says "cry later". The other mask on his left side is smiling and it says "Smile Now". Under the cross is a big word saying "Ballin". |

# APPENDIX E

# TUPAC'S MUSICAL CONNECTION TO SLAVE MUSIC

| Tupac's Song | Slave Narrative and Song Parallel | BPC Value |
|---|---|---|
| "Young Black Male" | "Looked Down De Road" | In both of these songs, the artists make the connection with survival, the struggle for survival, and the power to survive; especially for young Blacks. The pain is much, and the sorrow is plentiful, but if we can just hold on together, we can make it happen. |
| "Cradle to Tha Grave" | "By and By I'm Goin' To See Them" | In these two parallel songs, both Pac, and the slaves discuss the pain of loved ones gone. "Well, mournin' time will soon be over" is the same theme that Pac uses in his song when he says, "All my homies drinkin liquor, tears in everybody's eyes Niggaz cried, to mourn a homie's homicide." In these two songs we see the connection to death, accepting death, but wishing that loved ones would not have to pass. A theme that is seen in many other songs within BPC as well. |
| "Death Around The Corner" | "Ain't That Good News?" | Both of these songs deal with the ultimate rest, happiness, and life struggle: death. In the inner city, many youth see death as the ultimate resting place and a time of peace, at last. Death is glorified, the slave knew this too. The "Good-News" for the slave, was Heaven, and God, i.e. death. For Tupac, this was |

| Tupac's Song | Slave Narrative and Song Parallel | BPC Value |
| --- | --- | --- |
| | | the same. He wanted to leave the "messed up earth" and return home to his father in Heaven. "Tryin to keep it together, no one lives forever anyway Struggin and strivin, my destiny's to die." |
| "Heaven Ain't Too Hard 2 Find" | "Marching Up The Heavenly Road" | In both of these songs, the narrative changes for hope and peace; in a journey that will end in Heaven for those who wait. The slave narrative says, "O come a-long_Mos-es, don't get lost, Marching up the Heavenly road…" Don't loose hope or vision, your pain and suffering will be rewarded, is the ultimate message for the listener. For Tupac, he infused many of his songs with this same message. In this particular song, he encourages the listener to be ready and to hold on, "Heaven ain't too hard to find, you just gotta have faith…" |

This is derived and connected to Howard Odum (1968) and Mark Fisher's (1969) work in which both scholars look at Black and slave songs. I make the connection to Tupac's music.

The song "Hold on Just a Little While Longer" also parallels Tupac's message:

**Hold On**

Hold on, just a little while longer
Hold on, just a little while longer
Hold on, just a little while longer
Everything will be alright
Everything will be alright

Pray on, just a little while longer
Pray on, just a little while longer
Pray on, just a little while longer
Everything will be alright
Everything will be alright

Fight on, just a little while longer
Fight on, just a little while longer
Fight on, just a little while longer
Everything will be alright
Everything will be alright

# APPENDIX F

## CONTENT ANALYSIS OF:

## 2PACALYPSE NOW (1992)

| Category | Song | Reasoning |
|---|---|---|
| **Social** *This area is concerned with the social issues that Tupac raises, be it sexual, theological, violence, rape, murder, and/or the crime syndicate.* | [1] Young Black Male [2] Trapped *[5] Violent* [7] Something Wicked | [1] This song deals with both the reality of the urban Black male and the harsh life he is set to live. [2] This particular deals with the young black male being trapped both socially and in class. [7] Pac talking about the basic social issues of ghetto males. |
| **Class** *Any part class or social status.* | [6] Words of Wisdom | [6] Pac describes the issues at large in AmeriKKKa and the Black community at large; Blacks are held to certain class positions because of racist institutions. |
| **Political** *Environmental, geographical, criminal justice, and/or government are all included in this category* | [3] Soulja's Story [4] I Don't Give a Fuck [5] Violent [12] Rebel of the Underground *[6] Words of Wisdom* | [3] Crack, gangs, and the reality that no one is really caring politically [4] The mess of the political injustice is making young urban youth feel hopeless; cops, political figures who don't help or care at all; the military |

| Category | Song | Reasoning |
|---|---|---|
| | | [5] This song doubles as both social and political; Pac describes how cops and society are crooked, so why are people mad at blacks for doing what they have to survive?<br><br>[12] This song subtly deals with the "enemy of the state" that is subsequently young Black males, according to Tupac. Tupac talks about that rebel and how niggaz need to educate themselves to be that "rebel." |
| **Communal**<br><br>*This area is concerned with any area that deals with the community of the urban environment; be it friends, enemies, communal issues such as sex, drinking, gangs, and/or crime. This area also looks at how friendships are formed and sustained.* | [8] Crooked Ass Nigga<br><br>[9] If My Homie Calls<br><br>[11] Tha' Lunatic | [8] This song deals with the community of authenticity; being real, and what happens when you don't stay true to the "game." Pac warns his people on what to look out for in the "hustle."<br><br>[9] Basic connection to the community and how Pac takes up for his friends and homies that call on him.<br><br>[11] Pac talks about sex, and how women can take advantage of brothas and what to watch out for. |
| **Familial**<br><br>*The family and areas that concern the family which include social, political, geography, and class. This area also deals with the extended family in the 'hood that makes up a* | [10] Brenda's Got A Baby<br><br>[13] Part Time Mutha | [10] This song can double as social as well, but Pac really makes an appeal to the family here and how hard it really is when young girls have babies with no solid family connections. |

| Category | Song | Reasoning |
|---|---|---|
| *large part of the family.* | | [13] The reality of single-momz and how hard it is on the whole families; Pac gives case studies. |
| **Spiritual**<br><br>*This is the area that concerns itself with matters of a theological, Christ like, God like, deity, holy, and/or divine subject within Tupac's music.* | [1] Young Black Male<br><br>[2] Trapped<br><br>[10] Brenda's Got A Baby<br><br>[6] Words of Wisdom | [1] This song describes how society at large is more complex than made out to be. The "pull yourself up by your bootstraps" is bullshit and young Black males need help; God (implied) is really the only help.<br><br>[2] This is the continuation of track one. Here Tupac used the nitty-gritty to explain why some Black males behave the way they do and why that is so.<br><br>[10] Once again the nitty-gritty is used while using Cone's (1991) ideology of the Blues. Tupac used a story to tell a broader and deeper story that exists in the urban society.<br><br>[6] Classical words of wisdom; these are Tupac's proverbs. We can then reverse that and now better interpret David's Psalms and the book of Proverbs by seeing, at greater depths, Tupac's own wisdom and epistemology. |

# APPENDIX G

## TUPAC'S AFFECT ON THE HIP HOP CULTURAL CONTINUUM

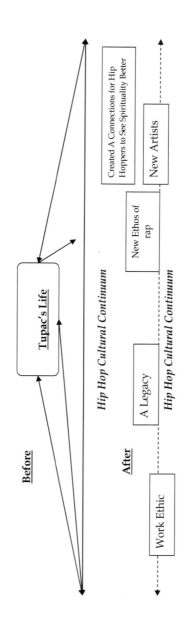

**FIGURE 21**

## TUPAC'S LIFE'S AFFECT ON THE HIP HOP CULTURAL CONTINUUM

# APPENDIX H

# SONG: SO MANY TEARS

I shall not fear no man but God
Though I walk through the valley of death
I shed so many tears (if I should die before I wake)
Please God walk with me (grab a nigga and take me to Heaven)

Back in elementary, I thrived on misery
Left me alone I grew up amongst a dyin breed
Inside my mind couldn't find a place to rest
until I got that Thug Life tatted on my chest
Tell me can you feel me? I'm not livin in the past, you wanna last
Be tha first to blast, remember Kato
No longer with us he's deceased
Call on the sirens, seen him murdered in the streets
Now rest in peace
Is there heaven for a G?  Remember me
So many homies in the cemetery, shed so many tears

Ahh, I suffered through the years, and shed so many tears..
Lord, I lost so many peers, and shed so many tears

Now that I'm strugglin in this business, by any means
Label me greedy gettin green, but seldom seen
And fuck the world cause I'm cursed, I'm havin visions
of leavin here in a hearse, God can you feel me?
Take me away from all the pressure, and all the pain
Show me some happiness again, I'm goin blind
I spend my time in this cell, ain't livin well
I know my destiny is Hell, where did I fail?
My life is in denial, and when I die,
baptized in eternal fire I'll shed so many tears

Lord, I suffered through the years, and shed so many tears..
Lord, I lost so many peers, and shed so many tears

Now I'm lost and I'm weary, so many tears
I'm suicidal, so don't stand near me

My every move is a calculated step, to bring me closer
to embrace an early death, now there's nothin left
There was no mercy on the streets, I couldn't rest
I'm barely standin, bout to go to pieces, screamin peace
And though my soul was deleted, I couldn't see it
I had my mind full of demons tryin to break free
They planted seeds and they hatched, sparkin the flame
inside my brain like a match, such a dirty game
No memories, just a misery
Paintin a picture of my enemies killin me, in my sleep
Will I survive til the mo'nin, to see the sun
Please Lord forgive me for my sins, cause here I come...

Lord, I suffered through the years (God) and shed so many tears..
God, I lost so many peers, and shed so many tears

Lord knows I.. tried, been a witness to homicide
Seen drivebys takin lives, little kids die
Wonder why as I walk by
Broken-hearted as I glance at the chalk line, gettin high
This ain't the life for me, I wanna change
But ain't no future right for me, I'm stuck in the game
I'm trapped inside a maze
See this Tanqueray influenced me to gettin crazy
Disillusioned lately, I've been really wantin babies
so I could see a part of me that wasn't always shady
Don't trust my lady, cause she's a product of this poison
I'm hearin noises, think she fuckin all my boys, can't take no more
I'm fallin to the floor; beggin for the Lord to let me in
to Heaven's door -- shed so many tears
(Dear God, please let me in)

Lord, I've lost so many years, and shed so many tears..
I lost so many peers, and shed so many tears
Lord, I suffered through the years, and shed so many tears..
God, I lost so many peers, and shed so many tears

## APPENDIX I

## FIVE STAGES OF RACIAL IDENTITY

1. Pre-encounter: this is where the young adult is still engaging with his or her own culture.

2. Encounter: The young people are faced with different cultures. Most of the time, they typically laugh at those who do things differently. But this is usually an awkward moment for the two cultures when encountering each other.

3. Immersion and Emersion: This is when the young person is immersed into a situation where they have to interact with other cultures; this is typically a negative experience (unless they have had a lot of exposure), which causes them to return to their culture of identity[1]. The process customarily stops here.

4. Internalization: When the young person is faced with the decision to either accept a new culture or immerse themselves into it, they must internalize the culture's patterns (norms, beliefs, values, and customs) at some level. When this happens, then number five is next.

5. Internalization-Commitment: Then there is type of friendship sought and a commitment by the two cultures and they begin to understand each other. This is rare.[2]

---

[1] Also See: Beverly D. Tatum (1999:54-59).

[2] These are important in understanding why Tupac was such a large attractant to young people. Simply put, people were able to identify with him both on a physical level and a sub-conscious level (c.f. Watkins 2005).

# APPENDIX J

# MATERIAL USED IN TUPAC ETHNOLIFEHISTORY

Below are the listings of materials used in Tupac's ethnolifehistory

| Archival DVD | Poetry | Interview Audio CD's | Other |
|---|---|---|---|
| 1) Tupac Vs<br>2) Thug Angel<br>3) Tupac Shakur:<br>4) Before I wake<br>5) Tupac Resurrection<br>6) 2Pac: Hip Hop Genius<br>7) Apprentice of Tupac Shakur | 1) The Rose That Grew From Concrete<br>2) Tupac Legacy (Volume 1) | 1) Tupac Shakur Speaks<br>2) Davey D 1992 Interview | 1) The Rose that Grew from Concrete (CD) various artists; Volume 1<br>2) The Rose that Grew from Concrete (CD) various artists' Volume 2 |

All 18 published CD's were used to study Tupac's music.

# APPENDIX K

# TUPAC'S INVOLVEMENT WITH THE LAW

| Date | Event |
|---|---|
| **December 1992** | Tupac files a $10 million lawsuit against the Oakland Police for alleged police brutality following an arrest for jaywalking |
| **April 1992** | Ronald Ray Howard, 19, shoots a Texas State Trooper and Howard's attorney claims that the young man was incited by Tupac's album 2Pacalypse Now, which was in the tape deck at the time.<br>Vice president Dan Quayle denounces Tupac and firmly states that his album has no place in our society |
| **August 1992** | Tupac has an altercation with some old friends in Marin City which results in the death of a 6-year old bystander and the arrest of Tupac's half brother, Maurice Harding, who was eventually released due to the lack of evidence. |
| **March 1993** | Tupac gets into a fight with a limo drive who accused Tupac of using drugs in his car. Tupac was arrested but the charges were later dropped. |
| **April 1993** | Tupac was arrested again for taking a swing with a baseball bat at a local rapper during a concert. He was sentenced to 10 days in prison. |
| **October 1993** | Tupac is arrested for allegedly shooting at 2 off duty Atlanta police officers where were allegedly harassing Black motorists. The charges were later dropped.<br>Columbia Pictures forces director John Singleton to drop Tupac from his upcoming film *Higher Learning*.<br>Tupac gets into an altercation with *Menace II Society's* director Allen Hughes. |
| **November 1993** | A 19 year old woman accuses Tupac of sexual assault |
| **March 1994** | Tupac begins serving a 15 day prison sentence for punching director Allen Hughes after he was dropped from the motion picture *Menace II Society*. |
| **September 1994** | 2 Milwaukee teens murder a police office and cite Tupac's song "Souljah's Story" as their inspiration |
| **November 1994** | Tupac's sexual assault trial opens. |
| **November 30, 1994** | While entering the lobby of the Quad Recording Studios in Times Square, New York City, Tupac is shot 5 times and |

| Date | Event |
|---|---|
| | robbed of jewels and cash estimated to be worth over $50,000. |
| **November 1994** | Tupac is acquitted of sodomy and weapons charges but found guilty of sexual abuse. |
| **February 14, 1995** | Tupac begins serving his 18 moth to 4.5 year sentence in New York's Rikers Island Penitentiary. |

## GLOSSARY OF HIP HOP LANGUAGE

**Beats**: The music that drives rap music; can also be termed as "having a good beat."

**Beef**: to have war, problems, issues, or anger with another person and/or gang.

**Bomb**: Really good; really good stuff.

**Burn**: To rip off or take without permission.

**Cap**: A gunshot.

**Capping**: To make fun of or to put down using clever wording; can also be called "Yo Mamma Jokes."

**Chill**: To take it easy and relax; to cease in a nefarious activity.

**Dope**: Really good.

**Flow:** To move or rhyme really well.

**Ghetto Kids:** Not a racial name (i.e. Black or Brown), but anyone that is young and living in the 'hood.

**Ghetto**: The bad part of town or to act or behave in a manner reflective of having no social skills.

**'Hood**: The inner city; the ghetto; a word that was taken from the word neighborhood, shortened to make it distinctly part of the inner city and urban context.

**Mark:** Someone who is known to be a sell-out or a two faced person.

**Simp:** Someone who is weak and does not stand up for themselves.

**Whack:** Really bad or awful.

**Yo:** What is going on, what is up, or how are you doing.

## SELECTED BIBLIOGRAPHY

Alexander, Frank, and Heidi Siegmund Cuda. 2000. *Got Your Back: Protecting Tupac in the World of Gangsta Rap*. 1st St. Martin's Griffin ed. New York: St. Martin's Griffin.

Alim, H. Samy. 2006. *Roc the Mic Right: The Language of Hip Hop Culture*. New York: Routledge.

Altheide, David L. 1996. *Qualitative Research Methods Series 38*. Thousand Oaks, CA: Sage Publications.

Anderson, Elijah. 1999. *Code of the Street: Decency, Violence, and the Moral Life of the Inner City*. New York: W.W. Norton & Company.

Anderson, Raymond D S. 2003. Black Beats for One People; Causes and Effects of Identification with Hip-Hop Culture. PhD. dissertation, Communications, Regent University, Virginia Beach, VA.

Annegret, Staiger. 2005. "Hoes Can Be Hoed out, Players Can Be Played out, but Pimp Is for Life"--the Pimp Phenomenon as Strategy of Identity Formation. *Symbolic Interaction* 28 (3):407-550.

Ardis, Angela. 2004. *Inside a Thug's Heart: With Original Poems and Letters by Tupac Shakur*. New York: Dafina Books.

Armstrong, Edward G. 2004. Eminem's Construction of Authenticity. *Popular Music and Society* 27 (3):335-349.

Bagwell, Orlando. 1994. Malcolm X: Make It Plain, edited by O. Bagwell. USA: PBS / A Blackside, Inc./Roja Production.

Baldwin, Davarian L. 2004. Black Empires, White Desires: The Spatial Politics of Identity in the Age of Hip-Hop. In *Thats the Joint! The Hip-Hop Studies Reader*, edited by M. Forman and M. A. Neal. New York: Routledge.

Banks, L. William. 1972. *The Black Church in the U. S.: Its Origin, Growth, Contribution, & Outlook*. Chicago: Moody Press.

Bastfield, Darrin Keith. 2002. *Back in the Day: My Life and Times with Tupac Shakur*. Cambridge, MA: Da Capo Press.

Bauman, Zygmunt. 2000. *Liquid Modernity*. Malden MA: Polity Press.

———. 2003. *Liquid Love*. Malden MA: Polity Press.

Bell, Daniel. 1973. *The Coming of a Post-Industrial Society: A Venture in Social Forecasting*. New York: Basic Books.

———. 1976. *Cultural Contradictions of Capitalism*. London: Heinemann.

bell, hooks. 1992. *Black Looks: Race and Representation*. Boston, MA: South End Press.

Bennett, Lerone. 1993. *The Shaping of Black America*. New York: Penguin Books.

Bernard, Russell H. 2000. *Social Research Methods: Qualitative and Quantitative Approaches*. Thousand Oaks, CA: Sage Publications.

Best, Harold M. 1993. *Music through the Eyes of Faith*. San Francisco CA: Harper Press.

Best Steven, Douglas Kellner. 1991. *Postmodern Theory: Critical Interrogations*. New York: Guiliford Press.

Betts, Raymond. 2004. *A History of Popular Culture: More of Everything, Faster, and Brighter*. New York: Routledge.

Black, C. Clifton. 2003. The Man in Black. J. Cash. *The Christian Century*, Oct., 8-9.

Blackwell, Albert L. 1999. *The Sacred in Music*. Louisville KY: Westminster Knox Press.

Blair, M Elizabeth. 1993. Commercialization of the Rap Music Youth Subculture. *Journal of Popular Culture* 27 (3):21-46.

Blake, Andrew. 1997. Making Noise: Notes from the 1980s. *Popular Music and Society* 21 (3):19-51.

Bosch, David Jacobus. 1991. *Transforming Mission: Paradigm Shifts in Theology of Mission, American Society of Missiology Series; No. 16*. Maryknoll, N.Y.: Orbis Books.

Bourdieu, Pierre. 1986. The Forms of Capital. In *Handbook of Theory and Research for the Sociology of Education*, edited by J. G. Richardson. Westport CT: Greenwood.

Boyd, Todd. 1997. *Am I Black Enough for You? Popular Culture from the 'Hood and Beyond*. Bloomington & Indianapolis: Indiana University Press.

———. 2002. *The H.N.I.C.: The Death of Civil Rights and the Reign of Hip Hop*. New York: New York University Press.

———. 2003. *Young Black Rich and Famous: The Rise of the Nba, the Hip Hop Invasion, and the Transformation of American Culture*. New York: Double Day.

Burnim, Mellone V. 2006. Religious Music. In *African American Music: An Introduction*, edited by M. V. Burnim and P. K. Maultsby. New York: Routledge.

Burnim, Mellonee V, and Portia K Maultsby, eds. 2006. *African American Music: An Introduction*. New York: Routledge.

Bynoe, Yvonne. 2004. *Stand and Deliver: Politcal Activism, Leadership and Hip Hop Culture*. Brooklyn NY: Soft Skull Press.

Cenedive, Drah. 2003. *2 Pac Lives: The Death of Makaveli/ the Resurection of Tupac Amaru*. Topeka, KS: Hard Evidence Publishing.

Chang, Jeff. 2005. *Can't Stop Won't Stop: A History of the Hip Hop Generation*. New York: St. Martin's Press.

Clarke, John Henrik, ed. 1969. *Malcolm X: The Man and His Times*. New York: The Macmillan Company.

Clay, Andreana. 2003. Keepin' It Real: Black Youth, Hip-Hop Culture, and Black Identity. *American Behavioral Scientist* 46 (10):1346-1358.

Cone, James. 1992. The Blues: A Secular Spiritual. In *Sacred Music of the Secular City: From Blues to Rap*, edited by J. M. Spencer. Durham, NC: Duke University Press.

Cone, James H. 1991. *The Spirituals and the Blues: An Interpretation*. Maryknoll, New York: Orbis Books.

———. 1997a. *Black Theology and Black Power*. 5th ed. Maryknoll NY: Orbis Books.

———. 1997b. *God of the Oppressed*. Maryknoll NY: Orbis Books.

Cook, Richard. 1999. The White Dj in Black Culture: He Is Norman Mailer's White Negro: Hip, Materialist and a Guru to Poor Youngsters. *New Statesman (London, England: 1996)*, Aug., 18-19.

Cox, Harvey. 1965. *The Secular City: A Celebration of Its Liberties and an Invitation to Its Discipline*. New York: The Macmillan Company.

Cube, Ice. 1990. *Amerikkka's Most Wanted*. Los Angeles, CA: Priority Records. CD.

D, Chuck. 1997. *Fight the Power*. New York: Delta Books.

D, Davey. 1991. The Lost Interview with Tupac.

Dark, Philip. 1957. Methods of Synthesis in Ethnohistory. *Ethnohistory* 4 (3):231-278.

Datcher, Michael, Kwame Alexander, and Mutulu Shakur. 1997. *Tough Love: The Life and Death of Tupac Shakur, Cultural Criticism and Familial Observations.* Alexandria, VA: Alexander Pub. Group.

Davis, Eisa. 2003. Scenes from Umkovu. In *Everything but the Burden: What White People Are Taking from Black Culture*, edited by G. Tate: Harlem Moon & Broadway Books.

Dent, Gina, ed. 1992. *Black Popular Culture*. 1st ed. Vol. 1. Seatle, WA: Bay Press.

Detweiler Craig, Barry Taylor. 2003. *A Matrix of Meanings: Finding God in Pop Culture*. Grand Rapids MI: Baker Academic.

Dillard, J L. 1972. *Black English: Its History and Usage in the United States.* New York: Vintage Books.

Donalson, Melvin. 2003. *Black Directors in Hollywood*. Austin TX: University of Texas Press.

Douglas, Kelly Brown. 1999. *Sexuality and the Black Church: A Womanist Perspective*. Maryknoll NY: Orbis Books.

Dre, Dr. 1993. *The Chronic*. Los Angeles, CA: Death Row Records. CD.

DuBois, WEB. 1961. *The Souls of Black Folk*. New York: Fawcett Publications.

———. 1966. *Black Reconstruction in America*. London W.C.1: Frank Cass and Company Limited.

Dyson, Michael Eric. 1995. *Making Malcolm: The Myth and Meaning of Malcom X*. New York: Oxford University Press.

———. 1996. *Between God and Gangsta Rap: Bearing Witness to Black Culture*. New York: Oxford University Press.

———. 2000. *I May Not Get There with You: The True Martin Luther King Jr*. New York: Free Press.

———. 2001. *Holler If You Hear Me: Searching for Tupac Shakur*. New York: Basic Civitas.

———. 2004. *The Michael Eric Dyson Reader*. New York: Basic Civitas.

Early, Gerald Lyn. 1997. Dreaming of a Black Christmas. *Harper's*, Jan., 55-61.

Edwards, Herbert O. 1975. Black Theology: Retrospect and Prospect. *Journal of Religious Thought* (32):46-59.

Fenton, William N. 1962. Ethnohistory and Its Problems. *Ethnohistory* 9 (1):1-23.

Fisher, Mark Miles. 1969. *Negro Slave Songs in the United States*. New York: Citadel Press.

Floyd, Samuel A. 1995. *The Power of Black Music: Interpreting Its History from Africa to the United States*. New York: Oxford University Press.

Forman, Murray. 2002. *The 'Hood Comes First: Race, Space, and Place in Rap and Hip-Hop, Music/Culture*. Middletown, Conn.: Wesleyan University Press.

Forman, Murray, and Mark Anthony Neal, eds. 2005. *That's the Joint! The Hip-Hop Studies Reader*. Vol. 1. New York: Routledge.

Foucault, Michael. 1984. *The History of Sexuality: An Introduction*. Vol. 1. New York: Vintage Books.

Frederick, E. Hoxie. 2000. What's Your Problem? New Work in Twentieth-Century Native American Ethnohistory. *Ethnohistory* 47 (2):469-510.

Fusco, Coco. 1995. *English Is Broken Here: Notes on Cultural Fusion in the Americas*. New York: The New Press.

George, Nelson. 1998. *Hiphop America*. New York: Penguin Books.

Gibbs, Eddie. 1994. *In Name Only: Tackling the Problem of Nominal Christianity*. Wheaton, Ill.: BridgePoint.

Gibson, Thomas. 2005. Letter to the President. USA: QD3 & Image Entertainment.

Gilbert, Derrick I M. 1997. Reflections on the Life and Death of 2pac: "Keep on Livin". In *Tough Love: The Life and Death of Tupac Shakur*, edited by M. Datcher and K. Alexander. Alexandria, VA: Black Words Inc.

Gobi. 2003. *Through My Eyes: Thoughts on Tupac Shakur in Pictures and Words*. New York: London.

Gottdiener, Mark. 1985. Hegemony and Mass Culture: A Semiotic Approach. *American Journal of Sociology* 90 (5):979-1001.

Green, Jared. 2003. *Rap and Hip Hop, Examining Pop Culture*. San Diego: Greenhaven Press.

Grout, Donald Jay, and Claude V Palisca. 2001. *A History of Western Music*. 6th ed. New York: W.W. Norton & Company.

Gruber, Enid, and Helaine Thau. 2003. Sexually Related Content on Television and Adolescents of Color: Media Theory, Physiological Development, and Psychological Impact*. *The Journal of Negro Education* 72 (4):438.

Gruver, Rod. 1992. The Blues as a Secular Religion. In *Sacred Music of the Secular City: From Blues to Rap*, edited by J. M. Spencer. Durham, NC: Duke University Press.

Gubrium, Jaber F., and James A. Holstein. 2003. *Postmodern Interviewing*. Thousand Oaks, CA: Sage Publications.

Guevara, Nancy. 1996. Women Writin' Rappin' Breakin'. In *Dropping Science: Critical Essays on Rap Music and Hip Hop Culture*, edited by W. E. Perkins. Philadelphia: Temple University Press.

Guy, Jasmine. 2004. *Afeni Shakur: Evolution of a Revolutionary*. 1st Atria Books hardcover ed. New York: Atria Books.

Hackford, Taylor. 2005. Ray. USA: Anvil Films.

Hall, John R. 1992. The Capitals of Cultures: A Nonholistic Approach to Status Situations, Class, Gender, and Ethnicity. In *Cultivating Differences*, edited by M. Lamount and A. Fournier. Chicago, ILL: Chicago University Press.

Hall, Stuart. 1992. What Is This "Black" in Black Popular Culture? In *Black Popular Culture*, edited by G. Dent. Seattle WA: Bay Press.

Harris, Jeff, and Bernie Kukoff. 1980. Different Strokes (Season's 1-3). USA: Sony Pictures.

Harvey, David. 1988. *Social Justice and the City*. Oxford: Basil Blackwell.

Hebdige, Dick. 1998. Postmodernism and 'the Other Side'. In *Cultural Theory and Popular Culture: A Reader*, edited by J. Storey. London, England: Pearson Prentice Hall.

Henry, Matthew. 2002. He Is a "Bad Mother*$'!#": Shaft and Contemporary Black Masculinity. *Journal of Popular Film and Television*, Summer, 114-19.

Heyward, Carter. 1999. *Saving Jesus from Those Who Are Right: Rethinking What It Means to Be a Christian*. Minneapolis: Fortress Press.

Hill, Rock. 2002. Researcher Points to Pop Culture for Educating Black Youth. *Black Issues in Higher Education* 19 (17):18.

Hodge, Dan. 2005. Tutorial # 2: Tupac's Relation to Hip Hop / Urban Youth. Pasadena: Fuller Theological Seminary.

Hodge, Daniel. 2003. Can You Hear Me Calling: Hip Hop/ Gangster Culture & the Future Urban Church. In *Fuller Theological Seminary's School of Intercultural Studies*. Pasadena: Fuller Theological Seminary School of Intercultural Studies.

Hood, Fred. 1980. *Reformed America: The Middle and Southern States, 1783-1837*. Alabama: University of Alabama.

Hooks, Bell. 1992b. Dialectually Down with the Critical Program. In *Black Popular Culture*, edited by G. Dent. Seatle, WA: Bay Press.

Hustad, Donald Paul. 1981. *Jubilate: Church Music in the Evangelical Tradition*. Carol Stream, Ill: Hope Publishing Company.

Iverem, Esther. 1997. The Politics of 'Fuck It' and the Passion to Be a Free Black. In *Tough Love: The Life and Death of Tupac Shakur*, edited by M. Datcher and K. Alexander. Alexandria, VA: Black Words Books.

James, Perkinson. 2004. Like a Thief in the Night: Black Theology and White Church in the Third Millennium. *Theology Today* 60 (4):508-530.

Johnson, James D, Lee Anderson Jackson, and Leslie Gatto. 1995. Violent Attitudes and Deferred Academic Aspirations: Deleterious Effects of Exposure to Rap Music. *Basic and Applied Social Psychology* 16 (1 & 2):27-41.

Jones, Lawrence. 1970. Black Churches in Historical Perspective. *Christianity & Crisis* 30 (18):226-228.

Joseph, James A. 1970. Has Black Religion Lost Its Soul? In *The Black Seventies*, edited by F. B. Barbour. Boston, MA: Porter Sargent Publisher.

Jospeh, Jamal. 2006. *Tupac Shakur: Legacy*. New York: Atria Books.

Kain & Abel, & Master P. 1996. *Black Jesus*: The 7 Sins: Priority Records.

Kaplan, David, and Robert A Manners. 1972. *Culture Theory*. New Jersey: Prentice Hall.

Keener, Craig S. 1999. An Ethnohistorical Analysis of Iroquois Assault Tactics Used against Fortified Settlements of the Northeast in the Seventeenth Century. *Ethnohistory* 46 (4):777-850.

Kelley, Robin D. G. 1994. *Race Rebels: Culture, Politics, and the Black Working Class*. New York: Free Press, Toronto.

———. 1997. *Yo' Mama's Disfunktional! Fighting the Culture Wars in Urban America.* Boston: Beacon Press.

Kelly, Robin D G. 2003. Reds, White, and Blues People. In *Everything but the Burden: What White People Are Taking from Black Culture,* edited by G. Tate. New York: Harlem Moon & Broadway Books.

Keyes, Cheryl L. 2002. *Rap Music and Street Consciousness.* Chicago IL: University of Illinois Press.

King, Roberta R. 1989. Pathways in Christian Communication: The Case of the Senufo of Cote D' Ivoire. PhD. dissertation, School of Intercultural Studies, Fuller Theological Seminary, Pasadena.

Kirk, J. Andrew. 2000. Following Modernity and Postmodernity: A Missiological Investigation. *Mission Studies* 17 (1):217-239.

Kirkland, David, Jeffrey Robinson, Austin Jackson, and Geneva Smitherman. 2004. From "the Lower Economic": Three Young Brothas and an Old School Womanist Respond to Dr. Bill Cosby. *The Black Scholar* 34 (4):10.

Kitwana, Bakari. 2003. *The Hip Hop Generation: Young Blacks and the Crisis in African-American Culture.* New York: Basic Civitas.

———. 2004. The Challenge of Rap Music from Cultural Movement to Political Power. In *That's the Joint! The Hip-Hop Studies Reader,* edited by M. Forman and M. A. Neal. New York: Routledge.

———. 2004. The State of the Hip-Hop Generation: How Hip-Hop's Cultural Movement Is Evolving into Political Power. *Diogenes (International Council for Philosophy and Humanistic Studies)* 51 (3):115-20.

———. 2005. *Why White Kids Love Hip-Hop: Wankstas, Wiggers, Wannabes, and the New Reality of Race in America.* New York: Basic Civitas Books.

Kohl, Paul R. 2004. The Lyrics in African American Popular Music. *Popular Music and Society* 27 (3):375.

Kraft, Charles. 1979. *Christianity in Culture: A Study in Dynamic Biblical Theologizing in Cross-Cultural Perspective.* 18 ed. Maryknoll, NY: Orbis Books.

Kraft, Charles H. 1991. *Communication Theory for Christian Witness.* Maryknoll, NY: Orbis Books.

Kramer, Jonathan D. 2002. The Nature and Origins of Musical Postmodernism. In *Postmodern Music Postmodern Thought,* edited by J. Lochhead and J. Auner. New York: Routledge.

Kreitzer, L. Joseph. 1982. Christ as Second Adam in Paul. Book; Archival Material, King's College, London.

———. 1993. *The New Testament in Fiction and Film: On Reversing the Hermeneutical Flow, Variation: The Biblical Seminar; 17.* Sheffield: JSOT Press.

———. 1994. *The Old Testament in Fiction and Film: On Reversing the Hermeneutical Flow, The Biblical Seminar; 24.* Sheffield: Sheffield Academic Press.

———. 2002. *The Dreaming Spires Version of Paul's Letters: (the Codex Oxoniensis).* Oxford: Alden.

Krueger, Richard A, and Mary Anne Casey. 2000. *Focus Groups: A Practical Guide for Applied Research.* 3rd ed. Thousand Oaks, CA: Sage Publications.

Kuçuradi, Ioanna. 2004. Rationality and Rationalities within the Framework of the Modernism-Postmodernism Debate. *Diogenes* 51 (2):11-17.

Lash, Scott. 1990. Postmodernism as Humanism? Urban Space and Social Theory. In *Theories of Modernity and Postmodernity*, edited by B. S. Turner. Thousand Oaks CA: Sage Publications.

Lazin, Lauren. 2003. Tupac: Resurrection. USA: MTV Films & Amaru Entertainment.

Le Gates, R. T.; Stout, F, and. 2000. *The City Reader.* Edited by R. T. S. Le Gates, F. 2nd Edition ed. London & New York: Routledge.

Lee, Spike. 1989. Do the Right Thing. USA: Universal Pictures.

Leland, John. 2004. *Hip: The History.* New York: Harper Collins.

Lewis, Craige G. 2004. The Truth Behind Hip Hop. USA: Ex Ministries.

Lewis, Lord. 2002. What Made Elvis Wiggle; the Culture That Shaped the Man Who Reshaped American Music. *U.S. News & World Report* 133 (2):59.

Light, Alan, Ed. 1998. *Tupac Amaru Shakur, 1971-1996.* Updated ed. New York: Three Rivers Press.

Lincoln, Eric C., and Lawrence H. Mamiya. 1990. *The Black Church in the African American Experience.* Durham & London: Duke University Press.

Linton, Ralph. 1936. *The Study of Man; an Introduction.* New York: London, D. Appleton-Century Co.

Little, Malcolm. 1964. *The Autobiography of Malcolm X.* New York: Grove Press Inc.

Loeterman, Ben, and Andrea Kalin. 2004. Slavery and the Making of America. USA: PBS.

Long, Sean. 2001. Tupac Shakur: Before I Wake. USA: Xenon Films.

Lynch, Gordon. 2005. *Understanding Theology and Popular Culture*. Malden, MA: Blackwell Publishing.

Lyotard, Jean- Francois. 1984. *The Postmodern Condition: A Report on Knowledge*. Minneapolis MN: University of Minnesota Press.

Mahiri, Jabari, and Soraya Sablo. 1996. Writing for Their Lives: The Non-School Literacy of California's Urban African American Youth. *The Journal of Negro Education* 65 (2):164.

Majors, Richard, and Janet Mancini Billson. 1992. *Cool Pose: The Dilemmas of Black Manhood in America*. New York: Lexington Books.

McWhorter, John H. 2003. Up from Hip-Hop. *Commentary*, Mar., 62-5.

Merriam, Alan P. 1964. *The Anthropology of Music*. Evanston, IL: Northwestern University Press.

Middleton, Richard. 2003. Locating the People: Music and the Popular. In *The Cultural Study of Music: A Critical Introduction*, edited by M. Clayton, T. Herbert and R. Middleton. New York: Routledge.

Miles, Jack. 2001. *Christ: A Crisis in the Life of God*. New York: Alfred A. Knopf.

Miller, Terry E, and Andrew Shahriari. 2006. *World Music: A Global Journey*. New York: Routledge.

Mitchell, Henry. 1979. *Black Preaching*. New York: Harper & Row.

Miyakawa, Felicia M. 2005. *Fiver Percenter Rap: God Hop's Music, Message, and Black Muslim Mission*. Bloomington, IN: Indiana University Press.

Miyakawa, Felicia M. 2003. God Hop: The Music and Message of Five Percenter Rap. Ph.D. dissertation, Indiana University.

Morgan, Marcyliena. 1998. More Than a Mood or an Attitude: Discourse and Verbal Genres in African-American Culture. In *African-American English: Structure, History, and Use*, edited by S. S. Mufwene, J. R. Rickford, G. Bailey and G. Bailey. New York: Routledge.

Mufwene, Salikoko S, John R Rickford, Guy Bailey, and John Baugh, eds. 1998. *African American English: Structure, History, and Use*. New York: Routledge.

Murch, Donna. 2003. The Prison of Popular Culture: Rethinking the Seventy-Fourth Annual Academy Awards. *The Black scholar* 33 (1):25-33.

Myra, Mendible. 1999. High Theory / Low Culture: Postmodernism and the Politics of Carnival. *Journal of American Culture* 22 (2):22-28.

Neal, Larry. 1970. New Space/ the Growth of Black Consciousness in the Sixties. In *The Black Seventies*, edited by F. B. Barbour. Boston, MA: Porter Sargent Publisher.

Neal, Mark Anthony. 1997. Sold out on Soul: The Corporate Annexation of Black Popular Music. *Popular Music and Society* 21 (3):117.

———. 1999. *What the Music Said: Black Popular Music and Black Public Culture*. New York: Routledge.

———. 2002. *Soul Babies: Black Popular Culture and the Post-Soul Aesthetic*. New York: Routledge.

———. 2003. *Songs in the Key of Black Life: A Rhythm and Blues Nation*. New York: Routledge.

———. 2005. *New Black Man*. New York: Routledge.

Nelson, Angela S. 1991. Theology in the Hip-Hop of Public Enemy and Kool Moe Dee. In *The Emergency of Black and the Emergence of Rap*, edited by J. M. Spencer. Durham, NC: Duke University Press.

Nettl, Bruno. 1983. *The Study of Ethnomusicology: Twenty-Nine Issues and Concepts*. Chicago, Ill: University of Illinois Press.

Nicholl, Don, and Michael Ross. 1975. The Jeffersons (Seasons 1-3). USA: Columbia Tri Star.

Niebuhr, Richard H. 1951. *Christ and Culture*. San Francisco, CA: Harper Collins.

NWA. 1989. *Straight Outta Compton*. Los Angeles, CA: Priority Records. CD.

Odum, Howard W. 1968. *The Negro and His Songs: A Study of Typical Negro Songs in the South*. 306 vols. Westport, Conn.: Negro Universities Press.

One, KRS. 2003. *Ruminations*. New York: Welcome Rain Publishers.

Ozersky, Josh. 2000. The White Negro Revisited. *Tikkun*, Sept./Oct., 3-61.

Palma, Brian De. 1983. Scarface. USA: Universal Pictures.

Peck, M. Scott. 1987. *The Different Drum: Community-Making and Peace.* New York: Simon and Schuster.

Perkins, Eugene U. 1987. *Explosion of Chicago's Black Street Gangs 1900- Present.* Chicago, Ill: Third World Press.

Perkins, William Eric, ed. 1996. *Droppin' Science: Critical Essays on Rap Music and Hip Hop Culture, Critical Perspectives on the Past.* Philadelphia: Temple University Press.

Perry, Imani. 2004. *Prophets of the Hood: Politics and Poetics in Hip Hop.* Durham, NC: Duke University Press.

Peter, Spirer. 1997. Rhyme and Reason. USA: Miramax Films.

Peters, Ken. 2001. Tupac Vs. USA: Dennon Entertainment.

Petracca, Michael, and Madeleine Sorapure, eds. 2001. *Common Culture: Reading and Writing About American Popular Culture.* 3rd ed. Upper Saddle River, NJ: Prentice Hall.

Pincus-Roth, Zachary. 2005. Pop Culture Takes Center Stage. *Variety*, March, 58.

Pinn, Anthony B. 1995. *Why Lord? Suffering and Evil in Black Theology.* New York: Continuum.

———, ed. 2003. *Noise and Spirit: The Religious and Spiritual Sensibilities of Rap Music.* New York: New York University Press.

Potter, Russell A. 1995. *Spectacular Vernaculars: Hip-Hop and the Politics of Postmodernism.* New York: State University of New York Press / Sunny Series.

Quinn, Eithne. 2005. *Nuthin' but a "G" Thang: The Culture and Commerce of Gangsta Rap, Popular Cultures, Everyday Lives.* New York: Columbia University Press.

Ramsey, Guthrie P. 2004. *Race Music: Black Cultures from Behop to Hip-Hop.* Berkeley, Calif.: University of California Press.

Rasmussen, Susan J. 1999. The Slave Narrative in Life History and Myth, and Problems of Ethnographic Representation of the Tuareg Cultural Predicament. *Ethnohistory* 46 (1):67-101.

Reed, Teresa L. 2003. *The Holy Profane: Religion in Black Popular Music.* Lexington, KY: The University Press of Kentucky.

Reese, Renford. 2004. *American Paradox: Young Black Men.* Durham, N.C.: Carolina Academic Press.

Richardson, Jeanita W, and Kim A Scott. 2002. Rap Music and Its Violent Progeny: America's Culture of Violence in Context. *The Journal of Negro Education* 71 (3):175-192.

Riffe, Daniel, Stephan Lacy, and Frederick G Fico. 2005. *Analyzing Media Message: Using Quantitative Content Analysis in Research*. 2nd ed. Mahwah, NJ.: Lawrence Erlbaum Associates, Publishers.

Ritzer, George. 2000. *The Mcdonaldization of Society*. Thousand Oaks, CA: Pine Forge Press.

———. 2000. *Sociological Theory*. 5th ed. New York: McGraw Hill.

Romanowski, William D. 1996. *Pop Culture Wars: Religion and the Role of Entertainment in American Life*. Downers Grove, Ill.: InterVarsity Press.

Rose, Tricia. 1994a. *Black Noise: Rap Music and Black Culture in Contemporary America*. Middletown CT.: Wesleyan University Press.

———. 1994b. A Style Nobody Can Deal With: Politics, Style, and the Postindustrial City in Hip Hop. In *Microphone Friends: Youth Music and Youth Culture*, edited by A. Ross and T. Rose. New York: Routledge.

Ross, Andrew, and Tricia Rose, eds. 1994. *Microphone Fiends: Youth Music and Youth Culture*. New York: Routledge.

Rux, Carl H. 2003. Eminem: The New White Negro. In *Everything but the Burden: What White People Are Taking from Black Culture*, edited by G. Tate. New York: Harlem Moon & Broadway Books.

Sample, Tex. 1984. *Blue Collar Ministry: Facing Economic and Social Realities of Working People*. Valley Forge, PA: Judson Press.

Sapir, Edward. 1949. *Language: An Introduction to the Study of Speech*, Harvest Books; Hb7. New York: Harcourt.

Schultz, Michael. 1972. Which Way Is Up? USA: Universal Pictures.

Scott, Jonathan. 2004. Sublimating Hiphop: Rap Music in White America. *Socialism and Democracy* 18 (2):135.

Seligman, Adam B. 1990. Towards a Reinterpretation of Modernity in an Age of Postmodernity. In *Theories of Modernity and Postmodernity*, edited by B. S. Turner. Thousand Oaks CA: Sage Publications.

Shakur, Sanyika. 1993. *Monster: The Autobiography of an L.A. Gang Member*. New York: Penguin Books.

Shakur, Tupac. 1991. *2pacalypse Now*. New York, NY: Jive Records, Amaru Records. CD.

———. 1993. *Strictly 4 My N.I.G.G.A.Z.* New York: Interscope Records. CD.

———. 1994. *Thug Life Volume 1*. New York: Interscope Records, Atlantic Records. CD.

———. 1995. *Me against the World*. New York, NY: Jive Records. CD.

———. 1995-1996. *All Eyez on Me*. Los Angeles, CA: Death Row Records. CD.

———. 1996, 2001. *Makaveli the Don Killuminati 7 Day Theory*. Beverly Hill, CA: Death Row Records Inc.

———. 1997. *R U Still Down? Remember Me?* New York, NY: Jive Records. CD.

———. 1999. *2pac+ Outlawz: Still I Rise*. Los Angeles, CA: Interscope Records. CD.

———. 1999. *The Rose That Grew from Concrete*. New York: Pocket Books.

———. 2000. *The Rose That Grew from Concrete*. Santa Monica, CA: Amaru Entertainmnet; Interscope Records. CD.

———. 2001. *Until the End of Time*. Santa Monica, CA: Amaru Entertainment, Interscope Records, Death Row Records. CD.

———. 2002. *Better Dayz*. Santa Monica, CA: Amaru Entertainment; Death Row Records; Interscope Records. CD.

———. 2004. *2pac Loyal to the Game*. Santa Monica, CA: Interscope Records, Amaru Entertainment. CD.

Shakur, Tupac, Eminem, Outlawz, and 50 Cent. 2003. *Tupac Resurrection*. Santa Monica, CA: Interscope Records, Amaru Entertainment, MTV Music. CD.

Shakur, Tupac, Afeni Shakur, Jacob Hoye, Karolyn Ali, and Walter Einenkel. 2003. *Tupac: Resurrection, 1971-1996*. 1st Atria Books hardcover ed. New York: Atria Books.

Shaviro, Steven. 2004. The Life, after Death, of Postmodern Emotions. *Criticism* 46 (1):125-141.

Shaw, Daniel R, and Charles E Van Engen. 2003. *Communicating God's Word in a Complex World: God's Truth or Hocus Pocus*. Lanham, MD: Rowan & Littlefield Publishers Inc.

Sheares Reuben, A. II. 1970. Beyond White Theology. *Christianity & Crisis* 30 (18):229-235.

Shenk, Wilbert R. 1999. *Changing Frontiers of Mission.* Maryknoll, NY: Orbis Books.

Silverman, David. 2000. *Doing Qualitative Research: A Practical Handbook.* Thousand Oaks, CA: Sage Publications.

Sims, Josh. 1999. *Dear 2 Pac: Fan Letters, Poems, and Art.* Los Angeles, CA: Destiny Merchandising LP.

Singleton, John. 1991. Boyz in the Hood. USA: Columbia Pictures.

Slobin, Mark, and Jeff Todd Titon. 1984. The Music-Culture as a World of Music. In *Worlds of Music: An Introduction to the Music of the World's Peoples*, edited by J. T. Titon, J. T. Koetting, D. P. McAllester, D. B. Reck and M. Slobin. New York: Schirmer Books.

Smiles, Robin V. 2005. From Black Power to Hip-Hop. *Black Issues in Higher Education* 21 (24):28.

Smith, Donald K. 1992. *Creating Understanding: A Handbook for Christian Communication across Cultural Landscapes.* Grand Rapids, MI.: Zondervan.

Smitherman, Geneva. 1977. *Talkin and Testifyin: The Language of Black America.* Boston, MA: Houghton Mifflin.

———. 1994. *Black Talk: Words and Phrases from the Hood to the Amen Corner.* Boston, MA: Houghton Mifflin.

———. 1998. Words from the Hood: The Lexicon of African-America Vernacular English. In *African-American English: Structure, History, and Use*, edited by S. S. Mufwene, J. R. Rickford, G. Bailey and J. Baugh. New York: Routledge.

———. 2000. *Talkin That Talk: Language, Culture, and Education in African America.* New York: Routledge.

Snapper, Juliana. 2004. Scratching the Surface: Spinning Time and Identity in Hip-Hop Turntablism. *European Journal of Cultural Studies* 7 (1):9-25.

Soja, Edward. 2000. *Postmetropolis: Critical Studies of Cities and Regions.* Malden, MA.: Blackwell Publishing.

Southern, Eileen. 1983. *The Music of Black Americans.* 2nd ed. New York: W.W. Norton & Company.

Spears, Arthur K. 1998. African-American Language Use: Ideology and So-Called Obscenity. In *African-American English: Structure, History, and Use*, edited by S. S. Mufwene, J. R. Rickford, G. Bailey and J. Baugh. New York: Routledge.

Speed, Lesley. 2001. Moving on Up: Education in Black American Youth Films. *Journal of Popular Film & Television* 29 (2):82.

Spencer, Jon Michael. 1990. *Protest and Praise: Sacred Music of Black Religion*. Minneapolis, MN: Fortress Press.

———. 1992. The Mythology of the Blues. In *Sacred Music of the Secular City: From Blues to Rap*, edited by J. M. Spencer. Durham, NC: Duke University Press.

———, ed. 1991. *The Emergency of Black and the Emergence of Rap*. Vol. 5, *Black Sacred Music: A Journal of Theomusicology*. Durham, NC: Duke University Press.

———, ed. 1992. *Sacred Music of the Secular City: From Blues to Rap*. Vol. 6. Durham, NC: Duke University Press.

Spirer, Peter. 2002. Tupac Shakur: Thug Angel, the Life of an Outlaw. USA: Black Watch Television, QD3 Entertainment, & Image Entertainment.

Starr, Larry, and Christopher Waterman. 2003. *American Popular Music: From Ministrelsy to Mtv*. New York: Oxford University Press.

Stephens, Ronald Jemal. 1991. The Three Waves of Contemporary Rap Music. In *The Emergency of Black and the Emergence of Rap*, edited by J. M. Spencer. Durham, NC: Duke University Press.

Stewart, Pearl. 2004. Who's Playin' Whom? *Black Issues in Higher Education* 21 (5):26-9.

Sullivan, Randall. 2002. *Labyrinth: A Detective Investigates the Murders of Tupac Shakur and Biggie Smalls, the Implication of Death Row Records' Suge Knight, and the Origins of the Los Angeles Police Scandal*. 1st ed. New York: Atlantic Monthly Press.

Tan, George. 1998. Tupac Shakur: Thug Immortal. USA: Xenon Pictures.

Tate, Greg, ed. 2003. *Everything but the Burden: What White People Are Taking from Black Culture*. New York: Harlem Moon & Broadway Books.

Terraciano, Kevin. 1998. Crime and Culture in Colonial Mexico: The Case of the Mixtec Murder Note. *Ethnohistory* 45 (4):709-801.

Tiersma, Jude M. 1999. Reading the Writing on the Wall: Missional Transformation through Narrative in Postmodern Los Angeles. PhD. dissertation, School of Intercultural Studies, Fuller Theological Seminary, Pasadena, CA.

Ting-Toomey, Stella, and Leeva C Chung. 2005. *Understanding Intercultural Communication*. 1st ed. Los Angeles, CA.: Roxbury Publishing.

Tippett, Alan Richard. 1973. *Aspects of Pacific Ethnohistory*. South Pasadena, CA: William Carey Library.

———. 1980. *Oral Tradition and Ethnohistory: The Transmission of Information and Social Values in Early Christian Fiji, 1835-1905*. Canberra: St. Mark's Library.

Truesdell, Keith. 1999. Chris Rock: Bigger and Blacker. USA: HBO Films.

Turner, Albert Uriah Anthony, Jr. 2004. Bad Niggers, Real Niggas, and the Shaping of African-American Counterpublic Discourses. Ph.D. dissertation, University of Massachusetts Amherst.

Turner, Bryan S., ed. 1990. *Theories of Modernity and Postmodernity*. Thousand Oaks CA: Sage Publications.

Tyson, Christopher. 2003. Exploring the Generation Gap and Its Implications on African American Consciousness: Urban Think Tank Inc.

Unknown. 2003. Why White Stars Are Ripping Off Rap and R&B. *Ebony*, June, 191-2, 194-5.

Vaughan, Don Rodney. 2004. Why the Andy Griffith Show Is Important to Popular Cultural Studies. *Journal of Popular Culture* 38 (2):397-445.

Wade, Bonnie C. 2004. *Thinking Musically: Experiencing Music, Expressing Culture*. New York: Oxford University Press.

Watkins, Mel. 1994. *On the Real Side: Laughing, Lying, and Signifying: The Underground Tradition of African-American Humor That Transformed American Culture, from Slavery to Richard Pryor*. New York: Simon & Schuster.

Watkins, S. Craig. 2005. *Hip Hop Matters: Politics, Pop Culture, and the Struggle for the Soul of a Movement*. Boston, MA: Beacon Press.

Weber, Robert P. 1990. *Basic Content Analysis*. 2nd ed. Thousand Oaks, CA: Sage Publications.

West, Cornel. 1988. *Prophetic Fragments*. Trenton NJ: Eerdmans Publishing Group.

———. 1990. The New Cultural Politics of Difference. In *Out There: Marginalization and Contemporary Culture*, edited by R. Ferguson. Cambridge MA: MIT Press.

———. 1993. *Prophetic Thought in Postmodern Times: Beyond Eurocentrism and Multiculturalism*. Vol. 1`. Monroe ME: Common Courage Press.

———. 1999. *The Cornel West Reader*. New York: Basic Civitas Books.

———. 2004. Finding Hope in Dark Times. *Tikkun*, July/Aug., 18-20.

West, Kanye. 2004. *The College Dropout*. New York: Roc-A-Fella Records, Def Jam Recordings. CD.

White, Armond. 2002. *Rebel for the Hell of It: The Life of Tupac Shakur*. New ed. New York: Thunder's Mouth Press.

White, Russell Christopher. 2002. Constructions of Identity and Community in Hip-Hop Nationalism with Specific Reference to Public Enemy and Wu-Tang Clan. Ph.D. dissertation, University of Southampton (United Kingdom).

Whitesell, John. 2003. Malibu's Most Wanted. USA: Warner Brothers.

Williams, Angelo Antwone. 1997. Crossroads Traveler. In *Tough Love: The Life and Death of Tupac Shakur*, edited by K. Alexander and M. Datcher. Alexandria, VA: Black Words Inc.

Yamaguchi, Kazuo. 1991. *Event History Analysis, Applied Social Research Methods Series; V. 28*. Newbury Park, Calif.: Sage Publications.

# INDEX

50 Cent, 17

Alexander, F., 17, 188
Alexander, K., 17, 188
Alim, S., 84
Altheide, D., 38- 40
Anderson, E., 79, 85- 88, 94, 97, 104, 124, 200, 277, 287
Anderson, R., 79, 85- 88, 94, 97, 104, 124, 200, 277, 287
Annegret, S., 79
Ardis, A., 18
Armstrong, E., 81, 106, 135

Bagwell, O., 110
Baldwin, D., 86, 140
Banks, W., 102
Bastfield, K., 2
Bell, D., 90, 126, 140
bell, h., 82
Bennett, L., 127
Bernard, R., 27
Best, H., 109-110, 116, 125
Betts, R., 103, 106, 111
Black, 3-4, 6-7, 11, 13, 18, 20-25, 38-39, 43-46, 48, 49, 50,-51, 57, 60- 62, 64, 67, 80, 83- 84, 88-89, 92-93, 95-96, 98, 105- 114, 116, 118-133, 135-136, 138-139, 143- 145, 149-155, 158-159, 163-167, 170- 171, 173-174, 176, 178-183, 187-197, 199, 201, 203, 207, 209, 213, 214- 215, 220- 225, 229, 231, 233, 242, 244, 246- 253, 255, 260, 264, 267-268, 291
Blackwell, A., 102, 247
Blair E., 69, 80-81
Blake, A., 93
Bosch, D., 284
Boyd, T., 24, 95, 96, 108, 116, 128, 139
Burnim, M., 51, 221, 226
Bynoe, Y., 108

Chang, J., 90

Chung, L., 59, 68, 77, 138
Clay, A., 24, 48, 72, 78, 95
Cone, J., 112-113, 120- 125, 127, 171, 174, 221, 224, 246-248, 250-257
Cone, J. H., 112-113, 120, 124-125, 127, 171, 174, 221, 224, 246-248, 250-253, 257
Cook, R., 140
Cox, H., 59, 61-62, 125, 286
Cube, I., 10-11, 44, 49, 69, 70, 93, 176, 183, 208

D, C., 26, 98, 117, 128, 143, 163, 173, 178, 188, 200, 208, 258, 279
D, D., 143, 258
Dark, P., 28-37
Datcher, M., 17
Dent, G., 127
Detweiler, C., 3-4, 270, 279
Dillard, J., 60, 83-84, 115, 140
Donalson, M., 113-114, 119
Douglas, K., 88, 116
Dre, D., 2, 82, 93, 118, 190
DuBois, W.E.B., 221
Dyson, M., 2, 15, 16, 18, 25, 69, 71-72, 90, 92, 94-95, 110-112, 124-132, 153, 157, 163, 169, 171, 177, 224, 229, 247, 249, 258, 262, 264, 286, 291

Early, G., 74, 103, 124, 247
Edwards, H., 121, 247, 267, 281
Eminem, 35, 81, 153

Fenton, W., 27, 29, 34, 37, 41- 42
Fico, F., 39
Fisher, M., 252
Floyd, S., 123, 127, 247, 251-252
Forman, M., 86, 92-94, 97, 125
Foucault, M., 114, 125, 135
Fusco, C., 121

Gatto, L., 145
George, N., 69, 114-115, 118, 136, 142-143
Gilbert, D., 128

gospel, 14, 16, 24, 89, 98, 107, 193, 212, 226, 234-236, 238- 239, 243-244, 255, 256, 260, 262, 264-268, 274, 277-279
Gottdiener, M., 97, 112
Green, J., 115
Grout, J., 46, 229
Gruber, E., 83
Gruver, R., 55
Gubrium, J., 34
Guevara, N., 91
Guy, J., 111, 153, 165, 192

Hall, J. R., 8, 78, 106, 236
Hall, S., 8, 78, 106, 236
Harvey, D., 102, 125
Henry, M., 176, 244
Heyward, C., 101
Hodge, D., 16, 48, 51, 61, 94, 95, 166, 205, 209, 267
Hood, F., 10, 20, 44, 101- 102, 113, 120, 124, 126, 134, 179, 183, 198, 209, 212, 287
Hooks, B., 126
Hustad, D., 55, 221, 235

Iverem, E., 170, 256

Jackson, A., 73, 106, 145, 181, 183, 264
Jackson, L., 73, 106, 145, 181, 183, 264
James, J. A., 39, 43, 73, 109, 112-113, 120, 124, 145, 171, 181, 192, 221, 246, 250
James, P., 39, 43, 73, 109, 112-113, 120, 124, 145, 171, 181, 192, 221, 246, 250
Johnson, J., 145, 252
Jones, L., 45, 90, 111, 127, 153, 162, 170, 178, 252
Joseph, J, 114, 164, 255, 258

Kain, A., 257
Kaplan, D., 60
Keener, C., 37
Kelley, R., 24, 80, 96, 139, 143-144, 213
Kelley, R.D.G., 24, 80, 96, 139, 143-144, 213
Kellner, D., 88, 109-110, 116
Keyes, C., 48, 50, 82-83, 85, 105, 141
King, R., 11, 16, 37, 93, 108, 111, 150, 171, 250
Kirk, A., 98
Kirkland, D., 124, 261
Kitwana, B., 14, 17, 24, 69, 71-72, 81, 85, 90, 94-95, 111, 115, 118-119, 179, 182
Kohl, P., 135
Kraft, C., 234, 246, 262, 272
Kraft, C. H., 234, 246, 262, 272

Kramer, J., 49

Lacy, S., 39
Lash, S., 82, 98, 116, 268
Lazin, L., 2, 144, 154, 167, 180, 260
Le Gates, R., 101
Lee, S., 96, 103, 132, 145, 207, 292
Leland, J., 82-83
Lewis, C., 124
Lewis, L., 124
Lincoln, E., 39, 114, 120, 126
Linton, R., 28, 31
Little, M., 24, 110, 174, 291
Long, S., 79, 166, 178, 200, 242
Lynch, G., 3, 14
Lyotard, J., 98, 105

Mahiri, J., 88, 135
Majors, R., 85
Mamiya, L., 39, 114, 120, 126
Manners, R., 60
McWhorter, J., 74, 124
Merriam, A., 47, 49-50, 52, 57-58, 237
Middleton, R., 97
Miles, J., 259, 280
Miller, T., 46
Missiological Essential, 284-287
Mitchell, H., 244
Miyakawa, F., 67, 279
Morgan, M., 48, 85
Mufwene, S., 83
Murch, D., 98
Myra, M., 102

Neal, A., 61, 79, 92, 97, 107, 118, 126, 144, 213
Neal, L., 61, 79, 92, 97, 107, 118, 126, 144, 213
Neal, M., 61, 79, 92, 97, 107, 118, 126, 144, 213
Nelson, A., 69, 72, 114-115, 118
Nettle, B., 52, 54
Niebuhr, R., 262, 270-271
nit grit 'hood theos, 273, 276
NWA, 45, 144

Odum, H., 83, 89, 252
One, KRS, 11-14, 47, 66-68, 71, 72, 79, 81, 98, 126, 138, 183, 201, 203, 208, 209, 215-216, 230, 232, 250, 264-265, 269, 279, 287, 289
Outlawz, 208-210, 223-225

Palisca, C., 229
Perkins, E., 69, 70, 91-92, 104, 132

Perry, I., 49, 71, 79, 141
Peter, S., 72
Peters, K., 16, 36, 50, 76, 113, 149-150, 153, 163-164, 169, 175-185, 224, 241, 247, 261- 262
Pincus, Z., 47
Pinn, A., 72, 120, 223, 244-245, 273
Postmodern, 22, 24, 93, 97, 111, 117, 120-121
Potter, R., 46-47, 82, 115-117, 279

Ramsey, G., 124, 249
Rasmussen, S., 29, 37, 42
Reed, T., 17-18, 71, 226, 248-249
Richardson, J., 145
Riffe, D., 39
Ritzer, G., 93
Robinson, J., 118
Romanowski, W., 93
Rose, T., 50, 69, 71-72, 85, 89, 90-92, 115, 117, 121
Rux, C., 80, 141

Sablo, S., 88, 135
Saint, 1-3, 23, 25, 36, 121, 146, 176, 186-187, 215, 218, 222-223, 245, 247-248, 262- 263, 281, 291
Sapir, E., 52, 59, 139
Scott, J., 12, 116, 145, 292
Scott, K., 12, 116, 145, 292
Seligman, A., 109
Shahriari, A., 46
Shakur, A., 1, 5, 12, 17, 21- 23, 35, 43, 53, 98, 137, 149, 152, 154-159, 162-167, 169, 172-173, 175-176, 178, 181-182, 184- 185, 187, 190, 200, 203, 209, 212, 256, 264, 270, 282- 283
　Shakur, M. *see* Shakur, A.
　Shakur, S. *see* Shakur, A.
　Shakur, T. *see* Shakur, A.
Shaw, D., 5, 19, 243, 262, 274
Shenk, W., 284-285
Silverman, D., 27
Sims, J., 18, 58
Smith, D., 81, 84, 87, 192, 263, 268, 270
Smitherman, G., 51, 60, 75, 83-84, 140, 213
Soja, E., 24
Southern, E., 78, 89, 103, 105-106, 221, 226, 251

Spears, A., 60, 213
Spencer, J., 104-106, 121, 135, 251
Spirer, P., 56, 72, 149, 165, 170, 173, 178, 200
Starr, L., 76, 103
Stephens, R., 72
Stewart, P., 96
Stout, F., 101

Tan, G., 151, 164
Tate, G., 80, 144
Taylor, B., 3, 4, 270, 279
Terraciano, K., 31
Thau, H., 83
Thug, 20, 24, 104, 128-129, 152, 175, 176-178, 183, 200, 202, 212, 215-218, 229, 231, 258, 260-261, 268, 274, 277-279, 284
Thug Life, 20, 24, 104, 152, 175, 183, 200, 212, 215-218, 229, 231, 258, 268, 277-279, 284
Ting-Toomey, S., 59, 68, 77, 138
Tippett, A., 20, 27-36, 42
Titon, J., 46
Turner, A., 39, 43, 140
Turner, B., 39, 43, 140

Van Engen, C., 243, 262, 274

Wade, B., 67
Waterman, C., 76, 103
Watkins, C., 40, 48, 92, 94, 118
Watkins, M., 40, 48, 92, 94, 118
West, C., 11, 14, 35, 86, 97, 102, 105, 111, 114, 117, 118, 131, 133, 153, 162, 176, 178, 180, 190, 247, 292
West, K., 11, 14, 35, 86, 97, 102, 105, 111, 114, 117-118, 131, 133, 153, 162, 176, 178, 180, 190, 247, 292
White, A. 127, 131, 136, 141, 144, 149-151, 156, 169, 174, 178, 179-183
White., 3, 8, 11, 13, 17-18, 71, 79-81, 84, 93, 97, 103, 108, 112-113, 118-120, 127, 131, 136, 141, 144, 149-151, 156, 169, 174, 178, 179-183, 213-214, 224, 243-244, 248-250, 252, 291
Williams, A., 129, 149

Yamaguchi, K., 27, 28

# VDM publishing house ltd.

## Scientific Publishing House
### offers
## free of charge publication

of current academic research papers, Bachelor´s Theses, Master's Theses, Dissertations or Scientific Monographs

If you have written a thesis which satisfies high content as well as formal demands, and you are interested in a remunerated publication of your work, please send an e-mail with some initial information about yourself and your work to *info@vdm-publishing-house.com.*

**Our editorial office will get in touch with you shortly.**

**VDM Publishing House Ltd.**
Meldrum Court 17.
Beau Bassin
Mauritius
www.vdm-publishing-house.com

Printed in Great Britain
by Amazon

36226286R00201